12

## THE COLOR OF RACE IN AMERICA
### 1900–1940

# The Color of Race in America
## 1900–1940

Matthew Pratt Guterl

**HARVARD UNIVERSITY PRESS**

Cambridge, Massachusetts

London, England · 2001

*Library of Congress Cataloging-in-Publication Data*

Guterl, Matthew Pratt, 1970–
The color of race in America, 1900–1940 / Matthew Pratt Guterl.
p. cm.
ISBN 0-674-00615-1 (alk. paper)
1. United States—Race relations.    2. United States—Ethnic relations.
3. United States—Intellectual life—20th century.
4. Race awareness—United States—History—20th century.
5. Ethnicity—United States—History—20th century.
6. Du Bois, W. E. B. (Wiliam Edward Burghardt), 1868–1963—Views on race.
7. Grant, Madison, 1865–1937—Views on race.
8. Cohalan, Daniel F.—Views on race.
9. Toomer, Jean, 1894–1967—Views on race.    I. Title.
E184.A1 G96 2001
305.8′00973—dc21        2001016970

*For Sandi,*
*and for Mom and Dad*

# Contents

# Illustrations

THE COLOR OF RACE IN AMERICA
1900–1940

# Introduction

I remember well when the shadow swept upon me. I was a little
thing, away up in the hills of New England, where the dark
Housatonic winds between Hoosac and Taghkanic into the sea. In
a wee wooden schoolhouse, something put it into the boys' and
girls' heads to buy gorgeous visiting cards—ten cents a package—
and exchange. The exchange was merry, till one girl, a tall new-
comer, refused my card, refused it peremptorily, with a glance.
Then it dawned upon me with a certain suddenness that I was different from the others . . . shut out from their world by a vast veil.
　—W. E. B. DU BOIS, *SOULS OF BLACK FOLK* (1903)

Color is not a human or personal reality; it is a political reality.
　—JAMES BALDWIN, *THE FIRE NEXT TIME* (1962)

When I was twelve years old, I first encountered the ambiguities of race. A group of slightly older boys on bicycles chased me through a small New England town, pedaling furiously and yelling "Nigger!" for the world to hear. It must have seemed strange to those who watched, to see a white boy marked as black. In the middle of an extended family vacation, my parents brought us to the house of a family friend in Peterborough, New Hampshire, a quaint hamlet of two-story wooden houses surrounded by pine trees. After carefully unpacking our bikes from the front of our Chevy Suburban, my brother and I left to explore the town center and the local Ames department store.

Later that day, I returned to Ames alone. "There he is!" The shout came from a rag-tag group of angry-looking boys. "Nigger!" In the mid-1970s my parents had adopted children from Vietnam, Korea, and the South Bronx, turning our household into a microcosm of the American Century. Growing up in a multiracial family in the Cold War United States, I was fa-miliar with the secret suspicions and fears of racism. An earlier well-inten-

1

tioned family vacation to a campground along the Virginia coast had taught us that the South—with its public glares, churlish finger pointing, and angry mutters—was hardly the place to go on holiday. But liberal New England, we all assumed, would welcome us.

And so that cry of "Nigger" surprised me, spurring me into instinctual flight. The boys followed, in rapid pursuit, until they had me trapped behind a string of stores. A quick glance confirmed that my tormentors were much like me—my own age, my own skin color. Their knuckles were gleaming brightly in the sun, a perfect, pure white from gripping their handlebars so tightly. Trapped, I avoided their stares, waiting for their fists to fall upon me, my eyes focused everywhere else—on a set of sand dunes nearby, or on the ground—half hoping that someone would come walking out of the nearest dune to rescue me.

"You're the Nigger's brother." One of them spat at me. "Get him out of town."

Him. My brother—my companion on that earlier trip downtown—was the son of an African-American enlisted man and a Vietnamese woman, one of the four adopted children in my family. The racist directive—remove the black child from our white town—hung there between the boys and me for a moment. Terrified and angry, I was filled with humiliation at my brother's blackness and, in turn, at my own vicarious blackness. I began to cry. Those tears shamed me into action, and I burst through the shining steel circle of their bicycles and rode off onto a path through the dunes. When I looked back just once, they were still standing there, comfortable in their whiteness and completely unconcerned with my cowardly escape.

The brother they called "Nigger" was not simply black to me, for I was then acutely aware of the Asian tilt at the corner of his eyes, and still vividly remembered the day he arrived from Vietnam, when he spoke not a single word of English. Nor could I understand what they had said about me. First they had called me "Nigger," and then "the Nigger's brother." I was white like them, but I was not white like them. It had never mattered so much before whether I was white or not. But at the moment of my encirclement, whatever I thought about race, or whatever I believed about my family, was irrelevant. What mattered, quite simply, was what those stronger, bigger, and more numerous boys believed.

"The conundrum of color," wrote James Baldwin, "is the inheritance of every American, be he/she legally or actually Black or White."[1] As Baldwin knew, whether we define ourselves (or are defined) as white, black, or something else, we all confront that conundrum in our everyday lives. My own sense of race and whiteness is most directly informed by my family—by my adopted brothers and sisters of color from Korea, from the South Bronx, and from Vietnam, and by our intricately interconnected lives. The experience of race, though, can differ from my own in degree and kind, ranging from W. E. B. Du Bois's traumatic slight by a young girl to the ghoulish inhumanities of the Holocaust and Jim Crow, apartheid and ethnic cleansing. Race is everywhere. The simple act of hailing a taxicab in midtown Manhattan is affected by the omnipresent thought of racial difference, as is the political assault on welfare, or the arguments about gun control and school violence, or even the placement and design of advertisements for cigarettes. And as my own brief travail in that New Hampshire town demonstrates, even where whites do not actually see people of color (or, conversely, where people of color do not see whites) the heavily racialized stuff of life is impossible to escape. Almost everything we in America do, or think, or say, is informed by race.

Race is a bizarre social invention, a public fiction masquerading as physical fact. In a nation where everyone is carefully—if sometimes unconsciously—scrutinized and then classified according to the imprecise dictates of certain visual cues (namely skin color), we all learn to assume that race exists as a public marker of supposedly real social, cultural, and genetic differences. This assumption is no recent phenomenon, and race has long been the *lingua franca* of American society and politics. Our "race problem," however, has usually been described as an issue between whites and blacks. The proliferation of heated debates, published essays, and much-ballyhooed books about race in America has invariably focused on the lives of black Americans, who are always presumed to be the past, present, and future "problem" of the United States. This public discourse on strife along the color line has been strengthened in recent years by a series of events involving white-black relations—the trial of O. J. Simpson, the congressional abuse of Anita Hill, the assault on the Haitian immigrant Abner Louima, the police beating of Rodney King and the subsequent riots in Los Angeles, and the killing of Amadou Diallo—that have received unprecedented press coverage.

But the "race problem" is not about black Americans: it is about race. Indeed, the overwhelming emphasis on relations between whites and blacks—on "the Negro problem" and "the color line"—obscures the diversity and racial heterogeneity of the American republic. The relatively open immigration policy of the past thirty years has seen the arrival of immigrants from Asia, Africa, South America, and the Caribbean—not from Europe, as was the case in the nineteenth and early twentieth centuries. Growing immigrant populations have benefited somewhat from the current climate of "identity politics," gaining a voice in contemporary debates about civil society. And older immigrant groups of European heritage, long presumed to have been completely assimilated into whiteness, have also rediscovered themselves in a social context in which "ethnic" identities—and not whiteness—are the source of political strength. As the historian Matthew Frye Jacobson has suggested, the "disavowal of whiteness has become pronounced in recent years, particularly around the question of affirmative action. The notion that Jews, Letts, Finns, Greeks, Italians, Slovaks, Poles, or Russians are not *really* white has become suddenly appealing in a setting where whiteness has wrongly become associated with unfair *dis*advantage."[2]

The ethnic escape from the bounds of whiteness comes at a time when American political culture has lunged rightward, cultivating a xenophobia directed against newer immigrants from "Third World" countries and an institutional racism focused on the impoverished classes of Afro-America. In the long night after the explosive arrival of Black Power and the race riots of the late 1960s and early 1970s, we have been treated to an extended debate on the supposed decline of traditional family values and the erosion of our citizenry's moral fiber. The impression given is that between 1950 and 2000 the United States suffered a precipitous, and wholly unprecedented, moral decline, a decline closely associated with the insidious evils of liberalism, especially the excesses of Affirmative Action and "welfare." Those who, in the heyday of American liberalism, argued in favor of expanding the powers of the state to help those most in need were, according to those "in the know" today, blind to the corrosive effects of their policies. The United States, we are told, needs only to shake off the detritus of the poor, the hungry, the gay, and the black to redeem its honor and restore the republic's political, moral, and cultural health to its Eisenhower-era vigor. The determined leaders of the religious right and their partisan allies have thus revealed a grand conspiracy against American life, one in which gay rights, feminism, and liberalism are dark, corrupting forces—sappers at the walls of Fortress America. And if some European ethnics have rediscovered their nonwhite "roots" in invented traditions of purported Old

World pedigree, many others have been completely seduced by whiteness and have shifted rightward, turning away from the traditional liberal alliance between the working class and Civil Rights groups and allying themselves with the emergent Republican majority.

Conceived in our age of racial discontents and confusions, this book is, to borrow a passage from Cornel West, "about what *race* matters have meant to the American past and of how much race *matters* to the American present."[3] Today, as the binary structure of racial identity—the white-black dyad—begins to give way before demographic trends predicted to make the United States a nation of myriad ethnic and racial groups with a white minority, the despair over the "disuniting" of the American community mirrors the fears and anxieties of the first thirty years of this century. Americans in that earlier age of "identity politics" grappled with analogous questions about personal selfhood, political citizenship, and social justice in a context of similarly pressing demographic, cultural, and economic transformations. Looking closely at the Progressive Era—and at particular Progressive Americans—we can learn a great deal about an earlier attempt to reestablish national unity in the face of cultural fragmentation, and even more about our own thirst for some mythic "American way of life" presumed to have died in the aftermath of open immigration, the Civil Rights Movement, and liberal reform.

Conventional history has Jim Crow and the one drop rule reigning supreme over the United States after the tumultuous 1890s—after the *Plessy* decision, after the so-called Redemption of southern political institutions, and after the devolution of Populism into racism. The North won the Civil War, as some would have it, but the South won the peace that followed. The dramatic rise of white supremacy and the resultant downturn in African-American prospects in the 1890s—named "the nadir" by Rayford Logan—brought with them institutions so brutal, so inhuman, that some termed them "worse than slavery."[4] From legal institutions to government bureaucracies, from national museums to publishing houses, from the Spanish-American War to Jim Crow, turn-of-the-century American political culture was characterized by a grim fascination with racial difference and "race problems." But "white" and "black" were not stable, easily defined identities in 1900, nor was the popular interest in race single-mindedly focused on color. In the northeastern United States, where "Old Stock" Americans clashed with European immigrants from Ireland, Germany, Italy, and Eastern Europe, race was marked by language, nationality, religion, and social status, as well as by color. Even as a color-coded negrophobia emerged in the New South, a different notion of racial difference emerged in the context of northern nativism. The story of race in modern America is thus far messier, and far less inevitable, than previously supposed.

If many turn-of-the-century Americans wrestled with problems of racial classification, all that changed in the twenty years following the Great War. During and after the war, newly aggressive advocates of social justice for "the Negro" gathered in New York, Chicago, and Boston and lashed out publicly against racism. The postwar Great Migration of African Americans into the urban North, and the accompanying arrival of other peoples of African descent from the Caribbean, shook nativism to its ideological foundations, supporting the emergence of the New Negro Movement and engendering the first truly national mass culture obsessed with "the Negro" as the foremost social threat. Together with the foreclosure of European immigration and the postwar growth of superpatriotism, the development of a racialized consumer society speeded the absolute assimilation of immigrant groups (previously understood as racially distinct) into the singular "white race." The result was a culture of racial thinking termed "bi-racialism" by the eugenicist Lothrop Stoddard, which encouraged Americans to focus on race-as-color and almost solely on whiteness and blackness, leaving them increasingly unable, or unwilling, to deal with national "race questions" other than the purportedly peculiar conundrum posed by "the Negro."[5]

African Americans and European immigrants were active participants in this history of race in Modern America—key players in the process the novelist Jean Toomer bitterly called "the hypnotic division of Americans into black and white."[6] In the fratricidal world of postwar African-American politics, the pitched battles among Marcus Garvey, W. E. B. Du Bois, Hubert Harrison, and Cyril Briggs revealed a shared assumption that a new "race-consciousness" was an indispensable part of the struggle for justice for "the Negro." More important, "race-consciousness" had come to mean color-consciousness. European immigrants also played an important role in the history of race. After the Great War and during the Red Scare, the urge to whiteness displayed by New Immigrants—the "riff-raff" whom novelist Owen Wister had once described as "dingy whites"—exploded into violence and race riots, leaving scores of African Americans dead or injured. That savage moment in the history of the United States signaled to all that the popular diffusion of "the Negro problem" and the whitening process were connected and had become a truly national dilemma. Bringing together African-American history and ethnic history, American history and world history, this book is as much about how white people thought about race as it is about how black people thought about race—and about how both groups understood and attempted to define and control racial difference in the context of a dawning "bi-racialist" sensibility.[7]

The road from a multiplicity of white races to the arrival of "bi-racialism" intersects the varied lives of four nominal New Yorkers: the Irish-American nationalist Daniel Cohalan, the eugenicist and white supremacist Madison Grant, the African-American advocate of social justice W. E. B. Du Bois, and the novelist and "American" pluralist Jean Toomer. Each in his own way, Cohalan, Du Bois, Grant, and Toomer were fascinated by questions of race, politics, and classification. All four wrapped their racial identifications in heavily gendered language and brought their own belief in manly authority, social status, and privilege to bear upon the refashioned notions of race, destiny, and history. Buffeted by the social changes brought about by the Great Migration, the Great War, and American empire, these four men encountered this "bi-racialism" from radically different vantage points.

The son of Irish immigrants to Manhattan, New York State Supreme Court Justice Daniel Cohalan was a quintessential Tammany Hall man and a ruthless politician. He was also a devout Irish nationalist—one of the faithful whose quixotic belief in an independent Ireland seemed, for a time, to be the grandest delusion of all. Indeed, along with the expatriate Fenian and jailbird John Devoy, Cohalan was instrumental in reviving the Irish-American nationalist movement during the early years of the twentieth century. The revival spurred by Cohalan's public work in New York culminated in the Irish Race Convention held in Manhattan in the spring of 1916, which celebrated the abundant virtues of "the Irish race" in America. His unsuccessful attempt to establish a metalanguage of "Irishness" illustrates the demographic and economic changes affecting the urban context and older, rapidly assimilating immigrant communities. And his failure to excite widespread support for "Irishness" reflects a common problem faced by postwar immigrant "race" leaders, who found their previously Irish constituencies absorbed with increasing finality into whiteness.[8]

If Daniel Cohalan's wartime thirst for Irishness reflected the larger history of the Irish in America, the contemporary struggles of W. E. B. Du Bois—the NAACP propagandist, editor of *The Crisis*, and eloquent spokesman for Pan-Africanism and social justice—likewise demonstrate the African-American dilemma. Du Bois called the story of his life an "illustration and exemplification of what race has meant in the world in the nineteenth and twentieth centuries."[9] Raised in New England and steeped in the works of Hegel, Herder, and the American idealist philosopher Josiah Royce, Du Bois spent most of the prewar period articulating his racial sentiments through the symbols and language of Romanticism and pluralism. Until the mid-to-late 1920s his graceful rhetoric persuaded many that the world-historical "Negro" had a unique destiny to fulfill, if only men and women of African descent might strive—and be allowed to strive—for civilization. As a Romantic pluralist, Du Bois sought social justice for African America in the context of the universal rights of "the fifty races of the world."

The Great War, the Great Migration, and the subsequent racial violence of the Red Scare changed everything for Du Bois, forever shaking his faith in civilization and in white folks. His Romantic pluralism gradually became the ashes from which his equally perceptive international socialism and unorthodox Marxism sprang. The reinvented Du Bois became perhaps the most insightful critic of the interrelationship of race, war, fortune, and empire in American culture.[10] His postwar life captures the drama of the African-American experience in the urban North. If the evolution of the world economy and the subsequent increase in the interconnectedness of the world helped to polarize the northeastern states around questions of whiteness and blackness, the unprecedented arrival of African Americans also encouraged this trend. Race riots, labor strife, residential and communal segregation, and the proliferation of African-American protest groups rubbed the raw racial nerves of Manhattanites, Bostonians, and Philadelphians. Inspired by the arrival of black folks in the urban North, protest leaders—participants in a New Negro Movement—helped to displace earlier understandings of race and to make blackness and whiteness integral parts of American politics.

That New Negro Movement emerged as a potent response to the champions of Nordicism, or white world supremacy. And no one life captures the rise of this Nordic vogue better than that of Madison Grant. In 1916, alarmed by the supposed dangers inherent in immigration, feminism, and the Great War, Grant produced the Ur-text of modern American nativism, *The Passing of the Great Race; or, The Racial Basis of European History.* The "white" Nordic working class, Grant thought, needed to have its race-consciousness awakened if the greatness of white America was to survive. Grant's emphasis on the peculiar martial qualities of "Nordics" likewise reflected a profoundly modern phenomenon—the discourse of "masculinity," with its emphasis on militarism, patriarchy, and preparedness.[11] Emboldened by the popularity of eugenics, Grant inspired his fellow "Nordics" both to celebrate their purportedly magnificent biological heritage and to recognize the dangers facing the republic.

Until the Great Migration and the New Negro Movement, Grant was more concerned with "dingy white" immigrants than with black folks. But after that migration, Grant—together with his protégé Lothrop Stoddard—forged a direct connection between the health of the political body and that of the physical body and adopted an authoritarian, black-white rhetoric reminiscent of Afrikaner nationalism and southern segregationism. This heightened negrophobia, the replacement for old-fashioned nativism, soon captured the imagination of white folks in the North. Indeed, Stoddard and Grant postulated a popular "White Atlantic" to match the "Black Atlantic" sensibilities of Du Bois, Garvey, and the New Negro Movement. In a world racked by revolution and war and troubled by a plethora of internationalisms—socialism, feminism, Pan-Africanism, Garveyism, and Bolshevism—Grant envisioned "absolute," or global, whiteness as the olive branch that would reunite labor and capital, pacify both immigrants and nativists, and erase the illusory differences between Anglo-Saxon and Celt. The dystopian visions of Grant and Stoddard, and the angry response to white world supremacy by Du Bois, Garvey, and others, reflected a new American sense of race as color, as a simple matter of blackness and whiteness.

The new "race-consciousness" posed particularly vexing problems for Americans who desired to be neither white nor black. In this context, the life of the devoutly mixed-race novelist Jean Toomer, much like those of W. E. B. Du Bois and Madison Grant, epitomizes the intersections of race, gender, and American political culture in the 1920s. Toomer is best known as the troubled writer whose prose poem Cane (1923) was celebrated as the first great work of the Harlem Renaissance. After the publication of Cane, Toomer protested its inclusion in the African-American literary canon on the grounds that, having several different bloods in his veins, he was not a "Negro." Few, however, understood his dilemma. Pinned between the rapidly organizing forces of whiteness and blackness, Toomer found it impossible to make himself understood or to escape the increasing southernization of northeastern American racial discourse. Toomer's failure to define himself as something other than white or black reminds us that knowing who and what you are, and having control over the terms of your own identity, are most precious human rights. And if Toomer—for all of his revolutionary attempts at rebuilding the architecture of race—was unable to offer an alternative to race itself, such a fact may reflect the difficulty of describing ourselves as something other than white or black today.[12]

The juxtaposition of these four lives reveals that the story of race can be politically complicated. Du Bois clearly plays the hero to Grant's villain in the awful tragedy of the African-American struggle for social equality. But Du Bois and Grant are also fitting representatives of the "bi-racialist" sensibility that classified Jean Toomer as a "Negro." Toomer would have accused Du Bois almost as readily as Grant of foisting blackness upon him after the success of *Cane*. Of course, Du Bois—and African America—participated in any debate about race with certain inescapable legal and political handicaps. Still, in a world where notions of blackness and whiteness empowered some people and disenfranchised others, it is important to note that newly "race-conscious" whites and blacks could both be involved, albeit unequally, in the exact same social process—the reconstruction of race—that sealed Jean Toomer's fate, or, indeed, the fate of Daniel Cohalan's precious Irish race.

These four men formed their own strongly held opinions about race in explicit dialogue with one another. Du Bois read the work of Grant and Stoddard closely and debated the latter in print and in person. Grant followed the rise of Du Bois with horror and sent newspaper clippings and other information on Garvey to his followers around the country. Toomer, Garvey, and Du Bois watched the explosive ascendance of Irish nationalism and from it drew very different conclusions about their own lives. Cohalan, Du Bois, and Toomer—three of the most inventive cultural pluralists in America—were key contributors to the extended debate about citizenship and self-governance in an increasingly diverse United States. And much like Du Bois, Grant, Cohalan, and Toomer, the nation's larger "ethnic" and "racial" communities shared ideas, corresponded across the color lines, and met in public and private venues to agree or disagree about the principles of democracy at home and abroad.

These lives—these separate worlds within America—came together in the aftermath of the Great War in the city of New York. As Manhattan became the dynamo powering the postwar advent of American supremacy, empire became a way of life and an integral part of the story of race in the

United States. The new media and financial capital of the world—home to hundreds of magazines, financial institutions, and radio stations—Manhattan was also the entrepôt from which the growing obsession with whiteness and blackness was exported, shipped around the world as if it were steel, or art, or the techniques of scientific management. Rubber factories sprang up in Liberia, Sumatra, and elsewhere, and were presented to the American public as distant evidence of "the Negro question." The occupation of Haiti by American troops during and after the Great War resulted in the imposition of Jim Crow justice and the importation of technology and fiscal capital into the tiny island republic by New York banks. Painters, sculptors, and writers cultivated a purportedly African aesthetic, drawing connections between "the Negro" in America and the African abroad. Business and advertising provided the economic and symbolic basis for the increasingly powerful link between the "Roaring Twenties" at home and informal colonization around the world. These connections between American life at home and empire abroad were as important for the New Negro Movement as they were for the prophets of Nordicism.

The Manhattan moment was, by and large, disconnected from the far reaches of the United States. In the Far West, in the Southwest, and in the deep South, popular sensibilities about race were informed by several regional factors, especially economic, cultural, and demographic differences. If the New South wrestled with a significant African American population in the context of an increasingly mechanized cash-crop agricultural economy, for instance, the racial dynamic of Texas and the Southwest was altered by an additional factor: the arrival of Mexican laborers.[13] In creole New Orleans, regional distinctiveness—the cultural legacy of French settlement and the desire of creole communities to preserve themselves as such—often competed with the American drive to include every drop of African blood in "blackness." The *gens de couleur libre*, as Rodolphe Lucien Desdunes named them, emphasized the mixture of "Latin" and "Negro" blood and culture that secured their classification as something different from "the Negro." Given a deepening regional confusion, attempts to legislate the lines of racial classification nationally and to deter miscegenation proved difficult, if not downright impossible, in the face of a continued lack of consensus about what, exactly, was meant by the term "race."[14] Making race in Manhattan, in other words, was not precisely making race in America.

But however powerful those regional economic factors may have been, the status of Manhattan as the cultural capital of America in the 1920s meant that the dominant national discourse on race did owe far more to the Northeast than to the New South or the Far West. In the simplest of terms, the centrality of Manhattan in modern American culture was assured by its role as the largest city in the United States, by its status as media capital, and by the hubris of the city itself. Hollywood films and national radio programs took their shape from the cultural patterns of the city of New York. "New York might or might not be America," the historian Ann Douglas has written, "but in the 1920s the city was cornering, expanding, and reinventing the nation's cultural market."[15] With unprecedented metropolitan chauvinism, the legions of advertisers, bankers, writers, and "men of character" surveyed the grand metropolis and simply assumed—perhaps rightfully so—that New York had no rivals in culture or in style.

The lure of whiteness and blackness in the 1920s and 1930s also owed a great deal to the intellectual and cultural legacies of the turn-of-the-century New South. Prior to the arrival of "the Negro" in the North, Jim Crow's influence on northeastern political culture was best reflected in D. W. Griffith's wildly popular film *Birth of a Nation,* first screened in 1915. *Birth of a Nation* inspired white citizens of the republic—both North and South—to recognize that "the Negro" was a threat requiring a unified response, and to bury the "bloody shirt" of southern secession and rebellion. The political reunification of the national polity, symbolized by the election of the self-styled southerner Woodrow Wilson, likewise encouraged an intellectual marriage of North and South. The racialized politics of Wilson and *Birth of a Nation* thus signaled the intertwining of two crucial components of the southernization of northern racial discourse: the wartime nationalism of the period between 1914 and 1918 and the related emergence of the film and entertainment industry. Nationalist mass culture focused American energies on "the Negro problem" and served as the foundation for a presumably American way of life. Shown to audiences in packed movie halls around the United States, and greeted with both enthusiasm and great disdain, *Birth of a Nation* helped to nationalize white male dominance by making it seem vital and necessary and by shrouding it in cherished myths of reunion and the "Lost Cause."

Despite the certainties of *Birth of a Nation* and the appeal of southern folkways, however, significant regional variations in racial thinking persisted through the early 1920s. Other contemporary films—such as the preparedness classic *Battle Cry of Peace*—offered "the Hun" as a more dangerous menace than "the Negro" and portrayed the dangers of an Anglo-Saxon world overrun with hirsute, brutishly barbarian immigrants from Italy and low-browed German infiltrators. D. W. Griffith, Woodrow Wilson, and others may have succeeded in reuniting the political culture of North and South, but smoothing away the racial distinctions between Anglo-Saxons and Celts proved a bit more difficult. Irish Americans, for instance, continued to articulate their own nationalist dissent from "Anglomania" in heavily racialized terms. In one particularly telling case, members of a secret Irish-American nationalist group, the Clan na Gael, followed a private screening of *Birth of a Nation* with a raucous tribute to "Irish stepdancing." Only after the Great Migration of African Americans in the 1920s would the southern tradition of negrophobia become the dominant mind set of the "world city" of Manhattan. The fear and anger of the chief architects of Jim Crow in the southern states would then provide citizens of the northeastern states with a crucial body of ideas and symbols, inspiring them to both race riots and primitivist fascination. No more fitting cinematic conclusion to this part of the story of race can be found in the Depression era than the novel and film *Gone with the Wind*, in which the Irish O'Hara family—blessed with "magnolia whiteness"—finds its destiny bound up with the Anglo-Saxons of the Old South and the ghosts of slavery.[16]

In sum, by the late 1920s and early 1930s American political culture was almost single-mindedly focused on "the Negro" and on race-as-color. If this white-over-black sensibility triumphed at a particular moment in the history of the northeastern United States, that same moment also witnessed the growth of a particular cultural center of global significance—namely the "world city" of New York. If "absolute whiteness" and "absolute blackness" were born during a remarkable period of Manhattan's history, that same period corresponded with an unprecedented stretch of national economic growth at home and economic and cultural expansion into Europe, Latin America, Africa, and South America. That same span also found national popular culture fascinated with the supposedly romantic legacies of the Old South. The rise of "bi-racialism" was thus an integral part of an epoch of national and world-historical significance, playing a vital role in the organization of America's imperial adventures as well as in the response to and awareness of those same adventures both at home and abroad.

# 1

# Salvaging a
# Shipwrecked World

When you are actually *in* America, America hurts, because it has a powerful disintegrative influence upon the white psyche. It is full of grinning, unappeased aboriginal demons . . . and it persecutes the white men . . . until the white men give up their absolute whiteness.

—D. H. LAWRENCE, *STUDIES IN CLASSIC AMERICAN LITERATURE* (1923)

As the years pass, the supreme importance of heredity and the supreme value of superior stocks will sink into our being, and we will acquire a true *race*-consciousness (as opposed to national or cultural consciousness) which will bridge political gulfs, remedy social abuses, and exorcise the lurking spectre of miscegenation . . . we have our task, and God knows it is a hard one—the salvage of a shipwrecked world!

—LOTHROP STODDARD, *THE RISING TIDE OF COLOR AGAINST WHITE WORLD SUPREMACY* (1920)

For Brooks Adams, a grandson of President John Quincy Adams and the youngest member of his generation of the renowned Adams family, the end of the nineteenth century was the end of one momentous cycle of history. Drained by years of "being civilized too much," the nervous force of the Anglo-Saxon race had run its course. The failure of the British to end the Anglo-Boer war and defeat the barbaric, dingy Boer race, Adams would later argue, was the clearest example of the effects of overcivilization upon the once manly Anglo-Saxon. When Max Nordau, the author of Adams's favorite work of dystopian history, *Degeneration,* declared that the age of *fin-de-race* had arrived, Adams sadly agreed: "I cannot disguise from myself that . . . my race is run. I have nothing more to hope from the world." On a fact-finding vacation in India in 1896 (he had gone to examine the state of the British Empire), Brooks seemed to have lost his faith entirely: "I do not believe," he wrote to his brother despairingly, "that we have the vitality left to escape. We bear every mark of premature decay . . . the worm is at the heart eating, eating."[1]

Adams's grim predictions were first offered publicly in his remarkable historical work *The Law of Civilization and Decay,* published in 1896. Much like his older brother, the historian Henry Adams, Brooks had long struggled to apply the laws of nature to human society, to understand the natural principles that determined the course of civilizations past and present. Troubled by the economic crash of 1893 and the subsequent fiscal panic, Brooks set out to define for his generation the roots of the great crisis at hand. Race and civilization, he argued, were one and the same. Each civilization passed through a series of stages, and in the last, fatal stage, the vital manhood of the race—the foundation of the civilization—was vanquished by fate: "In this last stage . . . the economic, and, perhaps, the scientific intellect is propagated, while the imagination fades, and the emotional, the martial, and the artistic types of manhood decay." Thus, he concluded, "when a highly centralized society disintegrates, it is because the energy of the race has been exhausted." Lashing out at the unimaginative and unmanly advocates of ruthless capitalism—"the Jew" was, for Adams, always a prime target—he bemoaned the hopeless diminution of civilization's most fantastic and manly elements, decried the death of the "martial and imaginative age," and yearned for a rebirth brought on by the "infusion of barbarian blood."[2]

Like Adams, most turn-of-the-century commentators were anxious and somewhat bewildered by the unprecedented social changes that swept them into modernity. During the 1890s, technological, economic, and cultural revolutions—what Henry Adams called "the sudden interruption of forces totally new"—changed American life forever.[3] Millions of immigrants and "Old Stock" Americans were thrown together, crowded into cities; transcontinental railroads crisscrossed the country and steamships traversed shipping lines around the world in growing numbers, facilitating an explosion of economic activity; the frontier closed, cutting off continental expansion; a war over the practical means of empire was begun and won; and the United States was transformed from an uncivil, rough-and-tumble backwater to a world power and the very seat of "civilization." The nation practically buzzed with electricity, or, rather, hummed like the dynamo the elder Adams had viewed with fear and excitement at the Paris Exposition of 1900.

In this moment of widespread social, economic, and cultural tumult, a vast tide of racial categories washed over American culture, its ambiguities and confusions hidden by multiple political motives. Several fundamental questions plagued discussions about "race problems" throughout the United States. What, exactly, was a race? Where, precisely, should the boundary lines of racial difference be drawn? What, specifically, marked race physically upon or within the body? Race, it was argued, could be marked by language, nation, skin color, relations between the sexes, arts and technology, social standing, government and laws, or religion. One popular encyclopedia, capturing the depth of the problem perfectly, listed several conflicting definitions of race without explaining or exploring the contradictions. Scientists, journalists, politicians, and cultural figures wavered between allegiance to one set of physical traits and to another, leaving a remarkable looseness of fit in the language of race. And as "the science of races" grew more sophisticated, "race charts" and "purely somatical classifications" became ever more confused and complicated, leaving at least one writer disgusted by the power of "expressions vagues qui ne servent qu'à obscurcir les idées." "Terms have been used which themselves need definition," complained the ethnologist A. H. Keane; "the meaning of some, such, for instance, as *race, clan, tribe,* still gives rise to constant, often to angry, discussion, amongst writers on ethnological subjects."[4]

## The Problem of Classification

Nowhere was the problem of racial classification more vexing than in the science of history. In an essay published in the inaugural number of the journal of the American Historical Association, the distinguished historian William M. Sloane used the "science of races" to lay the groundwork for a nationalist grand narrative. "The real merit of the evolutionary philosophy which has captured the thought of our day," he suggested, "lies in the fact that it has made possible a science of the humanities." And while Sloane admitted that illustration of "the laws of nature" had, in some disciplines, proved far more complicated than originally supposed, he also ardently concluded that, so far as the study of man was concerned, an "orderly arrangement of our knowledge concerning his motives and conduct" was within reach. "Evolutionary philosophy," or popular Darwinism, had encouraged Sloane to discount the "fickleness of personal will" and focus on the grandiose story of competition between the races and the interconnected history of rising and falling "civilizations." Another writer concluded, echoing Sloane:

> The New History is genetic. From effects it strikes at once at causes. Henceforth history must deal with physical origins . . . Accounts of warring rulers no longer constitute the history of mankind. Decisive battles of the world have been . . . inevitable for reasons far deeper than mere caprice of petty prince. The segregation process in nations, everywhere and at all times, has been upon physiographic lines. Invariably in vain have been the mightiest efforts of so-called world conquerors to overstep these boundaries, which Nature has so immutably set. We look beyond the will of man for an adequate cause for the distribution of peoples.

For Sloane, as for Brooks Adams, that simple shift of focus changed everything. "The doctrine of the unity of history," Sloane wrote, "has not merely been rehabilitated, but it has been so emphasized that the consequences are simply revolutionary . . . [for] to accept the doctrine of the unity of history is already to admit that no country is more than one wheel in the series which moves the hands on the dial-plate of human progress." Race—a world-historical, comparative framework—was to be the basis of all historical knowledge.[5]

Adams, Sloane, and their contemporaries were excited by the possibilities of Universal History, especially where it revealed the advent of a peculiarly "American" civilization. The dramatic entry of the United States onto the world stage after victory in the Spanish-American War, and the general despair over decaying, degenerating Europe, could easily be explained with a new narrative of world history and progress—one which concluded with the triumphant rise of "America." "Never," suggested Edward Ellis, the author of a popular history that covered the battle of Salamis, the battle of Manila, and everything in between, "has the importance of a knowledge of history been more generally felt than at the present time." Universal Histories used the "science of races" to weave together divergent pasts, tapping into a widespread and purportedly "recent" interest in "the most distant and most primitive races of mankind."[6]

All, however, was not well with the world. Indeed, the certainty of racial difference—manifest in the lavish illustrations, sweeping assertions, and grand conclusions of Universal Histories—hid a general unease about racial classification. Ethnology, in short, was unable to develop an agreed-upon principle of classification. John Clark Ridpath, the author of a massive ethnological encyclopedia entitled *Great Races of Mankind* (which he termed an "ethnic history of mankind"), drew up an extraordinarily complicated "race chart," splintering whiteness into hundreds of national and regional racial groups. Surveying his remarkable attempt at a unifying scheme of organization, Ridpath admitted that there were serious problems of classification in the "science of races":

> Another essential topic in ethnic history is that which considers the classification of the races and their arrangement into a whole according to manifest and established principles . . . We shall find in this part of the inquiry that at the present stage of our knowledge some uncertainty still exists relative to the best principle of division for classifying the different races of mankind. Nearly all of the physical and mental characteristics of men have been taken as the foundation of a classification of the races; but few of those characteristics have been found to be sufficiently constant to furnish an invariable and scientific principle of division. In the present work the color of the human body has been taken as the most invariable criterion of race character, and on that fundamental fact, assisted by other physical traits and by intellectual peculiarities of development, particularly by the great fact of language, the classification has been made.[7]

As Ridpath's admission suggests, the purpose of classification was the arrangement of "the whole"—a vision of the racialized world and Universal History. Any uncertainty regarding that project of classification posed a serious problem, leaving many (and the economist John Commons in particular) to hope that readers would not suffer from "confusion if we use the term 'race' not only to designate . . . grand divisions . . . but also to designate those peoples or nationalities which we recognize as distinct yet related within one of the large divisions." The scatterbrained focus on skin color, national history, and the "great fact of language" complicated the task of racial classification. "It is," concluded another author dryly, "a difficult matter to classify mankind."[8]

Interrelated demographic and economic factors were, in part, behind this problem of classification. In contrast to the comparatively steady demographic composition of the New South, tens of millions of Irish, Italian, and Jewish immigrants poured into northeastern cities between 1880 and 1920, inflaming "racial" sentiments and becoming the symbolic embodiment of the intensification of modern life under industrialism. Amid the grimy squalor of New York, Boston, and Philadelphia (cities where the African-American presence was small) the cultural, political, and economic authority of Old Stock Americans was increasingly menaced by those recent arrivals of questionable "whiteness" from Italy, eastern Europe, and Ireland. However, the overwhelming need for labor in the urban Northeast—even "alien" labor—outweighed the supposed dangers of immigration, and thus restrictionist legislation passed before the 1920s limited only Asian immigration and not that of "dingy" white Europeans. Satisfying the regional appetites of American capitalism, the arrival of these immigrants also inflamed nativist hatred and bigotry. By the turn of the century hundreds of thousands of "white" immigrants were either house servants to Old Stock Americans, factory workers toiling in the grim sweatshops and factories of Manhattan, or on the docks pushing, pulling, and lifting an ever increasing variety of goods into and out of the bowels of massive steamships. Patrician nativists may have complained that the vigor of Anglo-Saxon stock was sapped as immigrants stole away and then tainted the manly, hardscrabble labor central to the survival of the republic, but robber barons and politicians saw only dollars and votes. The resulting political antagonisms between nativists, Darwinian capitalists, and Old World nationalists shaped the racial discourse of the urban North.[9]

New South and urban North thus wrestled with very different "race problems" and labor problems—the "Negro problem" and the "Alien menace" respectively—and the language of racial classification shifted with the prevailing political winds of either region. This regional focus often led to some rather peculiar confusion. In the 1880s, for instance, an anti-Catholic group named the American Protective Association—a group that "had eyes only for the menace of the Irish"—actually drew support from African Americans in the North. An awareness of "the Negro problem" was, however, not limited to the South, and southern politicians did see the dangers of European immigration. Indeed, southern sympathy for restriction of immigration was based on a fear that "the Negro problem" would soon have an immigrant analogy in the North, and that immigrants might divide "white unity." Northern nativists, in turn, were in perpetual dread that Irish—and later Jewish, Italian, and Slavic—immigrants would cause racial degeneration, and were forever citing the miscegenation and violence that lingered throughout the southern reaches of the country. And, as David Roediger has adroitly demonstrated, immigrants in dirty and dis-

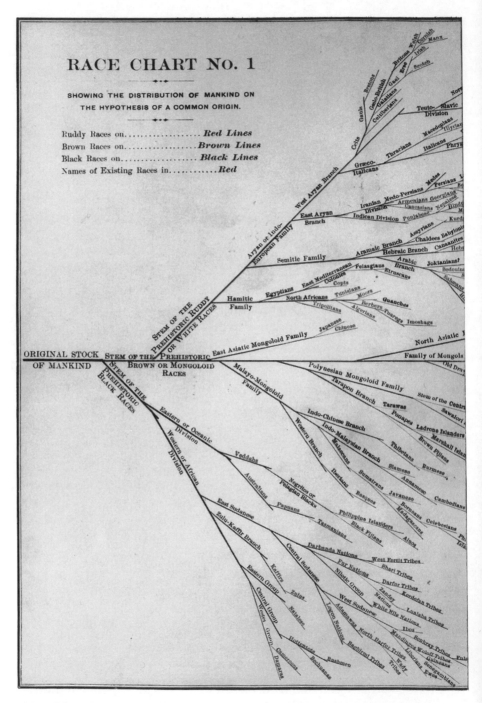

The problem of classification, as revealed in John Clark Ridpath's "Race Chart," published in *Great Races of Mankind* (1893).

ease-ridden cities routinely countered nativist assertions of racial difference with a determined focus on their own whiteness, on "the Negro," and
on slavery. "The Negro," then, was an omnipresent (if geographically and
politically distant) reminder of the myriad dangers posed by unrestricted
immigration—an object lesson in racial disharmony.[10]

For the moment, the North needed no further instruction in racial conflict. In Boston, New York, and Philadelphia, "Anglophiles" and Irish nationalists clashed, in the press and in the street, over the degeneration of
"the Anglo-Saxon" and the pitfalls of New York politics, Anglo-American
rapprochement, and the struggle to "save the soul" of Ireland. And this
prolonged, transatlantic conflict was understood as a "racial conflict"—as
a struggle between the destinies of "Celt" and "Anglo-Saxon." "We shall use
race and nation interchangeably," wrote the Anglo-Saxonist and Bostonian
John L. Brandt, who then admitted that "different nations have different
ideals, customs and religions that do not always harmonize." An unde-
clared race war threatened to disrupt American political culture as patricians sought to preserve Old Stock cultural authority, exacerbating fears of
a "clash of races" akin to that in Europe. Yet these tensions—which might
have encouraged a full-blown socialist labor movement—were ultimately
diffused or weakened by the urge toward assimilation and the desire for
"whiteness."[11] Again, as early as the mid-nineteenth century, Irish-American artisans and other working-class groups had shown their determination to be included in the American polity by carving out an ideological
space for themselves above "the Negro slave." By the end of that century,
immigrant groups—torn between racialized nationalist sympathies and
white solidarity—were suspended somewhere between the seductive inclusiveness of American whiteness and the evils of transatlantic Anglo-
Saxondom. Immigrant nationalist leaders may have secured their own
prominence by invoking the "Celtic" or "Jewish" race, but they also clung
to "whiteness" with great tenacity.[12]

Driven, in part, by these demographic factors, the quirks of racial classification were also fueled by the first stages of American imperialism. For
decades, belief in the "manifest destiny" of the United States to continue
the "restless, rushing wave of settlement" westward had been a cornerstone
of American nationalism. During the economic twists and turns of the
1890s, it became common to lament that those "frontier opportunities" for
imperial adventure had vanished, while yearning for a solution to the various "crises" posed by overproduction and underconsumption. If some excessively nervous Americans found solace from the modern world in the

arts and crafts movement, or, like Henry and Brooks Adams, in an appreciation of the medieval aesthetic, many others believed that an outward-
turned gaze would reveal new opportunities for the regeneration of manliness, civilization, and racial dominance. Like many of his contemporaries, Frederick Jackson Turner, the architect of the belief that the frontier
had been "closed," suggested that the "energies of expansion" could be
spent on "a vigorous foreign policy." And by 1900 Brooks Adams increasingly agreed.[13]

American jingoism soon found its patron saint in Theodore Roosevelt.
Challenged by the Spanish-American war, Roosevelt—a man Brooks Adams jealously dismissed in private as a "volatilized wom[a]n who [runs]
about in [a] motor car and can't keep still"—resigned his political office,
enlisted in the army as a cavalry officer, and charged headlong into American mythology. Dressed in a custom-fitted Brooks Brothers uniform, and
leading his ragtag collection of patrician ne'er-do-wells and social misfits
into battle, the charismatic Roosevelt came to embody the "manly" potential of expansionist American culture. For Teddy Roosevelt, violence and
strength were one and the same. "Did I tell you," he coyly asked his friend
Henry Cabot Lodge, "that I killed a Spaniard with my own hand?" Even
without a war in which to exercise one's manhood, Roosevelt averred, opportunities for "manly" work were manifest in the vibrancy of modernity,
or in the practical application of the ideal of the dynamo to the world. He
concluded his critical review of Brooks Adams's despairing work *The Law
of Civilization and Decay:*

> While there is a decrease in emotional religion, there is an immense in-
> crease in practical morality. There is a decrease of the martial type . . . ex-
> cept as it survives in the slums of great cities; but there remains a martial
> type infinitely more efficient than any that preceded it. There are great
> branches of industry which call forth in those that follow them more har-
> dihood, manliness, and courage than any industry of ancient times. The
> immense masses of men connected with the railroads are continually
> called upon to exercise qualities of mind and body, such as in antiquity
> no trade and no handicraft demanded. There are, it is true, influences at
> work to shake the vitality, courage, and manliness of the race; but there
> are other influences which tell in exactly the opposite direction.

Aside from domestic reform work and therapeutic sports, suggested Roosevelt, there was no better venue for the careful preservation of American

"hardihood, manliness, and courage" than war, "strife," and the steward-ship of empire.[14]

It was a propitious time to embark on an imperial adventure. By the 1890s the tendrils of empire and "civilization" circled the globe. The bick-ering nations of Europe, especially France, Great Britain, and Germany and to a lesser extent Portugal, Belgium, and Spain, had seized much of the world as their own, demystifying each and every "blank space of delightful mystery"—each "white patch" on the map of the world.[15] National pres-tige, military security, and economic profit were at stake, and war seemed always just around the corner. "The competitive parceling out of the world by superior peoples," one confident English essayist remarked dryly, "is, like all competition, a process which promotes health and energy; but it does not necessarily tend to peace."[16] The former British settler colonies, Australia and the United States, had now conquered their own unruly wild spots, slaughtering and confining the aboriginal peoples of their respec-tive continents, while the British themselves followed the same course in southern Africa. With white European supremacy nearly complete in the late 1890s, and with a renewed desire for newer markets and grander eco-nomic opportunities, diplomatic attention focused on China, an older civ-ilization thought to be on the decline.

In this context, America seemingly needed its own colonies. Inspired by Roosevelt, thirsting for an empire of their own, and troubled by a drasti-cally changed world, patrician Americans rallied around the banner of "civilization" and increasingly preached the manly virtues of "the race"—even if they disagreed on what, precisely, "race" meant. "Americans fearful about the dwindling potency of Victorian manhood," writes the histo-rian Gail Bederman, "found Roosevelt's formulations of racially dominant manhood exhilarating."[17] Anglo-Saxonism and the manly stewardship of empire quickly became integral parts of American popular culture, not just in novels, political cartoons, and world's fairs, but also in board games and in bestselling books like Trumbull White's *Our New Possessions,* sold door-to-door by salesmen representing the Empire Publishing Company. In the press and in Henry Adams's genteel parlor in Washington, D.C., the American acquisition of "coaling stations" in Hawaii and the Philippines was understood to be part of the eternal progression of the white light of Anglo-Saxon liberty and democracy.

With the advent of empire, Brooks Adams, at least, was convinced that the future no longer seemed so grim. "The seat of energy," concluded a reinvigorated and now moderately confident Adams, "has migrated from Europe to America." "Our Spanish war," he wrote to his brother, "marked the passage of the Atlantic by the centre of force, and velocity of movement. America is now the great point towards which all movement gravitates." In the process, Adams's Boston, home to American Anglo-Saxonism and one of the great economic hubs of the nineteenth century, lost its pride of place to Manhattan island. In Manhattan, the center of the emerging empire, the architects of the new consumer culture—advertisers, cultural critics, litterateurs, artists—grappled with the role of "America" in the progress of civilization. With supreme confidence, American banks, businesses, and technocrats wove the United States into the fabric of world commerce and political life. "The vortex of the cyclone," Adams wrote, "is near New York. No such activity prevails elsewhere; nowhere are the undertakings so gigantic, nowhere is administration so perfect; nowhere are such masses of capital centralized in single hands."[18]

Imperial confidence, however, was always fleeting. Old Stock Americans waffled between confidence and crisis, between a belief in the superiority of the Anglo-Saxon race and a fear that "the race" could be corrupted through miscegenous relations with immigrants and "Negroes," and through the mere fact of overlordship in tropical climates. As the imperial adventure introduced "civilization" to "savagery," the process of natural selection seemed to be breaking down, raising questions about the wisdom of empire. Larger historical issues, such as the traditional belief that the republic should be an isolated exemplar of virtue rather than a benevolent manager in world affairs, or the sense that labor contractors were bringing in "hordes" of immigrants to replace American workers, likewise posed questions that demanded answers. "Wherever we have inferior and dependent races within our borders to-day," wailed the prominent anti-imperialist and president of Stanford University David Starr Jordan, "we have a political problem—'the Negro problem,' 'the Chinese problem,' 'the Indian problem' . . . in the tropics such problems are perennial and insoluble . . . These people in such a climate can never have self-government in the Anglo-Saxon sense. Whatever form of government we adopt, we shall in fact be slave-drivers, and the business of slave-driving shall reflect upon us." Despite the despairing conclusions of anti-imperialists, however, American capitalism and *Imperialistus americanus*—and not the isolationists—emerged triumphant from the turn-of-the-century debates about empire.[19]

Throughout the Gilded Age, representations of "the Negro" encouraged widespread faith in herrenvolk democracy. But soon after Teddy Roosevelt's post-presidential safari to Africa, striking photographic images of the "Dark Continent" became increasingly popular in American consumer culture. Emblazoned with images of lion-hunting, tropical jungles, and "the white man's burden," tiny postcards purchased by the public spread these images from Manhattan to Los Angeles, as did the daily press, the Progressive monthlies, and the emergent profession of advertising. It had taken the major European powers just under thirty years to devour the vastness of Africa—to define, and then to make subject, each parcel of territory claimed in the name of "Civilization, Commerce, and Christianity." Now, watching their former president (the manly embodiment of jingoism) stride across the killing fields of Old World imperialism, many Americans recognized a connectedness between their own peculiar sense of destiny and mission and the nearly absolute domination of Africa and Africans by the larger white world. "Imperialism," suggests John Higham, "left a heritage of race-feelings that enriched the emotional appeal of Anglo-Saxon nativism."[20]

But the hullabaloo about TR and empire could not solve the problem of classification. Increased interaction and political conflict with people of color in the Philippines, China, and elsewhere did not encourage most Americans to think strictly in terms of color—or of whiteness more particularly—and Anglo-Saxonism, whiteness, and American nationalism continued to be very different things. Indeed, because the American empire over people of color came in the heyday of the "New Immigration" and in the face of increasing Irish-American nationalism, a general worsening of the problem of classification was perhaps inevitable. Even the garrulous Roosevelt, the patron saint of American chauvinism and general bullheadedness, constantly fudged racial distinctions, settling eventually for a heated disdain of "the hyphen" and a love of "the American," a racial amalgam of Anglo-Saxons, Teutons, and "properly Americanized" immigrants.[21] The "alien menace," in short, continued to complicate whiteness.

By the end of his second term in office, Teddy Roosevelt's presidency had assured the United States of a voice in world politics. With the conclusion of the Great War, however, Brooks Adams lost faith in Anglo-Saxon America yet again. Adams turned his family home into a museum of the race's past, organizing gifts, portraits, and furniture for public viewing in the future, with the grandest shrines reserved for his distinguished grandfather and great-grandfather and his beloved older brother, Henry.[22] When he looked back on the history of the Adams family, he saw only the faded glory of his own life, the youngest and least distinguished member of the youngest and weakest generation. He was living proof, he believed, that the end of Anglo-Saxonism was at hand, and that the end of his life would mark the completion of one cycle of history. In 1916, embittered, depressed, and, as always, prone to read dystopian works on race and history, he is likely to have read a new and exciting work by a young attorney from New York, entitled *The Passing of the Great Race,* a work that owed much to his own classic, *The Law of Civilization and Decay,* and that similarly bemoaned the ruthless advances of capitalism and "the Jew." Sitting in his father's library, surrounded by one of the most extensive private collections of political theory in the United States, a somber Brooks Adams might also have wondered why Madison Grant, the author of that wartime "blockbuster," repeatedly doubted whether the great old Anglo-Saxon race had ever really existed.

## Absolute Whiteness

In 1883, when Teddy Roosevelt was a young member of the New York legislature with an uncertain future in politics, he embarked on a personal adventure in the American West that changed his life. Hunting and fishing—life in the wilderness generally—reinvigorated him and restored his sense of "manliness." He triumphantly returned to public life as the manly champion of political vigor and outdoor sport, or "the strenuous life." Four years later Roosevelt put together the "Boone and Crockett Club," a gentlemen's hunting club that would soon include the likes of the naturalist George Bird Grinnell, the novelist Owen Wister, and the Manhattanite Winthrop Chanler. Within a matter of years the Boone and Crockett Club expanded its mission, becoming far more than a vehicle for the therapeutic rejuvenation of overcivilized patricians. Concerned that wild game was vanishing in the East and the West, Roosevelt and his fellow amateur naturalists worked to develop a national park in the West and to regulate hunting in the East. In both of these reform efforts, young Madison Grant—an eager attorney of colonial pedigree, ample means, and patrician temperament—was remarkably helpful, hobnobbing with legislators and drafting bills for consideration. Indeed, nearly forty years later, William Temple Hornaday would give Grant the lion's share of credit for the pivotal early successes of the Conservation movement.[23]

Tall and strikingly handsome, Madison Grant had been born and raised in a world defined by aristocratic privilege. His father, the wealthy Gabriel Grant, was a doctor "of Scottish abstraction," a battlefield surgeon and Congressional Medal of Honor winner during the Civil War, and an early public health care reformer in the city of Newark. His mother, Caroline Amelia Manice, belonged to a well-to-do family with roots back to the old Dutch colony of New Amsterdam, and hailing more recently from the Old Stock community of Jamaica, New York. The oldest of four children, young Madison—like countless other wealthy patrician children—was blessed with extensive private schooling. He also lived for several years in Dresden, Germany, and traveled throughout Europe and Asia on the traditional Victorian "grand tour." Together with his family pedigree, degrees from Yale (B.A., 1887) and Columbia (LL.B., 1890) gained him membership in the myriad upper-crust clubs of the Northeast, among them the Knickerbocker, Union, and Turf and Field Clubs. A sizeable inheritance also left him free to pursue a life of aristocratic ease and republican disinterestedness. Early efforts at political reform soon followed, as Madison and his younger brother DeForrest took up the banner of "progressivism" against the myriad evils of immigrant Tammany Hall. Soon Madison's penchant for genealogy and heredity—his pride in his lineage—would lend itself to activities in various scientific organizations involved in eugenics, breeding, and conservation. "A Park Avenue bachelor," John Higham once noted, "he was the most lordly of patricians."[24]

As the son of a northern Civil War surgeon and public health reformer, as a fellow Progressive and friend of Theodore Roosevelt, and as the mentor of a generation of eugenicists and conservative reactionaries, Grant, with his patrician activism, reflected a long-standing desire for order and authority among Old Stock Americans. Writing after Grant's death in 1937, Fairfield Osborn distilled the general essence of his life this way: "A man of distinguished appearance, over six feet tall and of very upright carriage, a meticulous dresser, he had a great self assurance, was formidable in discussion or debate, and had great tenacity in carrying through any project or idea." He was, an anonymous admirer would later write, "a man of forceful character and marked executive ability, intensely loyal and possessing a deep sense of honor." Grant's supposed tenacity is less revealing than the earnest desire for order—or for meticulousness—reflected in his always perfectly trimmed mustache and his stiff, precise "upright carriage." His warped Mendelian eugenics, made famous during the Great War, was similarly designed to impose order on a chaotic and unruly world through

A dapper Madison Grant, ca. 1925.

the construction of a simple racial taxonomy. This taxonomic project—the grandest public manifestation of Grant's character—received its most obvious expression in his algebraic assertion that "the result of the mixture of two races . . . gives us a race reverting to the more ancient, generalized and lower type . . . The cross between a white man and an Indian is an Indian; the cross between a white man and a negro is a negro . . . the cross between any of the three European races and a Jew is a Jew."[25]

After working to elect New York's reform mayor, William Strong, in 1894, Grant used his Boone and Crockett Club connections to become involved in the great Progressive Era tradition of institution-building—

colored, of course, by his aristocratic sensibilities. After some consideration, Grant proposed to Roosevelt that the Club support a wildlife park in the undeveloped southern tip of New York State (now incorporated into New York City as Bronx County). The result was the Bronx Zoo, an expansive park run by the New York Zoological Society, of which Grant was a founding member. Grant's amateur naturalism, rooted in his youthful collection of rare reptiles, now flourished, and a series of scientifically impressive publications and public honors followed. For the next twenty years, Grant, George Bird Grinnell, and other refined Americans would be the driving forces of the Conservation movement, preserving the redwoods, enacting national and state legislation to protect animal life, and developing an extensive system of national parks—efforts designed to "preserve to future generations some remnant of the heritage which was our father's." If some patrician Victorians found manly satisfaction in political reform movements, in a retreat to medievalism, or in a headlong rush into imperialism, Grant found a similar sense of worth, purpose, and authority in the preservation of the natural world—in the invention of "wilderness."[26]

The attorney and naturalist did not, however, limit his activities to conservation, and was remarkably active in other, somewhat less romantic, pursuits. Working to preserve the natural world, Grant believed, necessitated a careful study of race and breeding. His leadership role in the budding Conservation movement was thus accompanied by active involvement in the eugenics movement, the Immigration Restriction League, and, later, postwar superpatriotism. In this sweeping approach to naturalism, Grant was a typical Progressive—a true "joiner" if ever there was one. Perpetually nervous about the state of the republic, and inspired by the grand New England tradition of nativism, Grant embodied Richard Hofstadter's classic description of the Progressives as conservative anti-Semites, paranoid fascists, and zealous rivals of the upstart robber barons. His proto-environmentalism—from his early work with the Boone and Crockett Club to his "Save the Redwoods" campaign of 1919—was rooted in a fearful reaction to the frightening realities of the modern world. The growth of cultural institutions in the early twentieth century was an integral part of patrician efforts to resolidify cultural authority and social status. By attempting to control public representations of nature, for instance, Carl Akeley's dioramas at the American Museum of Natural History were part of a larger, concerted effort to dictate the rules of social relations through subtler, less overtly coercive means. Nearly every facet of Grant's life, from his work on genetics to his steadfast refusal to allow amateur photographers into what later became the Bronx Zoo, reflected a similar desire for social order and patrician authority.[27]

That insatiable hunger for cultural fixedness was most profoundly expressed in Grant's interest in racial classification, which grew out of the great turn-of-the-century debate over the "alien menace." By the 1880s Irish immigration had slowed considerably, and subsequent legislation restricting Asian immigration—driven through Congress by West Coast fears of a "Yellow Peril"—had quieted the vocal advocates of immigration restriction in American political culture. The nature of immigration, however, soon changed again, bringing ever-larger numbers of southern and eastern Europeans—largely Catholics, or "Slavs"—to the United States. Patrician concerns about this "New Immigration" reached a fevered peak with the publication of the terrifying conclusions of the United States Immigration Commission headed by Senator William Paul Dillingham, which had concluded that an astounding sixty percent of American employees were foreign-born. The idyllic Victorian past—a world of presumed pristine neatness and order—had been ruined by the scale and type of immigration. The hysterical public reaction to the findings of the Dillingham Commission—couched in multiple scientific volumes, including a *Dictionary of Races and Peoples*—hinted that the "alien menace" had, once again, become a political dilemma of the first order.[28]

In the face of this new threat, the glamour of applied science lent credibility to a wide variety of figures—scientists, novelists, agitators—who presumed to be public experts of one sort or another on "the alien menace." The New Jersey educator Henry H. Goddard, for instance, armed himself with legions of female "testers" whose "natural" intuitive abilities made them perfect for the task of classifying immigrants, and developed a taxonomy of types—a unilinear scale of intellectual ability—terming "moron" those "high-grade defectives" who were capable of functioning in modern life, but whose genetic material was dangerously flawed.[29] The "menace," Goddard and others argued forcefully, could be clearly seen in the faces and bodies of the new immigrants arriving at Ellis Island. The sociologist Edward A. Ross, bemoaning the loss of the "pioneering type" in the American genetic pool, suggested that "twenty per cent" of eastern and southern European immigrants were "hirsute, low-browed, big-faced persons of obviously low mentality. In every face there was something wrong—lips thick, mouth coarse, upper lip too long, cheek bones too high, chin poorly formed, the bridge of the nose hollowed . . . there were so many sugar-loaf heads, moon-faces, slit-mouths, lantern-jaws, and goose-bill noses that one might imagine a malicious jinn had amused himself by casting human beings in a set of skew-molds discarded by the Creator." Novelists and pulp fiction writers popularized stereotypes of the crafty, superstitious Italian and the German "brutish brute," or, in at least one case, used "Slavic"-sounding names for primitive beasts—the great pale apes of Edgar Rice Burroughs's *Tarzan of the Apes*.[30]

Something had gone terribly wrong, and Grant, in true Progressive Era fashion, set out to fix it with his first foray into middlebrow consumer culture—with the popularly written scientific treatise he entitled *The Passing of the Great Race*. Published in 1916, with a war raging in Europe and with questions about the future of the republic plaguing American politics, *Passing* captured one patrician generation's angst in language and symbols that were soon central to American political culture. Pressed deeply into the blue cover of the book, an irregular golden hexagon drew for prospective readers a frightening analogy between the lost "racial civilizations" of the past and the endangered American civilization built by men like Grant's father, the stalwart Civil War veteran to whom the book was dedicated. "If the Melting Pot is allowed to boil without control," Grant intoned, "and we continue to . . . deliberately blind ourselves to all 'distinctions of race, creed, and color,' the type of native American of Colonial descent will become as extinct as the Athenian of the age of Pericles, and the Viking of the days of Rollo." Grant's pantheon of heroes (Rollo, Pericles, and his own father) included all worthwhile champions of "honor," "virtue," and battlefield prowess—men, in other words. The masculinist legacy of the Civil War generation of heroes—assumed to possess sterling Mayflower pedigree—would soon be lost, Grant surmised, if the idea of "the melting pot" was allowed to triumph.[31]

Appearing after the Dillingham Commission and in the midst of a national craze for scientific precision and expert knowledge, *Passing*—Grant's public sermon on the "race question"—became a bestseller of great and lasting cultural importance. In the simplest of terms, Grant spelled out the roots of race-suicide: immigration, alcoholism, and a lack of historical perspective, failings that betrayed a dangerous lack of "race-consciousness." The zeal and passion of *Passing's* prose masked the cunning, authoritarian undertones of Grant's scientific practice. If Grant exposed the key threats to the republic, his eugenic solutions were decidedly antidemocratic. "It would not be a matter of great difficulty," he offered casually, "to secure a general consensus of public opinion as to the least desirable, let us say, ten per cent of the community. When this unemployed and unemployable human residuum has been eliminated, together with the great mass of crime, poverty, alcoholism, and feeblemindedness associated therewith, it would be easy to consider the advisability of further restricting the perpetuation of the then remaining least valuable types. By this method mankind might ultimately become sufficiently intelligent to deliberately choose the most vital and intellectual strains to carry on the race."[32]

*Passing* was Grant's attempt to get this message out—to convince his fellow patricians of the clear and present danger posed by unrestricted immigration, moral laxity, and the absence of race-consciousness. Building a better American meant breeding a better American or, perhaps more correctly, it meant making sure that the right people were doing the breeding. A scientific taxonomy and classification of race, popularized in the eugenic conclusions of *The Passing of the Great Race,* were thus to be the handmaidens of a much-needed return to hierarchy and order. So urgent was this task, and so important was *Passing* to the resurrection of patrician race-consciousness, that Grant was a tireless advocate for its sale, becoming a bother to booksellers throughout Manhattan, chiding them publicly when his book sold out, and routinely pestering his publisher about the stock, display, and advertisement of his masterpiece.[33]

In an age of widespread literacy, a powerful message required a potent science that everyone could understand. Science, many Americans had come to believe, could solve anything. Enamored of eugenics, the institutionalized science of breeding better racial stock, Grant sought to create public support for the rigorous application of the new science of inheritance, Mendelian genetics, to the American race problem. Genetics, as Grant and his contemporaries understood it, focused on "discontinuous variation"—those "characteristics inherited on an all or nothing basis"— that appeared in the wake of hybridization. Progressive Era interpreters of Gregor Mendel's experiments argued that when two "pure" strains, or races, were crossbred, the first hybrid generation contained the "traits" of both strains, with one trait proving dominant while the other became "recessive."[34]

Warping Mendel to suggest that the "traits" of inferior races inevitably achieved dominance in hybrid progeny, Grant sought to chart mathematically the future of all mixed-race offspring, developing what amounted to a streamlined racial taxonomy. In a grim stroke of genius, he reduced all the complicated, wordy discourse of the American science of inheritance down to the simplest of formulas: "Nordics"—the biologically and qualitatively "superior" stock of northwestern Europe—should breed only with other Nordics, and not with inferior stock from southern Europe, Jews, or "the darker races." The "cross between a white man and a Jew," Grant concluded, "is a Jew."[35] "Race-consciousness" and eugenics were the answer to America's problem. All the high-minded reform rhetoric about environment—or "nurture"—was, Grant argued, nonsense, for no amount of government regulation and workplace reform could change the genetic potential of inferior stock already in the United States. Legislating morality was impossible, he continued, but you could *breed* a better moral citizen if you had laws on the books against miscegenation and in favor of the sterilization and segregation of lesser, "immoral" races.

If Grant advocated eugenics to undo the physical damage done to Nordic America by "alien stock," he urged immigration reform to undermine the insidious interests of big business. Like Roosevelt and Brooks Adams before him, Grant understood the corrosive qualities of modern American political culture in the context of the history of immodest national expansion and exploitative labor relations. In order to facilitate the "haste" and "extravagance" of national expansion, Grant argued, "inferior" immigrant labor was brought in, degrading the value of hard, manly work among white Nordics. When most available work seemed tainted by the presence of "a polyglot mass of aliens," Nordics stopped having children. "For every immigrant arriving," Grant wrote, "one American was not born." Nineteenth-century Americans had failed to heed the warning of the founding fathers—men who, Grant suggested, were adamantly opposed to open immigration. Blinded by greed, industrial interests had brought in "inferior stock," were "extravagantly wasteful" in developing the nation, and had fostered the development of "colonies of foreigners" to suit their own needs and not the needs of the republic. The excesses of the House of Morgan could only be combated through moral reform, immigration restriction, and governmental regulation—though Grant gamely offered that a "repeal [of] our Contract Labour laws" and the use of exclusively male Chinese laborers bound to tedious servitude would help big business cope with the loss of "the immigrant."[36] Grant's eugenic sensibilities, then, were partly rooted in a Rooseveltian disgust with the injudicious excesses of American capitalism. The perils of immigration and the dangers of business excess, however, were hardly new problems in the 1910s.

War—the Great War in Europe—was a more immediate catalyst of Grant's eugenic fulminations. With "evolution" serving as one of the key organizing metaphors of the Gilded Age, late-nineteenth- and early-twentieth-century Americans (led by the irrepressible Roosevelt) envisioned war itself as "eugenic," assuming that the superior races inevitably triumphed over the inferior races in a hypermasculine Darwinian struggle for the survival of the fittest. In *Passing*, however, Grant based his arguments for a resurgent "race-consciousness" on the disastrous unintended consequence of the conflagration in Europe: the "suicide" of the Nordic race. In contrast to those who argued for the centrality of "struggle" in weeding out the unfit, Grant argued—as the American Museum of Natural History paleontologist Henry Fairfield Osborn put it—that "war is in the highest sense dysgenic . . . It is destructive of the best strains, spiritually, morally, and physically." Disaster appeared to be at hand, Grant surmised, for Nordics were killing Nordics in the Old World: "From a race point of view, the present European conflict is essentially a civil war and nearly all of the officers and a large proportion of the men on both sides are members of [the Nordic] race." Ironically, the same physical and psychological traits which Grant so admired in Nordic men—most notably their warrior instincts and physical prowess— left them ideally suited to warfare, thus making the Great War an exercise in "race suicide."[37]

European Nordics, overly obsessed with their national origins, were betraying "race" for nation. Grant ultimately rested his revolutionary understanding of the Great War as "race suicide" on the "sociological" understanding of "race" laid down by William Ripley. Following Ripley, Grant believed that genetic material alone—and not world-historical spirit, religion, language, or nationality—was constitutive of race; "racial lines," he argued, were "absolutely independent of both national and linguistic groupings." There were, Grant maintained, three races in Europe: the Nordic, the Alpine, and the Mediterranean. The pure white Nordic race, qualitatively superior to the terrible and dusky Alpine and Mediterranean races of eastern and southern Europe, could be found throughout the world in positions of power and influence. The Great War, then, was a tragedy of epic proportions, an "old story of mutual butchery and mutual destruction between Nordics . . . [and] the modern edition of the old berserker blood rage."[38]

In an interesting and important twist, the two groups whose status formed the bedrock of American racial discourse in the nineteenth century were not prominently represented in *Passing of the Great Race*.[39] The in-

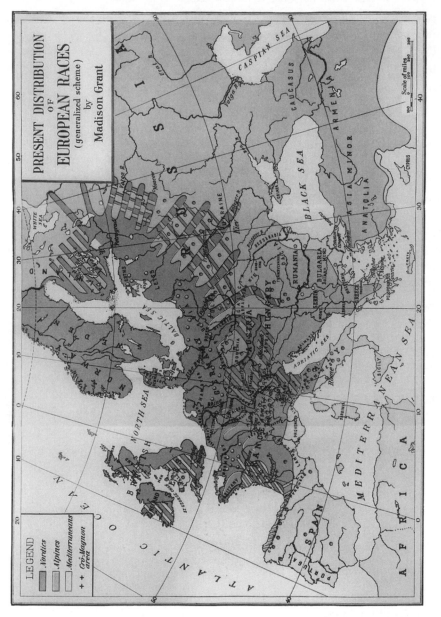

Madison Grant's early notion of transnational "Nordicism," published in *The Passing of the Great Race* (1916).

creasingly powerful (and assimilated) Irish in America found themselves subsumed—albeit somewhat unwillingly—into the folds of Nordicism, with Irish-American nationalism understood to be a sort of false "race-consciousness." Only the Irish in the far West of Ireland were of the "middle Paleolithic race."[40] African Americans were regarded with little, if any, fear. "The Negro problem," Grant suggested, seemed fixed in its "place" in the South, and so long as people of African descent remained there on rural, segregated farms they would be welcome in America. Indeed, Grant attributed the enviable fluorescence of race-consciousness in the South directly to the physical presence of African Americans, and expressed admiration for the legislative machinery of Jim Crow. The inclusion of the Irish in Nordicism and the reluctance to consider "the Negro" in Africa or in the American South as a threat mark Grant's work as decidedly different in tone and content from the "negrophobic" works of Thomas Dixon and D. W. Griffith. It also testifies to the continued disjunction between the symbolic economy of racial classification in the Northeast and that in the South in 1916.[41] Casting about for a northern equivalent of "the Negro," Grant erected clear and immutable boundaries between Nordicism and the newly arrived "Mediterraneans," or "Jews," but found northeastern political culture lacking the urgency of race professed in the deep South. The return of popular race-consciousness in the North might, he believed, help to secure the passage of national legislation that would end the influx of undesirables and protect the white working classes from competition with these purportedly fecund races.

Disgusted with those who still wrestled with the problems of classification, and in contrast to those Europeans who continued to focus on national differences, Grant spoke lovingly of whiteness in a singular, or more global and inclusive sense, and thus considered racial identity as far larger than national or regional identity. If, Grant argued, "racial lines" were "absolutely independent" of national and linguistic boundaries, then the *real* lines of racial difference "cut through [language and nationalism] at sharp angles and correspond[ed] closely with the divisions of social cleavage."[42] In short, racial classifications were one with the social boundaries created by economic stratification. "Race," he would offer confidently, "is the greatest of all privileges." Members of the Nordic race, if they hoped to secure their tenuous grasp on world domination and genetic magnificence, needed to recognize the transnational, transreligious, translinguistic, and transatlantic nature of their racial identity. *The Passing of the Great Race* was, in John Higham's words, "a defense of both class and racial consciousness, the former being dependant on the latter." A renewed "race-consciousness," then, was an awakened class-consciousness. But if Nordics were a transnational racial ruling class, then the Great War, tragically, was "class suicide on a gigantic scale." The biological, technological, cultural, and economic superiority of the Nordic world was ultimately assured only by a shared and heightened sense of "race-consciousness" that mimicked class-consciousness; "race," the prophet of the Nordic vogue later put it, "all is race."[43]

The arrival of absolute whiteness also signaled the emergence of a new masculine sensibility in American political culture, a fact not lost upon some women readers of *The Passing of the Great Race*. In the spring of 1918, for instance, Margaret Bradshaw purchased a copy of *Passing*. A woman of means and character, Bradshaw might have had a dozen reasons for the purchase: from an aristocratic penchant for racial chauvinism to an intellectual and literary interest in a book which was gathering considerable word-of-mouth buzz and which would soon be a postwar blockbuster. Or perhaps she—like many others—recognized the explicit eugenic pacifism of *Passing*, best captured in its much-repeated conclusion that the Great War was "race suicide."

After reading the book, however, Bradshaw could barely contain her disgust with its failure to live up to its eugenic pacifist credentials. In a seething letter to Grant's publisher, she lambasted Charles Scribner's Sons for issuing such a dangerous book, accusing both Grant and Scribner's of celebrating a distinctly masculine culture of violence and thus of provoking the Great War then raging in Europe. In response, the Scribner's publicist invoked race, commenting upon the transnational "race-consciousness," or Nordicism, that suffused Grant's work. *Passing*, the publicist averred, was one of the first "scientific" works of the twentieth century to argue for something akin to pan-whiteness, lumping nearly all of northern Europe into the "ivory whiteness" of the Nordic race. "I appreciate the point you make that he includes all the belligerents in this war in the Nordic Race," Bradshaw wrote in her second letter to Scribner's, "[but] the whole book extols aristocracy and apparently the aristocracy of physical force." Bradshaw further complained that Grant (unlike Brooks Adams before him) had described art and intellectualism—the hallmarks, she thought, of civilization itself—as the province of the decidedly inferior and unmanly Mediterranean race. Violence and masculine dominance, it seemed, were the supreme markers of racial superiority. The troubling correspondence with Bradshaw was eventually forwarded to Grant himself, who promised his editor, the literary giant Maxwell Perkins, that he would "try to smoothe down her ruffled, patriotic plumes."[44]

As Bradshaw recognized, the enthusiasm for Nordicism in the northeastern United States rested upon an unusually potent masculine ethos. In contrast to much of the previous literature on race, for instance, *Passing* offered "race-consciousness" as a wholly masculine endeavor, and in the process partly severed—or at least transformed—the foundational connections between womanhood and race. Turn-of-the-century Americans understood civilized "manliness" (which meant Anglo-Saxon manliness) in terms of strict self-control and the denial of all "base" or "primitive" instincts. The carefully delineated concept of "womanhood" was absolutely central to this Victorian racial sensibility. As guardians of the home and hearth, women purportedly inculcated values, character, and principle in their children, which would then be passed on, ensuring the continued progress of civilization. In short, women "nurtured" young people to proper racial maturity, and thus the concept of womanhood—its preservation, protection, and veneration—was the very foundation of civilization and evolution. This idealization and the evolutionary discourse that lay beneath it were a source of feminist strength and weakness in the 1890s: the basis of feminist claims to a redress of political grievances and the root cause of racial segregation in the woman's movement.[45]

Madison Grant's idealization of men—of the male body and of the connection between men's work and race-consciousness—may also have reflected a personal distaste for certain kinds of women. He was a lifelong bachelor prone to impassioned commemoration of the power of the male body, and his treatment of Margaret Bradshaw and his appreciation of the masculine realm revealed the mind of a man who would later smugly conclude that all "women are queer." In his pseudonymously published novel of 1931, *Hank, His Lies and His Yarns,* Grant would save his longest chapter for this exact subject, entitling it "The Man Who Understood Women." Therein, Bill, an unattractive balding man of recent wealth in a frontier town, hoodwinks the pretty Nell into a sexual relationship through complex trickery—trickery too complex for her, we are to assume, but deemed entirely appropriate by "the Major," the well-heeled and self-consciously handsome narrator who stands in for Grant. Women were, for Grant, odd and useless creatures and impossible to understand; hence *Passing* left them no place in the august work of race-consciousness.[46]

Abandoning sentimentality about race and womanhood, Grant's *Pass-*

*ing of the Great Race* was an astounding monument to the increasing homoeroticism and militarism of American culture. Again, the conflict in Europe was, in part, to blame. With the world torn apart by war, the turn toward military preparedness brought with it a veneration of male prowess in battle and American manhood. On a deeper level, however, the gendered bluster of turn-of-the-century jingoism—embodied in the still quite active Teddy Roosevelt—had bequeathed a strikingly potent intellectual legacy to the preparedness campaigns: an encyclopedia of images, keywords, and ideal "manly" types to inspire the younger generation of American patriots facing the Great War. Manhood, these youthful enthusiasts of the nascent 100 Percent Americanism movement argued, was the cornerstone of any civilization. Grant's strict adherence to this supposed iron law of American nationalism—his conflation of Nordicism with Americanism and manhood—was, then, a testament to the continued personal influence of his old friend Roosevelt, as well as to the broader gendered context of wartime American culture.

Discarding much of nineteenth-century racial science, Grant, in his obsession with Mendelian genetics and "the new science of race," emphasized—above everything else—the biological basis of race and race traits. The body, and not the home, was the foundation of the success or failure of the race. Biological capital was all that mattered. Nordicism, for Grant, was thus synonymous with masculinity: with the emergent conception of maleness that, in contrast to Victorian notions of manliness, included "barely restrained masculine violence" as a desirable male behavior. Nordics, Grant suggested, were not just physically perfect but also "domineering, individualistic, self-reliant and jealous of their personal freedom . . . chivalry and knighthood . . . are peculiarly Nordic traits." Nordics were warriors all, violent, lusty "blond giants . . . everywhere the type of the sailor, the soldier, and adventurer, and the pioneer." Not surprisingly, when Grant comments in *Passing* on the role of women he does so disparagingly, as if women, even Nordic women, were the equivalent of inferior races. "Women," Grant averred, "tend to exhibit the older, more generalized and primitive traits of the race's past . . . and retain the ancient and intuitive knowledge that the great mass of mankind is . . . bond and unequal."[47]

The emphasis on the power of applied science found in *Passing* intersected the wartime bureaucrat's love of professionals and experts. Indeed, in an age of experts, paperwork and data collection, Grant's text quickly became part of a public discourse on citizenship and fitness for self-governance. Military intelligence testing—the most public expression of the sentiments found in the educator Goddard's scientific examination of the "ill-bred" and supposedly defective Kallikak family—did more than reveal the paucity of "good stock" in the armed forces, for it also spread the news about what, exactly, "intelligence" meant to the zealous corps of expert psychologists. "The application of psychology . . . to war," boasted Robert M. Yerkes, chairman of the Research Information Service of the National Research Council, "advertised it widely and favorably and created an unprecedented demand for its services."[48] Watching Yerkes organize his psychological tests over the summer of 1917, Grant began to wonder whether eugenics—or, more generally, the "new science" of genetics—might have something of equal value to offer the wartime machine.

With the advent of American militarism, Grant jumped on the patriotic bandwagon, and offered his expertise in racial classification to the U.S. Army. Together with Charles Davenport, head of the Eugenics Research Office in Cold Spring Harbor, New York, Grant proposed an "Anthropological Committee" of the National Research Council, reorganized during the war as the Department of Science and Research of the Council of National Defense. Davenport and Grant labored to develop a complicated form containing a series of questions about a given enlisted man's body—focusing, for instance, on eye color, skin color, and head shape. The director of this remarkable venture would be in charge of all "racial and physical anthropometric matters in the army and navy," and would directly assist division surgeons with "racial problems"—problems that were understood only in terms of classification, and phrased as "Is this person to be classified as a white or a negro?"[49] Aided by a few carefully selected and well-trained physicians, Grant and Davenport mounted a massive taxonomic project: the systematic physical examination of tens of thousands of American troops for evidence of racial type. The data generated by this ambitious enterprise would, they hoped, be published after the war and would help generate public enthusiasm for a meaningful and lasting restriction of immigration.[50]

Nordicism would quickly become a postwar phenomenon precisely because it solved so many difficult political problems. In the midst of a terrible war fought in the Old World, and riddled with doubt about the ability of the republic to assimilate its immigrant population, patrician Americans increasingly preached the virtues of consensus. "No Hyphens!" they cried, arguing that loyalty and patriotism demanded an end to each and every manifestation of immigrant "difference." Immigrants, many hoped, would lose themselves in a powerful state patriotism, in loyalty not just to the English language, or to the nation, but to the race—to whiteness even more specifically. As one of the foremost leaders of the move to restrict immigration, Madison Grant brought his commitment to restriction and his thirst for eugenics together with a passionate enthusiasm for the "ivory whiteness" of the Nordic race. But Nordicism, despite its roots in Grantian eugenics and restriction, was also an integral part of the emerging consensual culture of "absolute whiteness," in which some crucial immigrant groups, especially the unruly Irish, were either no longer envisioned as racially different or no longer seen as a "problem." In short, Grant's petulant (and persistent) disgust with the assimilative qualities of "the melting pot" was transformed by postwar circumstance into a popular animosity toward "the hyphen"—toward those who resisted assimilation.

"The term 'Nordic,'" Grant once wrote to Lothrop Stoddard, "is a pet baby of mine." At the bottom of it all, *Passing* was a quintessentially "New York" work on nativism, catering to the selfish patrician anxieties of Manhattan's "Old Stock," composed largely of Dutch, English, and French "stock." But the wider circle of the Nordic pale and the seductive lure of masculine aristocracy would have a far broader appeal than Grant had ever imagined or desired. By the end of the Great War, *Passing* had a good deal of excellent press. The journal of the American Historical Association lauded the "solid scientific and historical truth" behind Grant's sweeping arguments, while the *Nation* celebrated the work for its "admirable reaction from the extreme socialistic views" of the postwar era. Sixteen thousand copies would eventually be sold.[51] Despite his own elitism, then, Grant's *Passing* helped to make that singular word "Nordic" popular for the masses of white Americans. During and after the postwar Red Scare, the term appeared with greater and greater frequency in mass culture and in scientific and political discussions of race and race problems. Conservative literary critics bemoaning the avant-garde sensibilities of "the Literary Mohawks" turned to Nordicism in defense of old-fashioned literary classics and modern questions of character. Young novelists F. Scott Fitzgerald, Ernest Hemingway, and Sinclair Lewis wrote subtle commentaries on the Nordic vogue sweeping through Manhattan and American political culture during the 1920s. Nordic Leagues sprang up in the North, and the increasingly powerful Ku Klux Klan readily used the "Nordic" as its ideal type—and these two organizations would later be deliberately confused by the satirist George Schuyler as "the Knights of Nordica."[52]

The postwar effect of this Nordic vogue was quite remarkable. Celebrating the optical qualities of race—"ivory whiteness" above all else—Grant's work, and the cult of Nordicism that soon surrounded it, made it possible for anyone who spoke English, looked "white," and subscribed to state patriotism (the new American religion) to lay claim to the civic privileges of Nordicism. This new sense of race was rooted not just in science, not just in an evolving political economy of racial difference, but also in a new visual sense of what race looked like. "The great lesson of the science of race," Grant argued, "is the immutability of somatical or bodily characters." The visual markers of race, in short, had been transformed, with the most noticeable markers of race being skin color and the shape of the head. But, forgiving Grant's oft-expressed enthusiasm for the "long-headed" Nordic, his desire to popularize the "bodily characters" of race, and to simplify racial identification and classification, came together most powerfully in his discussions of "ivory whiteness." "The Nordic race," he mused, "in its purity has an absolutely fair skin, and is consequently the *Homo albus,* the white man par excellence." The high priest of Nordicism had thus found a very popular message: the veneration of whiteness.[53]

Much like *Passing of the Great Race,* Nordicism achieved its greatest significance after the Great War and during what has been called the "Red Scare." Faced with the disturbing Bolshevik Revolution in Russia, and struggling to cope with a postwar economic downturn, patrician Americans began to see dissenters—alien "Bolsheviki"—everywhere. Radicalism and socialism lurked in the shadows, but especially in the working classes, whose rebellion against their betters would turn the world upside down. "The menace of Bolshevism," thundered Grant's disciple Lothrop Stoddard, "is simply incalculable. Bolshevism is a peril in some ways unprecedented in the world's history. It is not merely a war against our civilization; it is a war of the hand against the brain. For the first time since man was man there is a definite schism between the hand and the head. Every principle which mankind has thus evolved: community of interest, the solidarity of civilization, the dignity of labor, or muscle, of brawn, dominated and illumined by intellect and spirit—all these Bolshevism howls down and tramples in the mud."[54] Stoddard's fear and distrust of "Bolsheviki" was of a piece with the sense of the world as a living, hierarchical, economic system.

The institutional forces responsible for maintaining state patriotism during the war were pressed into service again in a more dangerous postwar conflict—a struggle "against chaos." The Department of Justice, the

Immigration Bureau, and local patriotic organizations stripped dissenters of constitutional rights, suppressed the advocates of "One Big Union," and stamped out radical cells throughout the country, whether they existed or not. Attorney General (and presidential hopeful) A. Mitchell Palmer brought the Red Scare to a fitting climax in 1920 with his breathtakingly antidemocratic deportation of thousands of a "alien radicals."[55]

As a congressional "expert" on eugenics, and as a trustee and active member of the American Defense Society (ADS), Madison Grant presided over the marriage of Nordic eugenics and superpatriotism to the institutional power of the postwar state. One of many groups devoted to exaggerated superpatriotism during the war, the ADS was Manhattan's answer to "the spirit of Bolshevism." Organizations like the ADS were not the lunatic fringe of American political culture; indeed, the remarkable postwar growth of such associations—the ADS membership rolls grew from 3,500 to 55,000 in 1918 alone—reminds us that anti-Bolshevism was at the center of postwar American life. During the Red Scare, the ADS, much like the larger American Protective League, infiltrated "radical" organizations, regularly sent information to the Military Intelligence Division, and orchestrated a more profound policing of American life. The postwar popularity of the ADS hinted that Grant's fellow patricians had awakened to the threat posed by the New Immigrant's "hereditary predisposition to undermine the Government"; "alien Socialists, Radicals, I.W.W.'s and Bolshevists," Grant admitted later, "served a very useful purpose in rousing Americans to the peril of an increase in their numbers."[56]

The program of the ADS closely reflected Grant's own concerns, blending interests in natural conservation, immigration reform, antiradicalism, and "Buy American" programs.[57] The connection between these facets of the late Progressive Era was a scientific thirst for efficiency, or, rather, patrician anger at the inefficient and wasteful development of America's natural, cultural, and biological resources. Grant suggested:

> In our haste to develop this continent since the Civil War, we have all been extravagantly wasteful in using our resources. We have killed all the wild game animals, we have cut down most of the forests, we have exhausted vast areas of virgin soil, we have polluted our streams and are destroying our coast fisheries, we have torn open the sides of the mountains for minerals, and are digging up our coal and draining off our oil at a prodigious rate. In order to do this in the shortest possible time, instead

of in the wisest possible manner, we have imported cheap alien labor and inaugurated an industrial era here. The result has been tremendous prosperity at the cost of the replacement . . . of the native American by a polyglot mass of aliens of every kind and description and the establishment of colonies of foreigners in our midst.[58]

Grant himself was an active member of two, remarkably different, ADS committees—one on Immigration and another on Natural Conservation. Biological capital, Grant believed, much like natural capital, needed the legal and institutional protection of the state. He encouraged other ADS leaders to contact his allies at the Immigration Restriction League, wangled concessions from federal officials about the appointment of a new Commissioner of Immigration in New York, agitated for the preservation of California's magnificent redwoods, and monitored the political sensibilities of his fellow New York patricians.[59]

Anti-Bolshevism required a defense of the capitalist order of things. Muting earlier anxieties about big business, Grant and the ADS organized hushed meetings with corporate executives, warned local and national officials of impending labor strife, and printed hundreds of thousands of anti-Bolshevist pamphlets to be given to employees with their paychecks.[60] Fearful of the demons of Bolshevism, patrician Americans reached out to assimilating immigrants and the working class even as they pushed dissenting elements of American society away. In contrast to those who professed devout patriotism to America, "hyphenated" immigrants—and especially Jews—were presumed to be racially distinct and bore the brunt of anti-Bolshevist Nordic authoritarianism. Nativism was now understood as class warfare; domestic economic strife was international racial strife bound up with national loyalties.

"Bolshevists," summed up Lothrop Stoddard, "are mostly born and not made." This theme of racial strife as class warfare emerged quite clearly at the Second International Congress of Eugenics, held at the American Museum of Natural History and organized by Grant and the paleontologist Henry Fairfield Osborn, especially in a public lecture by the aging French "racial anthropologist" and craniometrician Count Georges Vacher de Lapouge, a confidant of Grant's. "Anthropological analysis," Lapouge began, gesturing for effect at a massive landscape of the "glacial period" behind him, "reveals the existence of a superior white race and of inferior white races . . . It is the superior white race which, by virtue of its superior fitness, is now occupying the positions of social responsibility." "Be not mistaken," he howled, inflaming the old conflicts within whiteness, "the war of classes is a war of races."[61]

Political and popular culture increasingly emphasized the bounds of race, directing attention away from the gender strife of feminist radicalism. The ADS, for instance, routinely proposed "universal" military training (for boys only, of course), anxiously pointed out the supposedly racial threats to the nation, and confined a few carefully selected women to a nearly invisible auxiliary organization. Proliferating "Spider Web Charts"—some created by members of the ADS—exposed the dangerous connections between women's activism and the left, the "paired evils," as Nancy Cott terms them, "of feminism and socialism." "Right wing groups," Cott continues, "had a higher estimation of the coherence and power of the woman bloc than anyone else," and often accused feminists of "organizing women for class and sex war." To those who chose the American way of life—loyalty to Nordicism, to Americanization, to capitalism, and to patriarchy—the ADS and other like-minded organizations offered the olive branch of civic whiteness. To those who chose "hyphenism" or "pluralism," commonly equated with Bolshevism, feminism, and social revolution, they offered pain and suffering—represented most powerfully in the restriction of immigration and the antidemocratic excesses of the Red Scare. Dissent from the new order of things—fascistic patriarchy, pan-white supremacy, and postwar capitalism—indicated a lack of republican commitment, an absence of the qualities needed for proper citizenship. "Fascism," Bernhard Stern would later recall with Grant in mind, "discovered in patriotism an effective antidote to the spread of Communism."[62]

The "worship of the Nordic totem," as W. E. B. Du Bois called it, had become the supreme act of official patriotism and a fitting component of the Red Scare, paving the way for Grant's most cherished dream: serious restriction of immigration.[63] Temporary bills had been passed in 1921 and 1922, but only a permanent fix would satisfy the increasingly dominant conservative forces in American life. Grant, of course, was in the thick of the ensuing debate about immigration. As chair of the Eugenics Committee of the United States Committee on Selective Immigration, Grant had helped to write a report on immigration that argued for a drastic reduction of "aliens": cutting each group's potential number of immigrants down to two percent of the numbers of 1890. And the majority of white Americans agreed that "the alien menace" demanded sweeping national legislation on immigration, a different sort of attention from that required by "the Negro problem."

The confused interplay between "race," "nation," and "people," in the final bill owed more to the older report of the Dillingham Commission than to Grant. But whether hobnobbing with the influential Representative Albert Johnson, or offering sage advice to Harry Laughlin, the self-styled "House expert" on eugenics, Grant was one of the dominant forces shaping a permanent national policy on immigration. Pondering the reasons for restriction, House committee members huddled together on Capitol Hill, reading passages of *The Passing of the Great Race* to one another. Together with Charles Davenport, Grant controlled the flow of scientific information to Congress, trotting in Laughlin and Lothrop Stoddard, a member of the ADS's Committee on Revolutionary Movements, and ensuring that dangerous forces (notably Franz Boas) never got anywhere near the great debate. Legislators eventually submitted and passed unprecedented legislation—conceived in draft by Grant and others—linking immigration quotas to "national origins." And with the passage of this so-called National Origins Act in 1924, immigration from Southern and Eastern Europe, Asia, and the West Indies nearly ceased, prompting Du Bois to remark caustically that the "Nordic champions undoubtedly put one over on us."[64]

Grant's steady hand was also behind the passage of Virginia's Racial Integrity Law of 1925. In contrast to "national origins," however, the Racial Integrity Law replaced older classifications of "white" (resting on an ancestry fifteen-sixteenths "white") with ones in which any nonwhite blood rendered one, quite simply, not white at all. As before, Grant worked hard behind the scenes in determining the language of the legislation and in consolidating public support from very different quarters—the national Ku Klux Klan and members of Richmond's aristocratic "Anglo-Saxon Clubs."[65] The differences between the respective pieces of legislation—the Virginia law geared toward black/white relations, the federal legislation aimed at southern and eastern European and Asian immigrants—are significant. The logical gap between continued European immigration and American prosperity, it seemed, demanded that the influx of foreigners be stopped, but "the Negro" in the South was a different sort of problem, a problem that demanded legislation for social, physical, and biological separation. Through the mid-1920s, then, Grant continued to see significant differences in the racial dynamics of the industrialized North and the agricultural South, with the former burdened by an influx of undesirable labor brought into the republic at the behest of the robber barons, and the latter needing only tough legislation to protect against miscegenation with "Negroes." Regionally different racial dynamics thus continued, in Grant's mind, to require very different responses in 1924 and 1925—responses commonly understood as either nativist or negrophobic; discrimination within the pale, as it were, or without.

Even in the midst of the successful push toward the National Origins Act, however, there were signs that the segregation of "the Negro" was beginning to take national prominence over the perpetuation of the nativist tradition. When Harvard President A. Lawrence Lowell "surrender[ed] to the Bourbon South" and to the demands of Nordicism, simultaneously imposing a quota on the number of Jewish students admitted and segregating young African Americans from the freshman dorms, the response from Jewish intellectuals, well-heeled African Americans, and American pluralists was immediately forceful and, in the end, partly successful. The different types of discrimination, however, mirrored the differences between the National Origins Act and the Virginia Racial Integrity Law and hinted at a certain sensibility about race and the process of Americanization. In small numbers, it seemed, any European group could eventually be assimilated in the Nordic fold—into absolute whiteness; the same, apparently, could not be said for black folks. Many African Americans responded to the unequal discrimination against blacks and Jews at Harvard—and to the question of European immigration generally—by suggesting the opposite, by arguing that the "Negro problem" was inherently less difficult than that of "the Jew." Jews, many black leaders argued, were inassimilable, while "the Negro" was already "American." Du Bois, atypical among African Americans in his staunch pluralism, unwilling to privilege "the Negro" over "the Jew," and stunned by the apparent illiberalism of his alma mater, lambasted the entire process of Americanization—the streamlining of American culture to dispose of ethnic and racial anomalies within Nordicism—as the first step toward "the world rule of Nordic white through brute force." By raising the issue of color, and blackness and whiteness particularly, the Dormitory Crisis, as Du Bois understood, represented a possible threat to the very fabric of pluralism, to the very idea that the "fifty races of the world" could coexist in harmony in the United States.[66]

The Harvard Dormitory Crisis had also revealed the true contours of

American racial thinking: when push came to shove, the color line between "the Negro" and everyone else mattered far more to patrician Americans than the markers within whiteness. At certain critical moments in the history of the United States, that line between Americans of European descent and Americans of color had masked conflict within the pale of whiteness. In the seventeenth century, Virginia's aristocrats responded to the dangerous rebellion of Nathaniel Bacon—dangerous, in part, because it included several former slaves—with great force, afterward drawing clearer and clearer distinctions between whites and blacks, freedmen and slaves. Before the Civil War, Irish immigrants in northern cities had compensated for their increasing proletarianization and facilitated their assimilation by exposing the blackness of slaves in the deep South. Similarly, when faced with an influx of Chinese laborers deemed machine-like and effeminate, white wage laborers in California (many of them Irish) struck out at their darker competition and pushed for restrictive legislation that eventually closed the gate to Asian immigrants. And later, when African Americans moved in greater numbers into the industrial centers of post–World War II America, Italian and eastern European immigrants earned their whiteness by firebombing black homes, stoning black businesses, and fighting integrationist politicians with their votes, voices, and dollars. The Harvard Dormitory Crisis, then, was merely one sad chapter in the longer American story of white on black racism enabling ethnic assimilation. Could America, Du Bois once asked himself sadly, "have been America without Negroes"?[67]

The problems at Harvard hinted at a new wrinkle in the American social fabric. Indeed, the solution to one "race problem" and a rather significant shift in the demographic composition of the urban North would spark a prolonged interest in another deeper quandary—that of "the Negro." The Great War, having inhibited European immigration and spurred economic development, opened up a new opportunity for "the Negro." To replace their dwindling immigrant labor pool, industrial plants in Chicago advertised for black labor in the deep South. The promise of better wages and an idealized understanding of life in the North, together with repeated crop failures in the cotton South, inspired African Americans to head North during and after the war. "COME NORTH!" advertised Du Bois. "The demand for Negro labor is endless. Immigration is still cut off and a despicable and indefensible drive against all foreigners is shutting the gates of opportunity to the outcasts and victims of all Europe. Very good. We will make America pay for her Injustice to us and to the poor foreigner by pouring into the open doors of mine and factory in increasing numbers." Du Bois had found a thin silver lining in a very large cloud. For, after arriving in the great cities of the North, black Americans would encounter a horrifying wave of violence directed against them—violence rooted in fear, distrust, and blind hatred. And the shrieking advocates of immigration restriction soon shifted their focus to "the Negro problem." "The problems of national reconstruction," proffered Lothrop Stoddard, "are many. The closing of the gates to mass-immigration is merely a first step. Alien elements in our population must be assimilated. Political and cultural dissensions should be harmonized. Above all, our great negro problem must be realistically and constructively dealt with."[68]

Between 1919 and 1929 the tremendous growth of African-American communities in the urban North—composed largely of well-to-do northern black families and tens of thousands of poorer migrants from the deep South—shocked white Americans in New York and other cities. The virtual end of European immigration had inspired corporate forces to bring black folks northward, and then to segregate them into isolated neighborhoods and into the most menial, backbreaking, and pretechnological tasks in the industrial sector. But the resultant critical mass of African Americans in Harlem posed very serious problems for the social system of the North. Like southerners in the 1880s and 1890s (or South Africans in the 1920s), northeastern Americans had to grapple with "the Negro" at close range, in face-to-face situations, and in unprecedented numbers. The rules of social engagement needed to be rewritten, especially if these new arrivals in the North, unlike their supposedly docile southern counterparts, seemed unwilling to prostrate themselves before the might of Nordic America. For Rudolph Fisher's literary protagonist King Solomon Gillis, Harlem was frighteningly wonderful: he saw "Negroes at every turn; up and down Lenox Avenue, up and down One Hundred and Thirty-fifth street; big, lanky Negroes, short, squat Negroes; black ones, brown ones, yellow ones; men standing idly on the curb, women, bundle-laden, trudging reluctantly homeward . . . Negroes, predominantly, overwhelmingly everywhere." But for Lothrop Stoddard, for Madison Grant, and for many, many others, that same new ubiquitousness was shocking. "The negro," Stoddard concluded, pointedly using the lowercase "n," "is at once the most chronic and the most acute of our national problems."[69]

Having been marked as a newly "national" problem, the New Negro responded with unprecedented vigor. After wrestling their way into the old neighborhood of Harlem above Central Park, migrants from the deep South and the Caribbean did not placidly sit back and wait for social justice. Inspired by radical movements and encouraged by the relative safety of the urban North, "the Negro" in the North mobilized, marched, and protested against the worst excesses of American racism, and especially against the vicious race riots that exploded across the North during and immediately after the Great War. In the midst of the Red Scare, a youthful group of mass revolutionary movements, led symbolically by the Jamaican Marcus Garvey and his Universal Negro Improvement Association, launched a wholesale rhetorical assault on white world supremacy—a radical departure from earlier African-American protest groups. African Americans had served in the Great War (albeit not equally and under constant threat of racism, repression, and institutional discrimination), and, when faced with riots in Chicago, Knoxville, and Washington, postwar assertiveness was sometimes translated into a defense of the local community as black folks struggled against racial violence. "The New Negro," offered Cyril Briggs, head of the radical African Blood Brotherhood, "is willing to suffer martyrdom for the Cause . . . [and can anyone] deny that there is more wholesome respect for the Negro following the race riots in Washington, Chicago, Knoxville . . . than there was before those riots, and when there were only lynchings and burnings of scared Negroes and none of the fear in the white man's heart that comes from the New Negro fighting back?"[70] The New Negro, it seemed, was profoundly different from the "Old."

## Rising Tides and Darkwaters

The postwar excitement about nationalism and whiteness, and the emergence of "the Negro" as a northern problem, transformed American political culture. Having stopped the rush of European immigrants, and faced with a "rising tide" of increasingly politicized African Americans, patrician proponents of national unity softened their rhetoric about "alien Bolsheviki" during the 1920s and used "the African" or "the Negro" as a psychological mudsill for absolute whiteness. The man who put the pieces together was Madison Grant's leading disciple, Lothrop Stoddard. The son of the world-famous travel writer John L. Stoddard, Lothrop Stoddard had written a much ballyhooed Red Scare book, *The Rising Tide of Color*

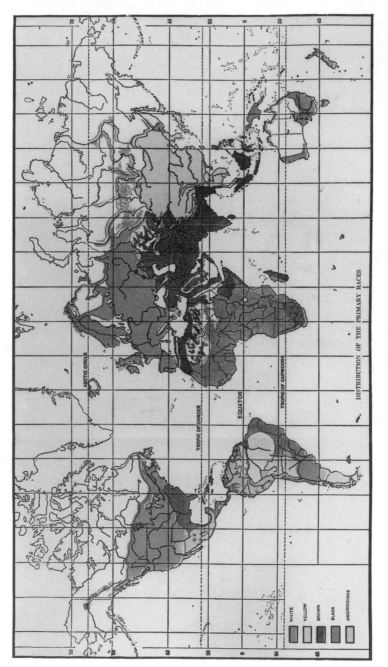

The world in colors: Lothrop Stoddard's map, published in *The Rising Tide of Color against White World Supremacy* (1920).

*against White World Supremacy* (1920), complete with a suitably fearful introduction by Grant, in 1920—a work written from his own personal notes and which, he believed, grew out of his lived experiences on the upper East side of Manhattan. Stoddard's incendiary prose belied his prim, neat appearance and his quiet appreciation of stamp collecting and pine-needle gardening. He wrote numerous works on world politics. The second work of his "trilogy" on race and color, *Re-Forging America,* would offer "the Negro" as the solution to "the problem of welding our heterogeneous population into a new organix [*sic*] synthesis."[71]

In *The Rising Tide of Color,* Stoddard had urged Americans to develop "a true *race*-consciousness (as opposed to national or cultural consciousness)," and had included a color-coded map of the racial world to make his point perfectly clear: race and color were one and the same. Given postwar fears of an emergent Japanese "brain proletariat" (especially after the unprecedented prominence afforded to the Japanese at Versailles and in the Washington Naval Conference), *Rising Tide of Color* was read with particular interest on the West Coast, where it inspired yet another "yellow peril" witch hunt.[72] But Stoddard's ideal world reconstructed around race-as-color would have to wait for its primary catalyst: the Great Migration. The arrival of African Americans in the North and West (and the subsequent agitation by some for social and political equality) had made it possible, Stoddard hoped, for that glorious "political, cultural, [and] spiritual unity" to emerge from debate about "the Negro problem." "The recent closing of our gates to mass-immigration," he later recalled, "had made such a welding possible."[73] All the potent, postwar streamlining measures against immigration had not, Stoddard soon believed, left American culture whole, and the republic suffered without the "unity we once possessed." The newly national "Negro problem," in other words, would pave the way for regional reconciliation and ethnic assimilation.

That "Negro problem," Stoddard concluded, was quite dangerous. Manipulated by Bolsheviks, radical "mulattos" and "foreign-born negroes" in the North were preaching revolution and shuttling younger radicals to Moscow, "where they are being carefully trained as Bolshevik apostles to their race." "The great negro quarters of New York, Chicago, and other Northern cities," Stoddard cried, "are seething with ideas and emotions which, by the power of mass contagion, may engender sudden and startling developments." Madison Grant, for one, also worried that African Americans' experience in France during the war—he noted the sexual conquest of supposedly all too willing French women in particular—would set their minds aflame with desire for social equality, economic revolution, and intermarriage. As an experimental solution to these varied problems, Stoddard (always a student of world politics and an admirer of the New South) coyly offered "bi-racialism," a total and complete separation of the races that paid tribute to Jim Crow generally and the Racial Integrity Law of Virginia particularly, and also to the merciless segregation of the races in South Africa.[74]

Written in the spirit of postwar superpatriotism, *Rising Tide of Color* and *Re-Forging America* predicted that the "conflict of color"—the coming battle of "the primary races of mankind"—would soon overshadow any threat from European immigrants. The darker peoples, Stoddard reminded his readers, outnumbered "the white world." The dangerous combination of the world conspiracy of Bolshevism, certain advancements in technological mastery by people of color, especially "the Oriental," and an incipient revolution against colonialism spelled the doom of "the white race." Complete with dystopian title and Grant's generous prefatory remarks, *Rising Tide of Color* was a real postwar phenomenon. In England, Lord Northcliffe described the book as "an international sensation": "I want every white man," he whispered on his deathbed, "to read it!"[75]

"Whoever will take the time to read and ponder Mr. Stoddard's book," offered President Harding to an eager crowd in Birmingham, Alabama, "must realize that our race problem here in the United States is only a phase of a race issue that the whole world confronts." Harding's proclamation rang true across in the United States, but especially in Harlem, where the notion that "the darker millions" could be truly dangerous and unified was greeted by New Negroes with open arms. Ironically, Stoddard's immensely popular treatises on race would feed the growing strength of African-American and Caribbean radicalism. "The tide that has started," the *Chicago Defender* predicted, "will continue to rise in spite of all Mr. Stoddard and the white races can do." All the postwar fears of Bolshevism as a racial threat were becoming color-coded, a process fueled by Stoddard's despair and Marcus Garvey's triumphant declarations.[76]

Stoddard's concern—and the general upper-crust interest in "the Negro" as a problem—was the patrician component of an emergent mass culture that grew directly out of the superpatriotism of the Great War and the 100 Percent Americanism of the Red Scare. The vigorous defense of capitalism engendered by the Red Scare had opened the door for an honest discussion of "class" in American life. That honest discussion, however, never occurred outside of the bounds of race, partly because advocates of 100 Percent Americanism so thoroughly quashed it, and partly because of the rising national interest in "the Negro." "A controversial war," suggests the historian Jackson Lears, "fought far from home, required unifying emblems to mobilize a disparate and contentious population." One such unifying emblem was absolute whiteness. The national popular culture of the postwar period and the 1920s slowly masked (or even erased) older divisions between ethnic groups—divisions which had formed the basis of much of nativism—in favor of a strictly white-over-black racial calculus. Between 1919 and 1929, then, American consumer culture reflected an ongoing transformation of the meaning of American whiteness. In the immediate aftermath of the Great War, threats of "Bolsheviki" and rumors of "the International Jew" led to widespread fears of social disorder and revolution. While the immediate response (the Palmer raids and the curtailment of fundamental civil rights) was swift and severe, the long-term reaction in the 1920s was perhaps even more effective. "Roaring Twenties" consumer culture—and mass culture more generally—focused on "the Negro" as a newer "mudsill," one more capable of uniting the disparate white peoples in the republic. Powered by the postwar Great Migration of African Americans northward and economic expansion abroad, the working parts of the new "culture of abundance"—advertisements, films, novels, and Broadway shows—all drew attention to the politics of skin color.[77]

Widespread representations of "the African" and "Africa" in films, fairs, and novels lent strength to connections between the presumed servility and technological inferiority of "the Negro" and white dominance of "the dark continent." Riots against African-American communities by white labor encouraged both whites and blacks to emphasize "the color line" above everything else. Black peoples, it was argued, were natural producers of raw materials—rudimentary cogs in an emergent world system that benefited only white consumers. American civilization, advertisers and political pundits then claimed, was an absolute democracy of consumers—people of any status, national origin, or social class could, if they had the means and were white, buy anything and everything they wanted.[78] People of color, therefore, should be safely tucked away in rural surrounds, crumbling ghettoes, and far-away places. This provocative use of "the color line" helped smother social unrest, though it also enabled and directed African-American protest in new and surprising ways. In sum, the focus on the labors of black folks around the world reflected a transformed sense of what it meant to be white in America and, more generally, what the relationship was between whiteness and blackness.

The focus on Africa, Africans, and race-as-color was part of a continued popular interest in America's place in the world. After the Great War, with American political culture increasingly celebrating the virtues of its white citizen-consumers, many came to see the United States as the jewel in the crown of what was termed "white world supremacy," and to see the growing American economy as an integral—if not indispensable—part of an anti-Bolshevist world economy that was organic, racial, and systematic. "Never in all history," offered one commentator, "has such an irresistible or marvelously concerted force been developed as that which the United States are bringing to bear upon the peoples which are geographically or politically within its reach." The attendant elements and causal factors of this "marvelously concerted force" were the explosion of U.S. economic productivity before and after the Great War, Americans' rapid entry into overseas imperialism as market expansionists, the triumph of Fordism and pervasive faith in business and technology, the widespread idealism of Wilsonian internationalism, the sense that the distances that separated cultures around the world were somehow shrinking, and the emergence of multinational business empires. Faith in "the culture of consumption," the cornerstone of postwar American civilization, thus rested upon a fervent belief in the rightful supremacy of what the literary critic Bram Dijkstra has called the "dark red blood of the capitalist superman." "Mr. Stoddard," wrote one critic in reply to *Rising Tide of Color* and *Re-Forging America,* "confuses race . . . with class."[79]

In this American world economic system, representations of races corresponded to classes in a color-coded global economy. Each race—white, yellow, brown, or black—had a place in the capitalist and colonial order of things. The resulting congruence of race, class, and place marked the geopolitical and world economic positions of both the West and "the darker nations," with the former invariably cast in the role of metropolitan entrepreneur and innovator and the latter as backward peasant. Africa and Africans were seemingly always at the bottom of the list. Thus the picture of Africa as "a land of enormous potential wealth . . . raw materials, and foodstuffs" drawn by Stoddard went hand in hand with the suggestion that black Africans—at home and abroad—were a natural, perfectly exploitable workforce. There were similarities, then, between the colonial divisions of labor found, for instance, on Liberian rubber plantations and the patterns that organized America's postwar industrial economy.[80]

The organic world economy rested upon a deep and fervent belief that economic, intellectual, technological, and cultural capital all resided in the West—and in America more particularly. This concentration of capital (very broadly conceived) could then be exported in one fashion or another to Haiti, the Philippines, and the American South. The resultant conflation of race, class, and color on a global scale served to justify the singularly American experiences in, for example, Haiti, where blackness and whiteness were further intertwined in a paternalist colonial setting. Thus the occupation of Haiti was marked by a desperate need to better the infrastructure of that tiny island nation—building railroads, improving roads—in order to facilitate enterprises of big business as well as to demonstrate the technological, cultural, and intellectual superiority of white Nordic America. The occupation of Haiti by the U.S. Marines, and the control of Haitian finances by American banks, was popularly understood to be an exercise in national benevolence, as if the military and financial parentage of Haiti's "half savage negroid people" protected the childlike descendants of African slaves from themselves. Indeed, accounts of the Haitian expedition grimly emphasized the survival of cannibalism and the uncivilized practice of voodoo.[81]

For those in America less concerned with world politics, reminders of the color-coded global divide between Nordics and Negroes could be found at home in mass culture. Technological advances in photography and magazine printing, for instance, allowed for the publication of crisp, clear images of Africa, and of Teddy Roosevelt's famous safari to the sub-Saharan regions of that continent. Vivid portrayals of Africa on songbook covers positioned white men and women "above" the primitive residents of the continent—in one case, literally flying above the "jungle" on an amateur anthropological survey of tribal customs. For more tangible evidence, proud Nordics needed to look no further than the young flying ace Charles Lindbergh to see (as his mother put it on the runway at Curtiss Field) evidence of the greatness of "the undemonstrative Nordic race." Lindbergh's mastery of the emerging airplane technology revealed Nordic manhood at its finest even as his penchant for personal eugenics in the selection of potential mates and his ardent anti-Semitism revealed its meanest side. The enthusiastic public response to Lindbergh's feat was part of a context that defined whiteness through technological sophistication and blackness through presumed primitivism. For further proof of the increasing interconnectedness of white and black, New Yorkers needed only to look at the prominence of the "primitive" artwork adorning the stone and metal of their proliferating Art Deco skyscrapers and the white walls of their museums, or found in the literature of the "Negro Renaissance." Freshly minted visual cues everywhere reminded Americans of the unparalleled importance of "the Negro" as a mudsill in American life—indeed, in Western civilization—and inspired an increasingly strict allegiance to the color line.[82]

Nowhere, however, was the popular importance of this racialized world economy more conclusively demonstrated than in advertisements for the rubber industry. In the modern world, rubber—harvested from trees on farms called plantations—was well understood to be "the handmaid of civilization." Prior to the Great War, the United States had imported its rubber from either British colonies or a few small South American rubber plantations. But after the war, with Europe in ruins, and with advocates of American superiority clamoring for overseas economic growth, skyrocketing rubber prices forced a reevaluation of the world market in the United States. "Almost overnight," one commentator wrote, "the American public learned, through its Department of Commerce, that the United States, though consuming fully seventy percent of the world's crude rubber, was wholly dependent upon sources of supply under foreign control." The solution, he continued, lay in extensive "investment of capital in rubber growing properties of our own . . . within territories under American political control."[83]

Had it simply been a matter of securing large quantities of rubber, Latin America would have been a logical place to start. After all, before the war, no less an authority than Harvey Firestone had proclaimed the superiority of South American rubber to all other types. And, as the historian Walter LaFeber has demonstrated, U.S. economic control of Latin America was fairly tight. But postwar rubber production was not just about rubber, or about corporate profits, or about the growth of the national economy: it was also tied to the racial dynamic in America. And so American mining and rubber corporations began investing in Africa and investing in color prejudice. A diverse interest in Africa—a popular anthropology of what one writer called "the cavernous blackness of Africa"—sprang up, accompanying the economic penetration of Liberia, southern Africa, and the "third world" more generally.[84] William Seabrook, the author of *Magic Island,* an exposé of "voodoo" practices in Haiti, pilfered two centuries of

continental writing about Africa to compose his widely advertised work
*Jungle Ways*, which purported to present "the unexpurgated truth about
the intimate life and customs—religious, magical, moral, sexual—of the
real savage."[85]

The interest in blackness abroad served an important purpose. As
W. E. B. Du Bois put it, the "discovery of personal whiteness among the
world's peoples" sealed the bargain between "whites" of all standing in
America, providing a high standard of living for white workers in the
United States at the cost of the deliberate, explicit exploitation of people of
color around the world.[86] A careful look at advertisements, literature, political discourse, and consumer culture reveals just how widespread this bargain must have been. During the 1920s, even as new immigrants waged
a war against black migrants for jobs and whiteness, representations of
black folks abroad and at home as hopelessly backward, happily servile,
and technologically uncivilized proliferated. Stylized representations of laborers on rubber plantations—the word "plantation" itself suggestive of
American slavery—emphasized (even at the cost of ethnological certainty)
the absolute blackness of America's new overseas proletariat. Advertisements, movies, and literature latched onto race, especially blackness and
whiteness, depicting black folks as either aged ex-slaves patiently tilling the
fields of the deep South or dangerous, libidinous creatures of the urban
jungle.

In particular, advertisements for the rubber industry forged critical connections between race, class, and place, and thus mirrored the race-as-
color-coded map of the world in Stoddard's *Rising Tide of Color*. An adver-
tisement for the Overman Cushion Tire Company painted the area "Where
Rubber Grows" black on a map of the world; Firestone's cartoon map of
"Worldwide Resources" planted rubber factories on every continent except
Africa and labeled the "Dark Continent" a rubber plantation. Promotional
literature for Firestone Rubber, picked up by millions at the 1933–1934
World's Fair in Chicago, contained striking representations of workers on
African rubber plantations. Visitors to the Firestone Building would also
have seen the "savageness" and "primitiveness" of Africa in the "Liberian
rubber plantation" diorama that must have contrasted quite nicely with
the self-conscious modernity of the Art Deco building itself.[87] The iconog-
raphy of the rubber industry thus described for white American consumers a biography of product authenticity: the quality of the rubber, in short,
was assured by the blackness of the laborers who harvested it.

Some of the companies that had earlier worked most closely with Madison Grant's American Defense Society to monitor employee radicalism were responsible for the most explicit advertisements of the 1920s, visually linking the rubber plantation in Africa to rubber consumption in the stylish modern metropolis of the New World. A remarkable series of ads for the U.S. Rubber Company—a long-time ADS ally—took great pains to draw connections between the quality of rubber and its cultivation under American direction by "black" workers. With an untamed jungle as a backdrop, four joined frames depict the transformation of the jungle (oddly enough, in Sumatra), and its primitive residents, into a streamlined plantation with machinelike Negro workers, and then the ultimate consumption of rubber tires in an exquisitely modern Art Deco metropolis: "Thousands of acres of jungleland . . . have been transformed into flourishing rubber plantations in order to serve the best interests of United States Tires." These interconnections, moreover, were the real selling point of the tires. Another advertisement, depicting a fatherly conversation between a man and a boy, proclaims: "United States Cycle Tires are *Good* Tires." "The rubber in those tires," the boy says, "came from Sumatra . . . The United States Rubber Company has a big plantation there—a hundred thousand acres—so they can grow their own rubber for tires and be sure it's good."[88]

To a certain degree, these simple advertisements—a revealing part of the mass excitement about black folks found in 1920s American culture—forged new associations with the larger world. The connection between black production abroad and white consumption at home highlighted the importance of whiteness and blackness in American life and made the world seem smaller, as full of potential as it was full of danger. "Nature's hidden powers," Lothrop Stoddard proclaimed, "yield themselves as at the touch of a magician's wand . . . Time and distance alike diminish, and the very planet shrinks to the measure of human hands." Technological advances in travel and communications, in photography, in film, and in the distribution of popular media had forced a cognitive shift, an awakening of the senses to the broader world. Du Bois, responding to one of his first radio listeners—he had spoken in Boston's Ford Hall on "The Civilization of White Folks"—could barely contain his sense of wonder at the shrunken world: "Imagine," he wrote, "you in Philadelphia hearing me speak in Boston? It is almost witchcraft, isn't it?" As the continents grew closer, race problems that might otherwise have seemed distant appeared closer than ever before, leading to an ever increasing urgency about race. The real benefit of this "new world," Lothrop Stoddard concluded happily, lay not in the application of technological development in Africa and Asia but rather in the *effect* such applications had on "the Nordic world" *at home.* "Shocked broad awake," he concluded, "the old stock is for the first time developing a real race-consciousness."[89] The conflation of race with class around the globe was likewise shaped by the migration of blacks northward in the United States and by the enormous body of southern ideas about the need for slavery and the failures of Reconstruction.

But these global connections forged by rubber advertisements—or by other aspects of consumer culture—also served a very particular social purpose. For in addition to producing those provocative advertisements, the U.S. Rubber Company worked closely with antiradical organizations like the American Defense Society to monitor employee organizations, to distribute pro-capitalist literature with paychecks, and to dampen any enthusiasm for cross-racial solidarity in an urban North then experiencing the transformative effects of the Great Migration. And the American Defense Society, in turn, was run by men like Charles S. Davison, Madison Grant, and Lothrop Stoddard—died-in-the-wool nativists convinced that the "conflict of color" was becoming more important in American life than the threats posed by "the International Jew" or the fecund "Mediterranean race." In the 1920s, then, an odd collection of corporate capitalists, advertising agents, and prophylactic superpatriots hoped that sustained attention on black peoples as "safe" labor more specifically, as rudimentary labor tucked away on plantations abroad or confined to the most menial of tasks at home—might soothe the anxieties of an ethnically pluralistic working class threatened by the arrival of black folks in northern cities and by the undeniable unevenness of social advancement in America.[90]

The gambit paid off. The deepening national popular fascination with whiteness and blackness, now connected to American economic activity abroad, eased class tensions within whiteness, masked ethnic differences, and reconceptualized the very idea of "the Negro problem" not just as a national problem but as a global one as well. But these "safe" representations of harmless darkies and primitive tropical laborers in the 1920s sat in stark contrast with the unprecedented vigor and vision of postwar "New Negro" radicalism. Once settled in the North, New Negro protest actually drew strength from a mass culture predicated on the measured abuse of "darker peoples" around the world. "The cause of 'radicalism' among American Negroes," suggested the West Indian émigré and popular streetcorner orator Hubert H. Harrison, "is international . . . [and] the international Fact to which Negroes in America are now reacting is not the exploitation of laborers by capitalists; but the social, political and economic subjection of colored peoples by white."[91]

In the process of exploring their commitment to this new race-consciousness, New Negro radicals crafted a uniquely creative critique of the new order of things in the world. New Negro "race men" pushed anticolonialism where the Irish—their nominal predecessors—had never dared to take it: into a critique of the world's economic culture, a culture which directly involved the United States and which increasingly victimized growing numbers of "the darker peoples" in Latin America, Africa, and the Caribbean. If the Firestone Rubber Company celebrated its technocratic "uplift" of African peoples, New Negroes argued that such work would be the death of "the white world": that "race-consciousness" as class-consciousness would be the inevitable result. If American Defense Society spokesmen feared the "mis-education" of darker peoples through imperial capitalism, New Negroes took pleasure in describing the "400,000,000 Negroes of the World" (as Marcus Garvey called them) as manly and well organized, as militaristic and capable of protest against "the white Leviathan." From the Black Star Line to the UNIA groceries, from the advertisements in the front pages of *The Crisis* to the Inter-Colonial Supply Company, people as different as Garvey and Du Bois, Hubert H. Harrison and Alain Locke offered their own version of "the culture of consumption," linking upward mobility, consumer capitalism, and race pride, but coloring it black instead of white. Indeed, the explicit association of capitalism with white world supremacy and technological advantage encouraged many New Negro radicals to propose a shadow world economy—a revolutionary black capitalism in which people of African descent were not just plantation workers in Liberia, or cotton pickers in Georgia, or bootblacks on 34th Street in Manhattan. Surveying the new world of social relations in light of the "new" race-consciousness, Lothrop Stoddard's erstwhile New Negro confidant, Hubert H. Harrison, concluded that the "shock" of worsening race conflict was at the root of the "white world's" vague unease and growing awareness that "Negroes [were] awake, different, and perplexingly uncertain" everywhere.[92]

## Victory and Defeat

The explosiveness and seeming omnipresence of African-American radicalism in the 1920s alarmed Madison Grant, and eventually encouraged him, much as it had Lothrop Stoddard, to give pride of place to "the Negro question." But if Grant's *Passing of the Great Race* had been ahead of the curve in its conflation of the hierarchy within whiteness with an inborn economic hierarchy in the pale of Europe, later Grant was slow to recognize the importance of race-as-color. The world had changed since the Great War, and Grant, now an old man, did not leap—as had his younger protégé Stoddard—to redraw the lines of race yet again, or to emphasize the conflict of the races as a struggle between Nordics and New Negroes. Out of touch with the political forces of the increasingly heterogeneous Manhattan, and refusing to bend on issues of pluralism, assimilation, and race, Madison Grant watched the advent of the New Deal from the sidelines and worried—even after the National Origins Act—about immigration. For someone with Grant's desire for order and hierarchy, however, American economic expansion and the proliferation of thought about "the Negro" could only increase awareness of the dangers posed by distant events and change the definition of what was dangerous. It was only a matter of time before the great patriarch of scientific racism shifted his attention to black folks.

Grant had long worried about the racial dynamic in the New South. "One race," he had concluded earlier, "must drive out the other or be destroyed . . . [and] unless some remedy is found the nation is doomed to mongrelism." As long as black folks remained quiescent in the South, however, he was satisfied. In *The Passing of the Great Race,* for instance, he had dismissed "the Negro" as a possible threat to capitalist America: "Negroes," he had suggested, "are never socialists or labor unionists." And as late as 1927 Grant had urged Lothrop Stoddard to attend to the problems of Asia because "the Negro" was not a "live issue." Stoddard, always fascinated by "the Darker world" and deeply indebted to Grant for the publication of *The Rising Tide of Color,* was moved enough by Grant's persistent anti-Semitism to publish a disturbing contribution to *The Forum* on what he termed "the Jewish Question."[93]

By 1930, however, Grant's traditional northern nativist animus toward Mediterraneans and Jews had been almost completely replaced by a dread of "the Negro." In his novel of 1931, *Hank, His Lies and His Yarns,* Grant offered the words of "Hank," the gruff, plain-spoken protagonist, as the purest common sense on matters of race and politics, democracy and equality. Casting himself as "the Major," Hank's educated chronicler, Grant offered lessons drawn from "long periods of solitude face to face with the realities of nature." The western frontier setting of *Hank*—a tribute to the turn-of-the-century work of another Boone and Crockett Club member, Owen Wister's *The Virginian*—also masked Grant's Depression-era anxieties about feminism, radicalism, and the possible repeal of Prohibition. In a chapter entitled "White Men," the Major asks Hank if he "believe[s] that all men are equal?" "Sure I do," Hank replies, to which the Major responds, "How many different people do you consider that there are in this world?" "Well," says Hank, counting on his fingers, "there is Greasers and Siwashes and they are pretty much the same; then there's niggers and there's Frenchmen and there's Dutchmen—they ain't so bad." "All these people," the Major responds incredulously, "are equals?" "Hell no," says Hank, "I am talking about the white men." Hank's strangely confused, or simpleminded, scheme of classification is buttressed by the new iron law of whiteness: all white men are equal, especially when in the presence of black folks.[94]

For Madison Grant, the crucial juncture was the onset of the Great Depression in 1929. The eternal economic collapse of the 1930s—much to "the consternation of Nordic ears"—gave rise to deeper rumblings of rebellion and revolution.[95] Grant was convinced that an economic downturn of such magnitude would make class conflict, or race conflict, inevitable. As terrifying proof, the perpetually nervous Grant needed only to consider the relatively successful organizational activities of the Communist Party of the United States of America (CPUSA) in the southern black belt and in Harlem. The CPUSA had aggressively sought to organize African Americans into sharecroppers' unions and political wedges, and marshaled its considerable strength behind a determined and quite progressive civil rights agenda. And while recent careful social histories have shown otherwise, Grant (and many white Americans) couldn't help imagining that black people were dangerously slack-jawed followers of the commands of the Comintern—or seeing in "the Negro" the seeds of a Depression-era war of the races.[96]

His new fear of "the Negro" as a proletarian threat appeared in its most sophisticated form in what Grant considered the crowning achievement of his life, a high school history textbook entitled *The Conquest of a Continent,* published in 1933. After pondering whether to include "the Negro" in his new book at all, Grant had come to the conclusion—after careful discussion with his aristocratic Klan contact and sometime protégé Earnest Cox, the leader of the "White America" society—that "now that we are through with immigration, the most important question remaining is the Negro." "Among the various outland elements now in the United States which threaten in different degrees our national unity," a confident Grant argued in *Conquest*, "the most important is the Negro." Social dynamics of recent vintage had, Grant believed, undermined the basis for the separation of the races in the South, converting "the Negro problem" into a national problem. The brashness of the African-American leadership class (especially the now thoroughly radical Du Bois) and the influx of dark-skinned and predominantly Catholic peoples from Latin and South America led Grant to reflect upon the dangers posed by even the smallest amount of Negro blood. A "mulatto menace," he averred, threatened to undo all the gains achieved by the National Origins Act: "We have facing us," Grant warned in *The Alien in Our Midst*, a collection he edited with Charles Stewart Davison, "a serious Negro problem with an ever-increasing number of quadroon and octoroon types which often pass for Cubans, South Americans, Portuguese or Italians, and it is by no means certain that the percentage of individuals with Negro blood in their veins is not increasing relatively to the pure Whites in spite of all statements to the contrary." As Norman Dike, a contributor to the collection, put it, light-skinned immigrants were shape-shifters, people without any "method of identification" capable of leaving "one locality without regret and taking up life wherever he finds it most promising." Continued restriction of immigration, then, served a twofold purpose—denying inferior stock admission to the United States while simultaneously denying anyone with even the smallest amount of Negro blood the ability to pass surreptitiously for a dingy white.[97]

In New York, Harlem posed a more immediate problem. From the mid-1920s, daily newspaper accounts of peculiarly "Negro" crimes—"Negro Bandits Equip Selves for Jazz Band," the *New York Tribune* blared—made the "mecca of the New Negro" seem irredeemably primitive and immoral. But demographic shifts also begat new and disturbing political alliances. In 1928 Al Smith—an Irish Catholic "wet," and thus a grave problem in Grant's eyes—secretly courted the African-American vote in New York, paving the way for the decisive presidential election of 1932, in which fifty percent of black folks living in Madison Grant's Manhattan voted for the Democratic candidate, Franklin Delano Roosevelt. "The Negro," it seemed, was becoming a factor in electoral politics. And in 1934 East Harlem, home to the largest Italian-American—and Italian-speaking—neighborhood in the United States, as well as to a growing Puerto Rican immigrant community, would elect Vito Marcantonio, whose leftward politics and much-celebrated use of religious amulets must have given Grant heartburn, to the House of Representatives. The northern end of the island of Manhattan, home to Grant's patrician family for two centuries, had become corrupted by a mix of the "worst sort" of peoples—"Mediterraneans," "Negroes," and "Latins." "The enormous Negro population in New York," Grant confided nervously to Cox, "is spreading and ruining real estate values in fairly good sections . . . one constantly sees on the street white and negro boys playing together and white and negro girls walking together."⁹⁸

*Conquest* was negrophobia tempered, or complicated, by nativism. But it was also more than that. Like Stoddard and like many Americans, Grant had been sensitized to world issues by the Great War, by the Red Scare, and by American economic expansion. His angst grew not just from purely domestic changes—the end of European immigration and the subsequent Great Migration of African Americans—but also from the threat of brown or black races out of place in the capitalist and colonial order of things. *Conquest,* published just five years after the Sixth World Congress of the Communist International suggested that blacks in the American South constituted an oppressed nation deserving of Communist support and organization, and conceived during the Depression and in the face of prolonged Communist agitation on behalf of African Americans, depicted the final battle of the war of the races as one between whites and blacks, Nordics and Negroes. Fearing an organized Communist menace in America, Grant trembled at the thought of Jews, Italians, and Negroes breeding Communist mulatto children—all with peculiarly "Negro" failings—in Harlem. The nightmare of Bolshevism had been transformed, and now threatened the very foundations of Nordic civilization. "It is the eleventh hour of capitalism," trumpeted Alain Locke, the Howard University philosopher and sometime debater of Lothrop Stoddard, "and the eleventh hour of Nordicism."⁹⁹

For all its grand conclusions about the racial basis of American culture, *The Conquest of a Continent* was something of an intellectual oddity when it was published in the midst of the Depression. Support for nativism had dwindled after the National Origins Act, leaving Grant and a few others to rumble on alone about the alien menace. The Depression revived those right-wing groups interested in old-fashioned nativism, Americanism, and antiradicalism—"the Quasi-Fascists," as the historian David Bennett later termed them.¹⁰⁰ But these right-wing groups were not as strong or as influential in the 1930s as their predecessors had been. Something rather profound had transpired. During the Great War and the "Roaring 1920s," Madison Grant's effusive Nordic chauvinism had been wildly popular among many mainstream Americans. By the early 1930s, however, only the far right maintained an abiding interest in the calling-cards of authoritarian antidemocracy: racial eugenics, forced sterilization, and state control of the gene pool.

Indeed, after bemoaning "the Negro problem" in the United States, Grant would find his strongest support during the 1930s in Hitler's Germany, where "the Jew"—and not "the Negro"—was the problem. His health failing, he oversaw the translation of his two scientific treatises on race into German for his readers in Hitler's Fatherland (his prized pupil, Stoddard, would soon head overseas to survey the grim truth of the coming Holocaust).[101] Grant would frequently show visitors a personal letter from Hitler himself, in which the Nazi leader described *The Passing of the Great Race* as his "Bible." In America, though, Grant's last offering, *The Conquest of a Continent*, met with a "chorus of jeers," its arguments so antiquated that one reviewer "expressed surprise that such books were still being written." Stoddard's *Clashing Tides of Color*, described as "grotesque in its anthropology and irresponsible in its historical reconstructions," met a similar fate, though one reviewer suggested that, at the very least, the 1935 work would bring Stoddard "further acclaim in Nazi circles."[102]

For Grant's enemies, he was now the embodiment of all that America was not. He had orchestrated the passage of sweeping immigration reform and had infused his precious Manhattan with "race-consciousness." Almost single-handedly, he had turned Nordicism into a popular euphemism for Americanism. But if the social order had been nearly restored in 1924, it had crumbled when "the Negro" had refused to stay fixed in the South and when the once-humming economy had come to a painful stillness. Troubled by the Great Migration and the Depression, he was increasingly in need of restorative visits to the Battle Creek Sanitarium. On his deathbed with nephritis in 1937, and concerned about the intrusion of cameras into his beloved Bronx Zoo, Grant had asked, "Are we winning?"[103] He had spent his entire life working to shore up the Gilded Age foundation laid by his father's generation, and to awaken Americans to the assumed preciousness of their heritage. And yet his efforts would be stymied time and time again. At the time of his death, all his determination and meticulous attention to detail, all the sweeping prose spent on racial thinking, left him largely alone and extraordinarily frustrated at the limitations of reform in the increasingly heterogeneous United States. In the end, the immigrants and people of color he so despised would come to dominate the economy, politics, and mass culture, remaking this country in their image and changing the very nature of what it meant to be American.

# 2

# Bleeding the
# Irish White

[I'd like] to introduce my Negro friends and my American Irish friends to one another in such a way as to make them better understand one another. For the situation of the Negro in America and that of the native Irishman in his own country throughout the past three hundred years have been strikingly parallel.

—LA TOURETTE STOCKWELL, "MAY I INTRODUCE—?"
(1936)

Only a super-ass would see even the slightest comparison between the Negro's degraded position in this country and the favored position of the English, the Irish, the Germans, the French, the Italians, and the Russians, all of whom are admittedly within the charmed circle of the dominant race.

—*CRUSADER* (1920)

Before the outbreak of the Great War in Europe, nationalists from Ireland envisioned the United States—and Manhattan in particular—as their base of operations in the transatlantic struggle against the British Empire. Subversives from India followed their lead, organizing several independence-minded groups in California and New York. By the time the United States entered the war, the "Irish question," and imperialism more generally, had become popular obsessions of American Progressive idealists and reactionary conservatives alike, and Manhattan had become a focal point for anti-imperialism. A similar anti-imperial awakening permeated African-American political culture—soon headquartered in Harlem—over the same period. During and after the Peace Conference, for instance, "Black Scare" radicalism exploded on the national and international scenes in the form of Marcus Garvey and the Universal Negro Improvement Association. Garvey, W. E. B. Du Bois, and many other African-American and

Afro-Caribbean political figures competed for the mantle of "Negro leader," and in the process added the threat of economic, social, and cultural revolution to black political culture. By the end of the Great War, then, events in the United States as well as in Ireland, Egypt, India, and Haiti had put the question of empire at the center of American internationalism, eventually making Manhattan, and not London, the center of metropolitan anticolonialism.

The most striking shared aspect of two quite different anti-imperial nationalisms—that of the Irish and that of "the Negro"—was the strength of diasporic sentiment buttressed by transatlantic connections. But if global debates over "the Irish question" and agitation surrounding "the Negro problem" made those two issues benchmarks for other nationalist organizations in the United States, race and racial difference soon set Irish-American and African-American nationalisms on very different paths. During the war, Irish-American nationalists drew upon more than fifty years of scientific discourse about "the Celt" to construct a transatlantic racial community predicated on the belief that the Irish and the Anglo-Saxon were biologically, culturally, and historically different. This racialized nationalism rested upon a broader belief that there were an abundance of white races, every one of them racially distinct, and that each of these white races possessed a unique national and world-historical destiny. Irish nationalism, then, derived its racialized qualities from an older, Romantic sense of racial difference in which "race," "nation," and "folk" were all loosely, but imprecisely, connected in history, language, and biology.

If, however, the "fundamental problem of the twentieth century" for the Irish was the conflict of the white races, for New Negro radicals, for Nordic voguers, and increasingly for American culture writ large, that "problem" was quite different. "The American race problem," concluded Cyril Briggs somberly, "is the problem of black and white . . . [and] before this problem of black and white all others sink into pale insignificance." Looking around the United States, and surveying the savage racial carnage in Houston, Chicago, and Knoxville, New Negro political leaders rightly sharpened the focus of American discussions about "race problems." Nourished by the northward migration of black folks, the angry radicals of the "Black Scare" reminded their supposedly Progressive contemporaries that they needed to look no further than the ramshackle clapboard huts of the Mississippi Delta, or the impoverished ghettos of the urban North, to find "huddled masses, yearning to breathe free." Many in America—especially Jewish liberals and patrician nativists—agreed. Lothrop Stoddard put it this way in 1914: "The world-wide struggle between the primary races of mankind—the 'conflict of color,' as it has happily been termed—bids fair to be the fundamental problem of the twentieth century, and great communities like the United States of America, the South African Confederation, and Australasia regard the 'color question' as perhaps the gravest problem of the future."[1]

This "conflict of color" changed everything for Irish-American nationalists. As the Great War began, a razor-thin line kept the Irish from being members of the white race; with the postwar dawning of a new sense of race and the emergence of worldwide anticolonialism partly based in New York, that line was quickly erased. The "looseness" and "elasticity" of the term "race" were soon replaced by a new taxonomy of races—roughly five instead of fifty. Du Bois named this reorganization of racial discourse "the discovery of personal whiteness among the world's peoples"; Lothrop Stoddard called it "bi-racialism"; the New Negro radical Hubert H. Harrison termed it "the New Race Consciousness."[2] Soon this notion that "the race problem" was simply a "conflict of color" and not a product of national competition, or that whiteness and blackness (and not Anglo-Saxonism and Irishness) marked racial difference, would become an integral part of American political culture. If, as many were coming to believe, the Irish weren't racially different from their oppressors in England, their struggle to "save the soul of Ireland" might not have the same anticolonial resonance. But despite the developing belief that the Irish were white, and regardless of the generations of white ethnic violence against people of color, and in the face of the whitening tide of hatred in 1919, postwar New Negro activists and Irish radicals still briefly found something in each other that they could have found nowhere else.

## To Save the Soul of Ireland

In the early afternoon of March 4, 1916, Monsignor Henry Brann stepped up to the podium in the great hall of the Hotel Astor, a French Renaissance–style structure built in Manhattan before the turn of the century. Brann's attentive audience that day was composed of two parts: a genteel, respectably dressed male audience—"delegates" they were called—were gathered around circular tables on the main floor of the hall; a mixed group of men and women clung to the balcony above, looking down upon the delegates. There were more than 2,500 people in attendance, all of them chosen for their devout faith in Irish nationalism. Facing his audience, Brann slowly held his arms out straight, turned his palms to the ceiling, and began to cry. "Oh God, eternal God," he shouted through the tears, "save Ireland: make her free and punish her enemies." With the end of Brann's short prayer for justice, the carefully selected audience erupted; the manly, civilized delegates cheered themselves "hoarse," the older men had "tears in their eyes," and the women in the balcony "wept for joy." It was a fittingly emotional beginning for the first Irish Race Convention, an event whose success turned on both the middle-class civility and the indisputable "Irishness" of its participants.[3]

Sitting among the delegates that day was Daniel Florence Cohalan. The son of immigrant parents, the young Daniel Cohalan had been an avid baseball player at Manhattan College, where he earned the law degree that would facilitate his easy rise up the political ladder of Tammany Hall. By 1914, the year in which a few well-placed Irish Americans began to consider the need for a convention, an older and wiser Cohalan had been elected "Grand Sachem" of the Hall, had been appointed New York State Supreme Court Justice, and had clashed with a young state senator named Franklin Delano Roosevelt over a possible seat in the Senate. Together with the aged Irish exile and veteran newspaperman John Devoy, the editor of the *Gaelic American,* Cohalan reorganized the extraordinarily secretive Clan na Gael, a nationalist group once associated with the dynamiter campaigns of the 1880s. With the first stirrings of war in Europe, "the Judge" (as he was commonly known) threw himself into the planning of the convention and into Irish-American nationalism. By the time he organized this first Irish Race Convention, Cohalan was perhaps the most powerful Irish nationalist on the American side of the Atlantic Ocean, presiding over a tightly knit group of hard-core revolutionaries and a considerable amount of cash. As wave after wave of nationalist fervor washed over him at the Race Convention, Cohalan must have savored the precise orchestration of the event, an event he had planned almost single-handedly, right down to his composition of the "Declaration of Principles" that the delegates would "spontaneously" adopt on Sunday, March 5.[4]

Cohalan's Irish Race Convention reflected many of the twists and turns of Irish-American nationalism. "Irish-American nationalism," suggests the historian Thomas Brown, "had its origins in loneliness, poverty, and prejudice. Compressed into ghettos, the Irish used their numbers and the group consciousness which the ghettos fostered to nourish, as nativists complained, 'their foreign feelings and their foreign nationality' . . . immigrants realized that in a hostile land their Irishness mattered more than their provincial differences. Life in America, said the Irish-American newspaperman Patrick Ford, lifted the Irishman out of 'the littleness of countyism into the broad feeling of nationalism.'"[5] Coming from a predominantly agrarian and rural Irish countryside, Irish emigrants to America— Cohalan's parents among them—had at first been shocked at the economic life of the urban United States. Settling in major cities meant becoming industrial wage earners, a task for which the agrarian Irish were poorly suited. Nevertheless, Irish labor quickly became prominent in mining, in factory work, and in unspecialized labor. Tightly knit Irish communities formed in Boston, New York, Philadelphia, Butte, and San Francisco. Missing their homeland, the Irish in America constructed a shared belief in their unwilling exile from Ireland. And that same shared belief ultimately gave grassroots nationalism in the United States a remarkable strength and longevity.

In the 1880s, blight and bad weather forced hundreds of thousands of Irish to head off to the United States during the great "second wave" of migration (over two million were to arrive between 1870 and 1920). The Clan na Gael and other less radical nationalist organizations, such as the Ancient Order of Hibernians and the Friendly Sons of St. Patrick, were able to greet immigrants newly arrived to the cold, industrializing world of urban America with the warm blanket of national sympathies. Settling predominantly in northern urban centers, the new immigrants were quickly assimilated into the Anglophobic world of the American Irish, a world in which "reorganized Fenianism"—as John Devoy, a former Fenian, termed it— was less a small subversive movement centered around the Clan na Gael and more a popularly shared religion. In this context, Irish-American leaders often invoked the "sea-divided Gael" to emphasize a shared sense of "Irishness," to claim cultural authority, and to mask widening socioeconomic divisions. "The nationalist rhetoric of emigration-as-exile," suggests the historian Kerby Miller, "obscured internal differences by implying that all Irish-Americans shared similar, externally imposed reasons for immigration . . . [while] the demands of Irish-American nationalists that the immigrants remain loyal to 'the *mother*land' . . . coincided with the needs of the Irish and Irish immigrant family and imposed strong communal pressures for ethnic solidarity and conformity on ambitious or assimilation-minded individuals." By the early 1900s Irish-American nationalism drew most of its impressive strength from the "homesickness and discontent" of the millions of working-class Irish men and women in American cities.[6]

While the Irish Race Convention of 1916 suggested a long-standing popular penchant for "Irishness," a closer look also reveals the guiding hands and manipulative nature of the Irish-American leaders. Showing an uncanny mastery of public relations, Devoy's *Gaelic American* had "predicted"—or prescribed perhaps—that the convention would be "no madcap gathering to voice the immature views, opinions, and resolves of well-meaning, unthinking men, but a National Congress, at which the intellect and mature judgment of the Race will consider the practical measures necessary to lift the Irish Cause to its proper place in the civilized world and ensure a fair hearing for Ireland's claim to Nationhood." A letter written to the Ancient Order of Hibernians president and Clan na Gael sympathizer Joseph McLaughlin comes fairly close to the mark in its conclusion that the convention was likely to consist of "conscripted 'delegates' under the veiled leadership of a few shrewd men." In similar discussions about the small cabal of clever nationalists running the Clan na Gael, Cohalan was singled out—and either praised or damned—for his role as the chief architect of the convention. Together with Devoy, Cohalan whittled the guest list down to "respectable" men who represented "all that is best in the Irish race" and who held the proper nationalist views. As McLaughlin put it, "the Convention will neither be the time nor the place to argue who is right, or who is wrong. We're right, and let the others keep away."[7] When the great day of the convention finally came on March 4, the end result of Cohalan's careful orchestration of the event was magnificent—from Brann's tearful opening prayer, to the waves of applause which followed the reading of the Declaration of Principles, to the two-hour delay caused by burly Clan toughs who forcibly removed some troublesome "Anglophiles."[8]

Nor did the orchestration end when the doors of the Hotel Astor closed. Devoy, a newspaper editor for over thirty years and a master of political spin, insisted that the attention to order and control had prevailed. "It was," he crowed, "the most orderly and best managed gathering ever held in New York . . . Everything moved like clockwork and not a cog slipped."[9] Press coverage of the event focused on the civilized nature of the partici-

**Daniel Cohalan (right) and Cardinal Gibbons at the 1919 Irish Race Convention.**

pants (though some Anglophile newspapers indicated surprise at the extent of the civility) and inevitably included a widely reproduced photo of hundreds of well-dressed and perfectly well-behaved Irish-American men seated at the Astor. In noting the attendance of a number of judges, Devoy, Robert Ford of the *Irish World*, and others hinted at the remarkable rise of "the Irish" from urban proletariat to lace-curtain bourgeoisie.

Race had been a fundamental component of Irish nationalism in America and Ireland since the 1840s. With the arrival of the famine Irish, the easy, uncomplicated whiteness of the power-wielding northeastern populace shattered, leading quickly to prolonged outbursts of Know-

Nothingism and, more important, scientific Anglo-Saxonism. Spurred on by the emergence of Fenianism and Darwinism, Anglo-Saxonism soon produced a body of knowledge about the supposedly glorious world-historical destiny of the Anglo-Saxon race and the bestial nature of those members of the Celtic race then clustered together in huddled masses in New York, Boston, and the West of Ireland. The Celt's place in evolution (the "missing link" between the ape and the Negro) and in history was a matter of great scientific debate in both New York and London, and popular images of the Irish as pug-nosed, low-browed beasts abounded. This depiction of the monstrous Celt was accompanied by representations of Irish men as "Paddys" (subversive, shiftless, and highly emotional and illogical) and Irish women as "Bridgets" (wage-earning, mannish, and humorously forgetful and clumsy). The lack of clear-cut gender distinctions—the manly Irishwoman, the emotional Irishman—hinted at the uncivilized nature of the Celt, which, in turn, underscored British political concerns about whether the Irish could ever govern themselves.[10]

The diasporic "culture of exile" developed by turn-of-the-century famine emigrants was thus, in part, predicated on the shared memories of the genocidal famine and the "sacrifice" of Irish manhood against the military might of the hard, cold Anglo-Saxon—memories made all the more fresh by the virulent Anglo-Saxonist scientific discourse on "the Celt." When the "young manhood" of Ireland met with violence at the hands of the English, or when the American Protective Association launched its "No Irish Need Apply" program in the 1900s, Gaelic-American nationalists responded by castigating the pervasive "gospel of Anglo-Saxon supremacy" and experienced a corresponding resurgence of popular racial faith and nationalist passion.[11] Still, if there was little chance for a truly interracial labor radicalism to develop among working-class Americans, nineteenth-century racialized nationalism proved quite able to connect the struggle to "save the soul of Ireland" with other protest movements, such as the African-American fight against Jim Crow.[12]

Turn-of-the-century sensibilities about "race" were torturously confused about the proper means of classification. If Anglo-Saxonism and Celticism were central components of Irish nationalism in Ireland and Romantic racialism in Europe, the American strain of both was complicated by another variant of the discourse of race: a focus on whiteness and blackness. As David Roediger and Eric Lott have suggested, whiteness was an integral part of American popular culture, and claims to racial privilege often worked to offset the troubling lack of self-mastery in industrializing America; class formation and race-consciousness went hand in hand. The Irish, for their part, attempted to leap directly from the "mudsill" to civilization by clinging to whiteness in well-publicized violent assaults against the small free black communities in the North and by representing blackness and slavery as the antithesis of modern urbanity in minstrel shows.

In the midst of the Civil War and again in the unrelenting heat of August 1900, the antagonisms between "Celt" and "Negro" in New York needed only a spark—in one case the threat of a general draft of the poorest into the Northern army, and in the other accusations that a black man had tried to shoot an Irish police officer—to touch off rough bloodshed. Such dogged negrophobia made nationalist sympathy between the Irish and the Negro difficult, if not impossible, to maintain over the long haul, and the Irish would continue to be well represented in race riots through the 1920s. Whiteness and Irishness thus complicated each other in nationalist discourse. On the eve of the Great War, with immigration hotly contested and with Anglo-Saxonism serving as the bedrock of Victorian political culture, imperial expansion, and Anglo-American rapprochement, the Irish could only be whitened so far, leaving them somewhere "between whiteness and Anglo-Saxondom." So long as the racial faith of Anglo-Saxonism and Irish-American nationalism remained solid, any and all attempts at the complete and total assimilation, Americanization, and whitening of the Irish race were doomed to failure.[13]

In the years prior to the Race Convention, that all-important racial faith was to intersect two new variations on the nationalist theme: a resurgence of racialized protest in Ireland and the wartime debate over immigrant assimilation in America. In turn-of-the-century Ireland, disenchantment with parliamentarianism (the constitutional agitation for a Home Rule Bill) and the limitations of physical-force nationalism in a peaceful decade led to the emergence of a powerful impulse to "de-Anglicise" Ireland through the careful recovery of "racial customs, language and tradition." What began with Douglas Hyde's lecture before the fledgling Irish National Literary Society in 1892, entitled "The Necessity for De-Anglicising Ireland," grew quickly into a popular aesthetic movement to arrest the decline of the "Gaelic spirit" in Irish society. Soon afterward, the velvet-clad poet William Butler Yeats, the wealthy Edward Martyn, and the Protestant matriarch Lady Isabella Augusta Gregory organized a "national theatre" to combat the "misrepresentation" of the Irish and to "show that

Ireland is not the home of buffoonery." With unabashed pride, cultural critics in Ireland soon spoke of Hyde's Gaelic League and Yeats's Abbey Theatre as "strong yeasts flung into the flaccid dough of an Ireland which is yet in the making" and began praising the virtues of Irish goods, culture, and language. The renewed zest of nationalism also encouraged the muckraking journalist Arthur Griffith to found the separatist political party Sinn Fein—which has been translated as "ourselves alone"—and the *United Irishman,* a newspaper devoted to the reclamation of Irish culture and political independence.[14]

What began, however, as an experiment in modern literature and genteel anticolonialism grew into an explosive national movement to preserve Irish manhood and liberate Ireland. Given the use of militaristic metaphors by Hyde, Yeats's own occasional literary outbursts of extreme nationalism (witness *Cathleen ni Houlihan*), and the lingering, shared hatred of the British, it was probably only a matter of time before the hard-line men of the Irish Republican Brotherhood (IRB) and younger dreamers, like the educational reformer Padraic Pearse, began infiltrating the Gaelic League and promoting rebellion. Pearse, in particular, was prone to highlight those aspects of Gaelic culture premised on martyrdom, racial rejuvenation, and liberation. The popular resurrection of the mythic figure of Cuchulainn—a Gaelicized, militaristic Prometheus and Christ figure—as the embodiment of vigorous Irish manhood was thus part of a broader, deeply subversive effort to overturn those racial representations of the Celt premised on emotionalism and cowardice. "The noble personality of Cuchulainn," Pearse suggested, "forms a true type of Gaelic nationality, full as it is of youthful life and vigour and hope." Or, as Yeats put it, "Manhood is all!" The reconstruction of Irish culture around race and modernism—part of the grand shift which Edward Said has called the "pronounced awareness of European and Western culture *as* imperialism"—was, ultimately, a most political act.[15] Increased radicalism was the result, and by 1915 Hyde had lost control of the ostensibly nonpolitical Gaelic League to Pearse and the IRB and Sinn Fein men were singing nationalist songs in Gaelic between acts of *Cathleen ni Houlihan* at the Abbey. With the formation of the Irish Volunteers, a citizen militia initially controlled by the IRB and created in response to Sir Edward Carson's Anglophile Ulster Volunteer Force, the Irish could drill, train, and flex their restored militaristic manhood to their hearts' content. The seeds of revolution, it seemed, were again sown in Ireland.

By the start of the twentieth century, conditions in America were also beginning to favor advocates of physical force over the conservative parliamentarians who had dominated Irish-American nationalism since the 1890s. Together with the Philadelphia whiskey distiller Joseph McGarrity and the aged Fenian and *Gaelic American* editor Devoy, Daniel Cohalan called a series of meetings in Atlantic City, Philadelphia, and New York which were to rebuild the Clan and begin to organize a response to the burgeoning spirit of *fin-de-siècle* Anglo-Saxonism. Lambasting parliamentarians and "Anglomaniacs" in the pages of the *Gaelic American,* and having 40,000 members by 1910, the Clan was quickly able to support, and then to a certain extent control, the course of nationalism in Ireland from Philadelphia and New York. The ties between the IRB and the Clan na Gael were, at this point, remarkably tight and often personal. Devoy and the Irish Republican Brotherhood leader Tom Clarke were close friends, as were McGarrity and Pearse, and these personal ties often meant that vital Clan funds were sent first to the IRB and then to organizations dominated by hard-line republicans and other staunch advocates of complete independence, such as Pearse's St. Enda's School, the Gaelic League, and Sinn Fein. With Clan strength increasing, with deeper tensions emerging in Europe, and with Ireland and Irish culture electrified, it seemed a propitious moment to enkindle rebellion.

For grim-faced Irish-American nationalists like Cohalan, getting guns to the Irish Volunteers in Ireland—the embodiment of Irish manhood—was of central importance. Padraic wrote to Devoy: "The one great duty of the hour . . . is to get guns and ammunition into the country. It is up to the American [Committee] to act *at once* and *on a large scale.* You are as much alive to the need as I am. Every penny you command must be expended now and the goods sent to us with as little delay as possible. A supreme moment for Ireland may be at hand. We shall go down to our grave beaten if we are not ready for it." Clan na Gael leaders responded quickly, if somewhat creatively, to the cry for dollars, playing on Irish America's romantic memories of the home sod. "Each man's sincerity," wrote Joseph McGarrity in an open letter sent to Clan members, "will be tested by the sacrifices he is prepared to make at this turning point in Ireland's history . . . [The] hand that will now withhold the sum it should freely give cannot be depended upon to strike a blow for Ireland." The San Francisco *Leader,* comparing those millions of Italian Americans who went back to Italy "to make the supreme sacrifice for their fatherland" with the Irish in America, asked, "Where the Italians gave much blood, can we not give a little gold?" In the United States, then, "Irish" manliness was tied to fiscal, and not physical, sacrifice.[16]

Another problem for the Clan and the IRB was the powerful Irish Parliamentary Party leader John Redmond, a man universally detested in physical-force circles, who was intent on gaining control of the Volunteers. Devoy, apoplectic at the thought of Redmond's dominance, likened the fratricidal conflict over the Volunteers to a "war" and concluded that the parliamentarian wanted to "gobble the Volunteers and render them useless." By the start of the Great War, with Redmond supporting the allied cause—and with the Clan and the IRB in constant contact with German officials and seeking military aid—Redmond made the startling claim that "95 percent of the Irish Race in America" supported his position on the war and Home Rule, and then, amazingly, urged the Volunteers to fight on behalf of England in the war. A more direct threat to Irish manhood could not possibly have been envisioned; Robert Ford invoked the idea of "race suicide," saying that a positive response to Redmond's appeal "would simply mean the complete wiping out of the remnant of our race."[17]

Cohalan, McGarrity, Devoy, and other Irish Americans also had to navigate the New World context while engaging in a struggle to "preserve the tattered remnant of Irish manhood" in the Old In addition to fears of "Irish youths . . . slaughtered on European battlefields," Irish-American nationalists had to grapple with the now pronounced conviction in some circles that, as the playwright Padraic Colum put it, "there is no Irish race in America nor anywhere outside of Ireland." In Ireland, many had slowly come to believe that Americanization programs had forced the Irish to "let go" of their "racial distinctiveness." "What is an American Gael?" said George Bernard Shaw in an interview; "I have asked professors of ethnology in vain. I never heard anybody in Ireland or Scotland call himself one. I saw that an American Gael was arrested recently for interrupting [Irish playwright J. M. Synge's] 'The Playboy.' His name was Rosenberg . . . I warned the Irish players that America is governed by a mysterious race, probably one of the lost tribes of Israel, calling themselves American Gaels. It is an especially dangerous country for genuine Irishmen and Irishwomen."[18] As if the comments of acerbic cultural critics in Ireland weren't bad enough, more than a few Americans also began to question what claim the Irish anywhere had to racial distinctiveness. Sinclair Kennedy, for instance, took Henry Cabot Lodge's depiction of the Irish in America as "honorary Anglo-Saxons" one step further by describing them as merely "disgruntled Anglo-Saxons." Madison Grant's *The Passing of the Great Race,* one of the most popular books of the late 1910s and early 1920s, argued that only the Irish in the far west of Ireland were "non-Nordic" and of the "middle Paleolithic race"; all those in America were, quite simply, white Nordics. And Grant, unlike Kennedy, glided over the ins and outs of the *assimilation* of the Irish to suggest that "the Celt" was a nationalist myth, and that the Irish had always already been biologically Nordic and racially white.

Popular science and the wartime thirst for national unity were not the only factors involved in the increasing whiteness of the Irish in America. The economic parity achieved by most Irish communities in the 1910s, and the resultant softening and gradual elimination of racialized represen-tations of the Irish, took a toll on nationalist discourse. Indeed, the general sense of national reconciliation that developed in the 1910s, and that cul-minated in the election of Woodrow Wilson—a southerner at heart—as president in 1912, masked the regionally different philosophies of race. This national reconciliation, the political scientist Michael Rogin has ar-gued, emerges clearly in D. W. Griffith's negrophobic and nationalistic film *The Birth of a Nation,* and directly involves the assimilation of European immigrants: "As blacks became the sign of negative American identity, Progressives took immigrants to the national bosom."[19] As the war con-cluded, and as consumer culture matured, "the Negro"—and not "the Celt"—became a national obsession. The intensifying focus on "the Ne-gro," soon to be exacerbated by the Great Migration and the "Black Scare," turned northeastern racial discourse away from its traditional Anglo-Saxonism and toward a unified sense of race-as-color, or as whiteness and blackness.

Irish-American nationalists also mounted their defense of Irishness and their attack on Anglo-Saxonism and the British Empire in the face of the rapid wartime growth of the American state and the attendant interest in state patriotism. The Great War came at the tail end of the Progressive Era, a diffuse, middle-class "moment" ambivalently committed to the ethi-cal and moral reformation of American capitalism. This reformist spirit merged with the necessities of war to engender several patriotic societies and institutions as well as to encourage the expansion of certain branches of government. The Committee on Public Information (the "Creel Com-mittee"), for instance, developed a sophisticated network of public speakers and devoted much time to the production and diffusion of "100 Percent American" propaganda. With non-official nationalisms increasingly viewed as traitorous and indeed dangerous, the Military Intelligence and Naval Intelligence bureaus grew exponentially, and began investigating certain "subversive" groups, paying particular attention to German-American, Indian-American, and Irish-American nationalists, as well as to the Anglophobic ties that bound these groups together. Hyper-patriotic organizations, such as the American Protective League and the American Defense Society, flourished during and after the war and sent a constant stream of reports to agencies of the official, "100 Percent American" nationalism.[20] To a certain extent, Irish-American nationalism thrived in this repressive atmosphere; surveillance and attempted control, it was thought, marked the maturity, or the dangerous qualities, of subversive nationalisms. But the personal thrill gained from state repression was hardly worth the cost of constant supervision. Cohalan, for one, was suspected of near-treason after some damning correspondence was found in the German foreign office during the "Von Igel" affair, and Devoy's *Gaelic American* was banned from the mails after attacking Wilson.[21]

At least four different problems, then, converged on Irish-American nationalism at the advent of the war in Europe—all of them connected to the idea of an Irish race. First, Clan na Gael leaders had to broaden the membership base of their organization in order to raise sufficient funds for a rebellion in Ireland—a rebellion they and the IRB leadership began quietly planning immediately, and which they hoped would rejuvenate the Irish race. Second, nationalists needed to convince Irish, British, and American politicians that "the whole Irish race" was not, as Redmond's allies in America assumed, willing to "be lined up on the side of humanity and civilization," and that the Volunteers would not fight for Britain.[22] Third, Devoy, Cohalan, McGarrity, and others needed to get Americans of "Irish blood" to act "Irish" quickly and on a large scale, and thus perform their Irishness in the face of critics in Ireland and America who no longer believed they constituted a race apart from the "white world," or who suggested that only a small hard-core group of subversives harbored "republican" sympathies. Finally, all these tasks faced opposition from the surging spirit of hyper-patriotism known as "100 Percent Americanism," a spirit which had strong support from President Woodrow Wilson and former President Theodore Roosevelt and which construed any "hyphenism" or cultural pluralism as "moral treason" against the state.

For Cohalan, the solution was simple: only an unprecedented mass convention of "the Irish race" in America could handle these problems, and then only if it was precisely and very secretly organized and publicly proclaimed a success. At a small Clan na Gael meeting presided over by Devoy and Cohalan in December of 1915, it was decided that a "public conference" should be held to refute Redmond. "Such a conference," Devoy wrote to fellow Clan members, "will afford a rallying point for the union of the entire Irish Race at home and abroad."[23] From that point forward the resurgence of Irish-American nationalism was scripted by Cohalan, who envisioned the spectacle of the Race Convention as the very public reawakening of "the race." As such, the convention was a complete success; the Irish problem became a matter of even greater international concern for progressive politicos and the dispersed "children of Erin" alike. Several complicated messages were unmistakably communicated: the Irish parliamentarian John Redmond did not speak for the exiled children of Erin, the Irish were civilized and not savage, and nationalism was a manly activity. Most important, Cohalan had begun the last great defense of the racial distinctiveness of the Irish in America.

Cohalan's convention also produced an organization that—at least on the surface—stood in stark contrast to the heavily gendered and secretive Clan na Gael. Indeed, despite its behind-the-scenes domination by Clan members, the Friends of Irish Freedom was remarkably inclusive, allowing the active participation of many previously excluded from Clan activities. Women, for example, were encouraged to involve themselves in FOIF functions and affairs. And compared with the ardent Catholicism of Clan meetings and rallies, the FOIF was relatively nondenominational (though the convention did have a preponderance of Catholic speakers on the dais of the Hotel Astor). The FOIF also served not just as a political organization but also as a social and cultural forum, hosting dances for young adults and conducting weekend lectures on Irish history, art, and poetry. Built on fiscal "sacrifice," the FOIF found itself obliged to open its arms to all significant wage earners of "the Irish race," and in 1916 that included women as well as men, the young as well as the old, the Catholic as well as the Protestant. This inclusiveness allowed Cohalan and the Clan leadership controlling the FOIF to gather together Irish Americans who might otherwise have been lost to "the melting pot" and teach them the virtues of "the cause" and "the race"—thus garnering their precious dollars for small arms and political lobbying. And when significant numbers of Irish Americans—40,000 in the aftermath of the convention—joined the Friends of Irish Freedom it only seemed to prove, as the FOIF leader Katherine Hughes had written earlier, that the Irish throughout the world "were one in race-feeling, as no other group in the world is one."[24]

The FOIF's public mask of inclusiveness was, however, often no more than a thin veneer. From the start, the convention's precision required more than ideological consensus, and thus only the "best sort" of Irishmen and Irishwomen were to be invited. In this fashion the tarnish of rowdiness, excessive drinking, and other lower-class "pursuits" was to be kept off the gleamingly perfect convention that Cohalan and Devoy orchestrated. Similarly, no Race Convention organized by the hyper-masculine Clan na Gael, or indeed seeking the preservation of "Irish manhood" in the face of possible conscription, could claim to be egalitarian in the fullest sense of that word.[25] If Irish-American nationalists like Cohalan and Devoy sought to identify and crystallize particular racial traits, such as the "fighting" nature of the Irish, they simultaneously gendered those traits: "fighting" was clearly a masculine activity. The convention itself was a thoroughly gendered space, with well-dressed Irishmen sitting directly in front of the speaker's dais in the great hall, while Irish-American women, dressed in white, Victorian blouses, were segregated in the balcony. Later, the well-supervised dances that came after FOIF meetings would teach young men and women the intricate rules governing sexual relations and the qualitative difference between manhood and womanhood. The steadfast masculine nationalism of Pearse and the IRB may have been somewhat muted in the American case, but the "good Irish wife" was nevertheless still central to Cohalan's pluralist protests.

During and after the Great War, Irish-American nationalism—and the connected Irishness of "the Celt"—was as strong as it had been in years. What is most interesting about the aftermath of the first Irish Race Convention is not just that race once again appeared in Irish-American nationalist rhetoric, but the somewhat peculiar way in which race was spoken and symbolized. Most delegates chose to articulate a full-blown cultural pluralism at the convention, weaving together Romantic racialism with American patriotism, and to eschew any direct or explicit claim to whiteness. There were thus surprisingly few references to the whiteness of the Irish at the convention, and nearly all of these were ambiguous about whether or not the Irish were, exactly, white. Indeed, for the next several years, until the end of the war and the opening of the Versailles Peace Conference, references to the whiteness of the Irish would be muted, implicit, or pointedly absent in the rhetoric of Irish-American nationalism.

In their quest to celebrate "Irishness" in the face of superpatriotism, Irish-American nationalists—and Cohalan in particular—latched on to the vision of a harmonious, romantically racialized society known as cultural pluralism. Cultural pluralism emerged just prior to the Great War as an alternative to the idea of America as a "melting pot" wherein the racial cultures and habits of immigrants were boiled away, leaving only "Americans." By the war's beginning, the "younger generation" of American intellectuals, led by the Harvard graduate Horace Kallen, had begun to conceive of a pluralistic America that was "a multiplicity in a unity, an orchestration of mankind."[26] This was a vision of social harmony predicated not on the explosive celebration of pan-whiteness but, rather, on the acute differences between "the white races"—between the Irish, the Anglo-Saxon, the Jew, and the Teuton. Instead of a melting pot, then, America was to be a concert of racially distinct groups, with the peculiar "genius" of each race contributing to the larger symphony of American civilization. The question of whiteness could be left aside.

Attempts to reconstruct the Irish race thus went hand in hand with a sometimes outrageous defense of immigrant pluralism—of "the little hyphen that unites in holy friendship the name of Ireland and the name of America." Daniel Cohalan joyfully celebrated "the alert Welshman" and "the dreamy Portuguese" among other groups, and carefully inscribed biological and historical differences within whiteness. At the League for Foreign-born Citizens in 1917, Cohalan emphasized the role each race's innate characteristics had to play in the American polity and in civilization. "No strength—moral, intellectual, or physical—which you have brought here from lands beyond the seas," Cohalan preached, "should be permitted to waste unused or undeveloped. Here is the great country into which you have come . . . Our national character is being formed, our national tastes are adjusting themselves and we need the best that every race and every strain of blood brings to us from abroad to make the most of our unique opportunity and to influence, for the better, the history of the world." If the advancement toward civilization rested upon America's ability to "liberate and harmonize the creative power" (in Randolph Bourne's phrase) of the many different races in the republic, then, as far as Cohalan and others were concerned, the continued existence of the Irish race was an absolutely central component of that advancement. The reconstruction of Irishness, the articulation of pluralism, and the staging of an Irish Race Convention were thus decidedly patriotic acts.[27]

With race, or Irishness, an integral part of wartime and postwar Irish-American patriotism, journalists, orators, and political figures of nationalist stripe rewrote American history to suit their needs. They argued that there were Gaels on Columbus's voyages, insisted that Ireland had been the bastion of "civilization" during the dark ages, provided "scientific evidence" that the Irish were prominently represented in the American Revolution, documented that George Washington loved the cause of Irish independence, and described the food served at the first Puritan Thanksgiving dinner as typical Irish fare.[28] At each step of the way, the peculiar racial genius of the Irish had ensured the continued progress of American civilization. The Irish, for instance, were a spiritual race, capable of seeing fairies and sprites, and the loss of this capability in an industrializing, increasingly homogenized America was tragic. All the more reason, then, for a public recovery of "Irishness."[29]

Cohalan offered his own impressions of what made the Irish so important. The Irish, he argued, were "a fighting race," and a vital masculine component of American military history. Many Irish Americans agreed. An emphasis on the martial qualities of the Celt was most common after the formation of the Volunteers and in anticipation of the Easter Rising, but it could also appear in discussions of the Irish contribution to the American war effort in Europe. The War Department, looking for volunteers to chase down Pancho Villa, placed advertisements in Irish-American weeklies depicting an Uncle Sam desperately in need of "the fighting race." Sacrifice and martyrdom emerged in Irish-American rhetoric as potent, racially regenerative experiences. "No men of any race," suggested Cohalan, "have shed their blood more freely, or even recklessly, than have the men of our breed."[30]

In Ireland those seeds of rebellion sown so carefully during the early 1900s were harvested immediately after the convention, when the Irish in Ireland staged a massive revolt against their British overlords. The Easter Rising of 1916 took place in a context deliberately primed for both success and failure. Cohalan, McGarrity, and Devoy had known about the planned rising for months, and the convention had deliberately invoked images of heroic Irish manhood and steadfast, supportive Irish womanhood in anticipation of the event. In Dublin, small bands of IRB men and Volunteers took possession of a few poorly chosen sites, and Pearse, along with Tom

Clarke, the socialist agitator James Connolly, and a few others, took the imposing neoclassical General Post Office as a headquarters. When the British finally came, it was not to wage war against a "civilized" enemy but rather to suppress an uncivil racial rebellion. That suppression tore Dublin apart and resulted in the execution of nearly all the leaders of the Rising. Indeed, there is some indication that Pearse and the others may have known from the start that the Rising was doomed, but chose a deliberate, manly racial sacrifice to purify the soul of Ireland.[31]

But across the Atlantic the culture of "enforced patriotism" in wartime and postwar America allowed very little room for enraged Anglophobia. Searching for a groundswell of Irish-American public support, FOIF leaders had to deal with the very different threats of state repression and ethnic irrelevance. "Did they die in vain?" asked the Irish American John Kelly, in an address to a Friends of Irish Freedom gathering. "Has our race lost its pride, its tradition, and its ideals? Are we so Anglicized that we can only think of making money?" "These men," wrote Devoy passionately, "perceived that nothing but a stand-up fight and the shedding of Irish blood in Ireland and for Ireland could clear away the noxious overgrowth of imperialistic cant and selfishness which . . . had been smothering every ennobling nationalistic ideal that had preserved the spirit of the Irish people through the centuries of British domination . . . one phase of the Irish Republican task was to save the *soul* of Ireland." But nearly every articulation of nationalist outrage in America was colored by the need to satisfy the most ardent "100 Percenters"—were you Irish or were you American, and how could you possibly be both?[32]

After the execution of the leaders of the Easter Rising, the FOIF held an "Irish Memorial Mass Meeting" in Manhattan. The bizarre decorations in Madison Square Garden for the event embodied that stark juxtaposition of selves in pluralism:

At one side of the stage was a great Celtic cross, on which was inscribed the names of the martyrs . . . A huge canopy of St. Patrick's green was spread beneath the dome and extended down the sides of the great building. Irish and American flags were strung around the boxes and an Irish Republican Flag . . . was suspended side by side with the flag of the American Republic from the roof in front of the stage. The centerpiece of the decorations was an immense electric American flag, which, when the audience began to sing the "Star Spangled Banner" at the opening of the meeting flashed with red, white, and blue lights and continued to wave over the speaker's dais until the meeting closed.

Here, at last, the paths of nationalists in Ireland and America diverged completely; in the aftermath of the Rising, nationalism in Ireland gained popular support which resulted eventually in the Sinn Fein electoral victories of 1917, while nationalists in America increasingly suffered under patrician superpatriotism and were forced, as John Devoy put it angrily, "to use the soft pedal."[33]

The "Irishness" of the Celt in America continued to hang in the balance until the war was over and the urgency of state patriotism had subsided. Once the gaze of 100 Percenters had been turned toward Bolshevism and the postwar menace posed by "the international Jew" and "the New Negro," the conservative stripe of Irish-American nationalism—which had shied away from socialism or communism in the twentieth century—made the Celt seem friendly, or even harmless, in comparison to other "alien" groups. Nor were Irish Americans able to speak in a uniform voice after the war, for the wartime cohesion provided by Cohalan and Devoy dissolved with the arrival of the Provisional President of Ireland, Eamon De Valera, in 1919.

De Valera, a gaunt former mathematics instructor and one of the few surviving leaders of the Easter Rising, had escaped from a British prison and made his way secretly to America aboard a tramp steamer. Once in the United States, he spoke constantly on the need for American support and the insistence of the Irish people for independence, and opened a sharp-tongued debate on the Americanization of the Irish. A split soon developed between Cohalan and De Valera over the best way to spend the funds raised by the third Irish Race Convention (held in 1919 in Philadelphia) and over the role of Irish-American nationalists in Irish politics. Simply stated, a large part of the dispute boiled down to De Valera's and Joseph McGarrity's belief that FOIF funds should go directly to Ireland, Sinn Fein, and the IRA, versus Cohalan's belief that the money should be spent lobbying for American recognition of the Irish republic. On a deeper level, however, De Valera put his finger on the difficulties of Irish-American pluralism: the impossibility of advocating both 100 Percent Americanism and Irish-American nationalism. Publicly challenging Cohalan, De Valera claimed that he "alone" was "answerable to the Irish people," and asked where Cohalan stood on the matter; Cohalan's forced reply—"I am in this work as an American whose first and only loyalty is to my own country"—was reprinted nationally in FOIF circulars and *Gaelic American* editorials, and reflected the ultimate paradox of pluralism. De Valera put "race first"; Cohalan, the supposed leader of the Irish race in America, put America first.[34]

There were other significant changes afoot. The wartime focus on Irishness and evasion of whiteness ended rather abruptly when, after the armistice, it seemed as if Wilsonian idealism, coupled with the lure and loathing of Bolshevism and the general thrust of the Peace Conference, might lead to Irish liberation. This became especially clear during the Peace Conference when postwar discussions of the Irish as a wronged "white race" took place within the context of larger attacks on British policy in Ireland, India, and Egypt.[35] When the time came to argue Ireland's case before the court of world opinion after the war, Irish nationalists in America practically leaped to claim the penultimate gift of whiteness, the right to self-government. From late 1918 onward, it was thus a matter of course to find in the rhetoric of the Clan na Gael or the Friends of Irish Freedom references to the Irish as "the only white race in slavery," or, better still, as "the only white race in America whose homeland remains subject to a foreign power."[36] When Irish Americans spoke of whiteness and placed their own struggle in a global, anticolonial context, they moved away from the understanding of their struggle as a "battle of two civilizations," one Anglo-Saxon and one Celtic. Invoking whiteness to differentiate between the "Hindoo" and the Celt, or between the struggle for Ireland's freedom and the struggle for Indian independence, postwar Irish-American nationalism—despite its vigorous postwar attacks on empire—was a willing participant in the sweeping return of whiteness and the reemergence of the complicated balancing act between whiteness and Irishness. And given the increasing centrality of "absolute whiteness" in science, politics, and popular culture, it was more and more difficult to conceive of the Irish in America as racially distinct from the Anglo-Saxon.

The twists and turns of postwar Irish-American nationalism and the resurgence of "whiteness" in its rhetoric did not at first undercut the formation of a potentially revolutionary anticolonial movement in the United States. On the night of August 2, 1920, in the midst of a massive, thirty-day Universal Negro Improvement Association convention in Manhattan, Marcus Garvey, "Provisional President of Africa," ascended the platform at Madison Square Garden and spoke to a crowd of 25,000. Greeted by a standing ovation and dressed in a "gown of purple, green, and gold," Garvey had to wait nearly five minutes before quiet descended and his words could be heard. "I hold in my hand," Garvey bellowed dramatically to the crowd, "a telegram to be sent to Edmund De Valeria [*sic*], President of the Irish Republic." He then read the telegram aloud: "25,000 Negro delegates assembled in Madison Square Garden in mass convention, representing 400,000,000 Negroes of the world, send you greetings as President of the Irish Republic. Please accept the sympathy of Negroes of the world for your cause. We believe Ireland should be free even as Africa shall be free for the Negroes of the world . . . Keep up the fight for a free Ireland." At the conclusion of the telegram, the UNIA delegates "shook the big building" with an extended burst of applause. "We new negroes," Garvey continued, "we men who have returned from this war, will dispute every inch of the way until we win." When the *New York Times* announced the next day that the "Cheering Negroes" gathered in the Garden had sent "Sympathy To Irish," the deeper implications of the event were revealed: Marcus Garvey, his movement now ostensibly allied with one of the most powerful forces in world politics, was very, very dangerous.[37]

While Garvey connected his diasporic protest to that of the Irish during the summer and fall of 1921, the Lord Mayor of Cork, Terrence MacSwiney, also a Gaelic revivalist and the editor of *Fianna Fail,* died slowly in Brixton prison. MacSwiney had been arrested by British authorities in August at what was thought to be a "Republican Court." His subsequent hunger strike—and the refusal of British authorities to be flexible in the face of that painful act of resistance—brought renewed international attention to the agonizingly slow and apocalyptically violent birth of the Irish republic. For the duration of that hunger strike, all those interested in the "Irish question" spoke of MacSwiney's protracted death as the human embodiment of the tragic situation in Ireland, which had recently exploded into the widespread guerrilla strife of the Anglo-Irish war. When he finally died on October 24, 1921—seventy-four days after his hunger strike had begun—MacSwiney quickly entered the pantheon of Irish martyrs, joining the eighteenth-century Christ-figure Robert Emmet and the poets and dreamers of the Easter Rising of 1916. After a solemnly ritualized and well-publicized funeral laid MacSwiney to rest, the ruthless war against "perfidious Albion" grew even hotter, more fanatical, and hopelessly bloody.

Much like the furious response to John Redmond's "treacherous" support of the English war effort four years earlier, MacSwiney's hunger strike reinvigorated Gaelic-American nationalism in the United States. In 1920 the political powers of Cohalan and Devoy may have been neutralized by an all too public dispute with Eamon De Valera, but other organizations kept the "fight for Irish freedom" in the minds and hearts of Manhattan's advocates of social justice. On the New York docks that August, the American Women's Pickets for the Enforcement of America's War Aims (an Irish-American group loosely affiliated with Cohalan's Friends of Irish Freedom) organized several massive strikes against British shipping lines, eliciting impressive support from the New York Irish and even a few sympathy strikes in Boston, Philadelphia, and elsewhere. On Friday, August 27, 1920, with MacSwiney slowly failing, 1,500 Irish-American longshoremen tossed aside the concerns of their union leadership and refused to work, choosing instead to march loudly, waving nationalistic banners and invoking the specter of "the labor problem" by calling for "England's head bowed on the altar of labor." "The imprisonment of MacSwiney," the *Times* concluded soberly, "seemed the chief cause of protest."[38]

The wildcat strike that bright and warm August day was not just another reflection of the agitation on the docks in support of MacSwiney and Ireland, for on that particular day nearly two hundred "Negro longshoremen" broke away from their work on a nearby British steamer to march with the strikers. If those intrepid African-American laborers chose to ignore, or perhaps just set aside, over one hundred years of Irish-American violence against black folks, they did so partly at the request of the flamboyant "President-General" of the Universal Negro Improvement Association, Marcus Garvey. On the morning of the strike, Garvey sent a personal representative down to the docks to encourage African-American support for the Irish. Irish-American nationalists responded in kind, cheering the "Negro longshoremen" who struck with them and, later, venturing into Harlem. Prominent Irish Americans—including Dudley Field Malone, the former collector of the port of New York and erstwhile confidant of Woodrow Wilson—met with Garvey at the squat, brick-faced headquarters of the UNIA, named Liberty Hall, that stood at 138th Street and Lennox Avenue. Once there, Gaelic activists promised financial support for the UNIA generally and for Garvey's magnificent venture, the Black Star Line, specifically, and vowed that the causes of Irish and African liberation would be forever linked. That same week in late August, at the massive UNIA convention being held in Manhattan, Garvey read aloud a second telegram he had sent to Ireland, this time to "Father Dominick, Confessor of the Lord Mayor of Cork"—a telegram which urged Dominick to "Convey to MacSwiney [the] sympathy of 400,000,000 Negroes."[39]

## A New Negro Manhood Movement

Marcus Garvey was, by his own unabashed admission, a wonder of self-mastery and a man of the modern world. The son of a local printer in Jamaica, the well-educated Garvey reached adulthood at nearly the exact moment that the United Fruit Company began its ruthless infiltration and destruction of the local peasant economy. After traveling throughout the Caribbean, in 1912 Garvey went to London, the seat of the British Empire, where he first encountered Pan-Africanism through Dusé Mohamed Ali, the Afro-Egyptian editor of *The Africa Times and Orient Review,* and honed his incendiary speaking style on the corners of Hyde Park. Staying in London between 1912 and 1914, Garvey may have first encountered "the Irish problem" through the debate over Home Rule, or through the militarization of Ireland's activists in the form of the Ulster Volunteer Force and the Irish National Volunteers. It is also probable that Garvey (avid newspaper reader that he was) watched the brutal repression of the Irish Transport and General Worker's Union in Dublin closely during the "labor lockout" of the summer of 1913. After returning to Jamaica and founding the Universal Negro Improvement Association and African Communities League, Garvey took his fledgling protest organization not to London but to Manhattan, the seat of American capitalism and the home of the same United Fruit Company which had so ruthlessly harnessed Jamaica's independent farmers and countryfolk.[40]

No figure in the surge of postwar radicalism known to us as "the New Negro Movement" drew more powerful connections between anti-colonialism in Ireland and the liberation of Africa than Marcus Garvey. Cyril Briggs's African Blood Brotherhood—with its deliberate emulation of the Irish Republican Brotherhood and its tightly defined roles for black men and women in the revolutionary struggle for freedom—could wax Gaelic with equal force. But for sustained vigor and popularity, and for the creative manipulation of nationalism, Garvey was unique. The general facts of Garvey's interest in Ireland are known, if rarely discussed: Garvey named his Liberty Hall in Harlem after the Dublin building which housed the head office of James Connolly's Irish Transport and General Worker's

Union—a Georgian structure singled out by the British for destruction during their bombardment of Dublin during the 1916 Rising. On occasion, Garvey argued that the green stripe on the pants of UNIA uniforms and on the African tricolor signified sympathy for the Irish cause, and, again, he may have used the phrase "race first"—one of many possible interpretations of "Sinn Fein"—to demonstrate similar feelings. There were also more tangible events like the wildcat strike on the Manhattan docks and the meeting with Dudley Field Malone. And on at least one occasion, Garvey claimed—excitedly and very publicly—to have been sent on a "secret mission . . . on the order of De Valera."[41]

In addition to the widespread spirit of anticolonialism that grew out of the Great War—a spirit tied to the perceived postwar decline of Western civilization and the Russian Revolution—the gendered coding of nationalism helped cement ties between New Negroes and other anticolonial movements in America. Indeed, as racial difference (the sense that the Irish were part of "the white race") increasingly pushed Irish-American and African-American nationalisms apart, a shared interest in manliness may have helped build solidarity. Irish nationalism, in both its American and Irish incarnations, was deeply gendered, leaving room for women's direct involvement in nationalism only as "helpmates." For New Negroes, the ideological matrix of race and gender in the postwar era brought together the imperatives of civilized manhood and domestic womanhood. The variant of postwar African-American radicalism that Hubert Harrison named the New Negro Manhood Movement produced a mountain of prescriptive literature on women's and men's roles, arguing, for example, that the manliness of black men was revealed in their protection (and control) of black women, or that black women should devote themselves to the maintenance of a Christian home. UNIA rhetoric was a response not only to the stereotypical representations of black women as asexual and masculine and black men as overly emotional, but also to the thirty years of criticism from African-American "Women's Era" activists. And to a certain extent the masculinism of anticolonial protest allowed Garvey and others to reconfigure sexual relations and cultural authority within the black community along lines more acceptable to men in general, and black men in particular.[42]

Proponents of a New Negro Manhood Movement argued that black men were self-sacrificing protectors of race and womanhood, and that "world's work"—from anti-imperialism to black capitalism—was race work, or men's work. When Garvey, Cyril Briggs, and others invoked death and sacrifice in the service of "the race," the gendered qualities of New Negro radicalism emerged at their clearest. "The time has come," Garvey declared in August of 1919 after suggesting that "sinister forces" were out to get him, "for the Negro race to offer up its martyrs upon the altar of liberty even as the Irish had given a long list from Robert Emmet to Roger Casement." Nor was Garvey alone in his appreciation for the politics of martyrdom, Irish martyrdom in particular, and New Negroes as different as Briggs and W. E. B. Du Bois were united in their respect for the symbolic importance of male death in the service of race-patriotism. The New Negro Movement, argued Briggs—a hated enemy of Garvey—was a "great resurrection of Negro manhood from the pit of degradation into which it had been cast by the white race."[43]

The Great War proved a good context for the growth of manly anti-colonialism. Indeed, the retributive, barely repressed anger expressed in New Negro radicalism was part of a broader reconstruction of masculinity in postwar America, as Gail Bederman has noted. New Negro radicals, participating in a remasculinized American culture, as many did after the war, argued that race and manhood were all that mattered. As in the broader American culture, an older, civilizationist rhetoric of "uplift" and "womanhood" persisted—Garvey's propaganda was nearly always laced with it to a certain degree—but the Garvey movement, and the New Negro Movement more generally, was a "manhood movement" above all else.[44] By 1919, arguably the take-off point for masculinist organizations like Garvey's UNIA and Briggs's African Blood Brotherhood, New Negro radicals had, despite their antiwar sentiments, linked black male experience in battle with racial self-determination, celebrating the "good humor, nerves of steel, and unconquerable corp d'esprit [sic]" evinced by black soldiers in the war and depicting the New Negro as a gun-toting advocate of real social justice in America. Even Du Bois's pro-Allies stance, criticized severely by the younger generation of New Negro radicals, shared some of the gendered peculiarities of wartime black nationalism, as the *Crisis* editor hoped, in the words of his biographer, to achieve "full citizenship through carnage." "We return from fighting," wrote Du Bois, "[and] we return fighting." *World's Work* magazine, concerned about the "intense" pride that military service engendered in "the Negro mind," argued that race riots in the postwar North were a logical result of the new, postwar manliness of "the Negro" and suggested that widespread national segregation—laws backed by "more knowledge and power than ever before"—might help.[45]

The manly anticolonialism of Garvey, Du Bois, Briggs, and others merged quite easily with traditional contours of black nationalism. The masculinism of turn-of-the-century Victorian civilizationist rhetoric and the millennial flavor of Ethiopianism, for instance, often electrified Garvey's rhetoric in particular. Much like Irish-American nationalism, African-American nationalism originally drew upon European Romanticism for its corpus of ideals, and later couched its protest in social Darwinist, civilizationist terms. This "classical black nationalism," as the historian Wilson Moses has shown, predated Irish-American nationalism by decades, originating in the 1700s, running through the life of "the peculiar institution," and maturing in the 1850s. If the "one-drop rule" and slavery made it easy for any of the "white races" in America to disparage the potential of "the Negro" for civilization, the shared experience of slavery undermined "ethnic divisions" between Africans and made it easier for "striving" educated African Americans to speak—without hesitation—of a unified "Negro race" in America and, indeed, around the world (even if such a thing was always mere fiction). "Across all frontiers," the *Crusader* hummed, "the Negro Race is one!"[46]

The success of the Irish in organizing a rebellion and in marshaling fiscal support from around the world gave Garvey and others reason to build real, tangible connections between Irish and African-American nationalisms. With its race conventions and its sponsorship of IRB revolution, Irish-American nationalism had become the standard by which all other subversive nationalisms in the United States were to be judged. The Easter Rising, the literary renaissance of Yeats and Hyde, and the race conventions of Cohalan and McGarrity had also marked the struggle to "save the soul of Ireland" as unique, as somehow different and more dangerous than previous unofficial nationalisms. The Irish, in both their American and European incarnations, were using the United States as the base from which to achieve Irish independence. Garvey envisioned the UNIA operating along similar lines. And, moreover, the Irish struck out at the British in 1916, proving that the Irish race had not been emasculated by "700 years" of British tyranny (Garvey, like Cyril Briggs, was fascinated by the prospect of violent resistance to empire). Irish-American nationalism was also very active in certain parts of Harlem through the early 1920s. The Harlem Branch of the Gaelic Society met monthly just two blocks from the corner of 125th Street and Lennox Avenue—near the focal center of the African-American community in Harlem—and also launched several successful protests against immoral depictions of Irish womanhood at the Harlem YMCA.[47] In other words, there were Gaelic Leaguers speaking on street corners within earshot of Liberty Hall, and there were local, personal connections forged on the dusty, cobbled streets of Harlem.[48]

The carefully cultivated anticolonial connections of the New Negro Movement were never confined to the Irish. A bevy of anti-imperialist organizations met frequently under the auspices of various Progressive venues, such as the Irish Progressive League, the Anti-Imperialist League, and the YMCA in Harlem. Groups like the Clan na Gael and the Friends of Irish Freedom had loose but important relationships with similarly named organizations, such as the Friends of Freedom for India, the Friends of New Russia, and the Friends of Negro Freedom. Dudley Field Malone and Frank P. Walsh, one of the Irish-American delegates to the Peace Conference, were executive officers of the FOFI and helped put out several pamphlets in support of Gopal Singh, a "Hindu held for deportation" at the request of the British. Lala Lajpat Rai, leader of the India Home Rule League of America, met with Oswald Garrison Villard of the NAACP, and Madame Bikhaiji Rustomji Cama published excerpts from *Gaelic American* editorials in her *Bande Mataram*.[49] Large meetings were held in which Indian, Irish, or New Negro activists spoke before mixed audiences. It was this broader anti-imperialism which encouraged Garvey to incite a sympathy strike on the Brooklyn pier, and which saw Dudley Field Malone and other Progressives approach the UNIA at Liberty Hall. The Department of Justice quickly took note of this phenomenon and, at the behest of the British government, began infiltrating and, ultimately, repressing these organizations.[50] While the Irish in America never seemed entirely enthusiastic about the subversive connections forged across "the color line," Garvey, Du Bois, and others leapt at the chance to shake the foundation of "white world supremacy." And these connections between various anti-imperialist organizations served several purposes, not the least of which was to establish beyond a doubt that black radicalism was a remarkably dangerous postwar phenomenon.[51]

Manhattan was a natural focal point for New World radicalism. As the seat of an economic empire, New York City had various material and capital connections around the world that few other cities could match. Additionally, there was, as historians have suggested, a unique Emersonian—or postcolonial—quality to the civic culture of New York. In the aftermath of the Great War, with American innocence spoiled and "Old Stock" patricians increasingly on the defensive, the battle waged in the 1910s—the battle of "the two generations"—seemed decided in favor of the younger radicals. As the "tide" of immigrants washed ashore at Ellis Island, the cultural politics of the younger generation of American radicals, many of them children of immigrants or immigrants themselves, found their positions strengthened by sheer numbers, by the infusion of Irish, Italian, and Jewish immigrants into Jersey City and New York City. Moreover, Manhattan was never just the social and political stronghold of the Irish, it was also the home of socialism, communism, and Zionism. Altogether, the cheeky confidence of younger radicals, the postcolonial qualities of American cultural nationalism, and the openness and relative flexibility of American egalitarianism—despite the *herrenvolk* nature of each—proved fertile ground for international protest movements and, more important, for the connections forged between anticolonialisms.[52] And those foundations of protest culture combined with the structural transformation of the world economy to make the docks of Manhattan and Brooklyn a likely port of call for anti-imperialists of every stripe. Anticolonial activists saw in Manhattan a natural base of operations, and, not surprisingly, Garvey's worldly protest found a home in Harlem rather than London or Jamaica.

The postwar anticolonial awakening was not, however, unique to Manhattan. For Egyptians, Indians, and the Irish, London continued to be a seat of protest against the British Empire. France's "colonial self" was soon present in the form of Blaise Diagne, the Senegalese representative in Paris. Indian nationalists, already suffering under patterns of colonial dominance modeled on Britain's experience in Ireland, heightened Britain's anxieties by invoking the specter of national self-discovery modeled on Ireland. And the Irish themselves, with some ambivalence partly driven by racial difference, returned the favor and conceived of India as "a larger Ireland." Indeed, some Gaelic agitators moved to India and worked on behalf of Indian nationalism, leading the British to legislate against "the Sinn Fein virus." Garvey's UNIA, whatever its shortcomings, had branches throughout the American South, the west coast of Africa, the Caribbean, and South Africa, and the Pan-African Congress movement of Du Bois and Diagne brought together activists from around the world in the European metropolitan centers of empire. No wonder, then, that it seemed as if things were falling apart, or that Lothrop Stoddard feared the "rising tide of color" and suggested that "the white world" was "shipwrecked."[53]

But if Manhattan's New Negroes—from Du Bois to Garvey to Briggs—were united in their appreciation of the struggles of the Irish in Ireland, they never forgot that the Irish were white, and that Irish Americans had a history of racial violence against African Americans. Du Bois, while insisting, "I shall at all times defend the right of Ireland to absolute independence," reminded one letter-writer that "there can be no doubt of the hostility of a large proportion of Irish Americans towards Negroes." Working-class ethnic violence against "the Negro" actually increased during and after the war, as African Americans moving northward for jobs and returning home invigorated by war and Europe challenged "white" economic mobility and manhood.[54] To a certain extent, then, the question was not whether the Irish were white, but instead just how white were they? Garvey argued:

> The English people have spread and scattered the universal propaganda against the Irishman, trying to impress the world that the Irishman is not fit to govern himself. In spite of that propaganda the Irish have been fighting for seven hundred years. What they have done to the Irish they will do to the Negro. But to our advantage, while the Irish are only 4,000,000, we are 400,000,000 . . . [and because] of the position of England to Ireland and Ireland to England, they are all cousins if not brothers. They are all one people, and it is only a matter of national limits that caused them to be fighting one against the other. It is not a matter of injustice done because of race . . . we cannot say that Ireland's fight is just like ours.

"The Englishmen, the Frenchmen, the American," Briggs likewise argued, collapsing the previously racialized differences between nations in Europe and immigrants in America, "are all whitemen first and Englishmen, French, and American after."[55]

New Negroes were thus of two distinct minds about the Irish, celebrating their every success in the struggle for freedom and castigating them for their repeated and continued violence against "the Negro" in America. For every editorial or public speech which concluded that "White Irishmen are equally, and in some instances, more oppressed than Negroes," there was another arguing the opposite and suggesting that "white Irishmen" were, in fact, more often directly responsible for the plight of "the Negro." And even those New Negroes who truly sympathized with the Irish and who hoped to establish a "trans-racial" alliance of oppressed people—such as A. Philip Randolph—were increasingly marking the Irish as "white."[56] Time and time again, the New Negro critical discourse on "the Irish question" hit upon a disjunction between Irish claims to be racially distinct and popular arguments to the contrary. Were the Irish "absolutely" white? If so, was the Irish problem really analogous to the Negro problem? That question became more difficult to answer affirmatively—even by the most zealous advocates of Irishness—once Irish Americans succumbed to the lure of pan-whiteness and once an Irish republic had, in imagination and in law, been established. Indeed, when the Anglo-Irish war ended, the achievement of an Irish Free State and the subsequent civil war over the Anglo-Irish treaty split American organizations, making future "race conventions" improbable, and further undermining the very possibility that the Irish constituted a race apart.[57] The uproar surrounding Lothrop Stoddard's public appearance in Boston with the Ku Klux Klan's Grand Goblin, A. J. Padon Jr., would have made sense to the Irish race in America—and to the anti-Catholic Klan, no doubt—but Stoddard himself would have been more focused on the threat posed by a deeply racialized and color-coded "under-man" and could hardly have understood why the "American Gael" clung so fiercely to anything but whiteness.[58]

Irish-American nationalism had been part of a Romantic view of the world, in which there were fifteen, thirty, or even fifty races all progressing toward unique destinies and possessing peculiar racial traits. Postwar African-American radicals, however, despite drawing connections between their own struggle and that of the Irish, increasingly saw no racial difference between Anglo-Saxons and Celts: both, they thought, were members of a singular "white race," or, as Cyril Briggs put it, were "within the charmed circle of the dominant race."[59] Indeed, even as anticolonial sentiments drew the causes of Ireland and African America together, Irish Americans and African Americans were forced further apart by race. To postwar race leaders in Harlem, the predicaments of the Irish in Ireland and "the Negro" in America were strikingly similar: a shared interest in anticolonialism and antiracism tied to a deep antipathy for "perfidious Albion"; a desire to overturn a series of racial representations which were deeply gendered and tightly tied to colonial oppression; a hope that Wilsonian idealism and the postwar drive for colonial self-determination might overturn the dominance of white over black, or Anglo-Saxon over Celt; and a sense of global dispersion and racial community that made their struggles similarly diasporic and geopolitically complex. Despite the lofty rhetoric of shared struggle, "absolute" whiteness of the Irish in America and the subtle differences between Irish and black anticolonialism forced NAACP propagandists, soapbox socialists, Liberty Hall Zionists, Clan na Gael subversives, and Irish politicians to deal publicly with the differences between Celt and Negro, between "the Irish question" and "the Negro problem," and between Irishness, whiteness, and blackness. Faith in the distinctive racial "Irishness" of the Celt in America was gradually eroded by the new idiom of race-as-color—by the new set of symbols, words, and meanings that marked biological and historical difference.

# 3

# Against the
# White Leviathan

Sitting in the Viktoria Café, on the Unter den Linden, Berlin, Matthew looked again at the white leviathan—at that mighty organization of white folk against which he felt himself so bitterly in revolt. It was the same vast, remorseless machine in Berlin as in New York.

—W. E. B. DU BOIS, *DARK PRINCESS* (1928)

Race, W. E. B. Du Bois argued in his essay "The Conservation of the Races," was the stuff of which civilization was made. Delivered in 1897 before the fledgling American Negro Academy, a group of educated African Americans comprising the luminaries of the Washington set—including Bishop Alexander Crummell (a lifelong inspiration to Du Bois), the Yale man William Ferris, Kelly Miller, and Archibald and Francis Grimké—"Conservation" argued aggressively for the importance of "the Negro" in American life. Black folks, Du Bois suggested, had something to contribute to the sweep of world history. Echoing the idealist philosophies of his former Harvard professor Josiah Royce, Du Bois articulated a version of racial pluralism, or the belief that the peculiar successes of American civilization rested upon its ability to harness the innate racial gifts of its increasingly diverse citizenry. "We are the people," Du Bois claimed, "whose subtle sense of song has given America its only American music, its only American fairy tales, its only touch of pathos and humor amid its mad money-getting plutocracy . . . [and] we believe that the Negro people, as a race, have a contribution to make to civilization and humanity, which no other race can make." For Horace Kallen and the Irish American nationalist Daniel Cohalan, cultural pluralism was a political philosophy developed for "the white races" in opposition to the corrosive effects of the melting pot and, later, 100 Percent Americanism. For Josiah Royce it was an attempt to preserve regional cultural differences in the face of national "proletarianization" and "homogenization." Du Bois's nascent pluralism combined these interpretations—though he anticipated Kallen's work by over a decade—and added a crucial dash of racial chauvinism. Including the Negro in the concert of races, and arguing in favor of the preservation of "spiritual, psychical differences," Du Bois suggested the interrelatedness of white and black, Teuton and Negro, and foreshadowed much of the rhetoric of the Harlem Renaissance long before most of its future participants had even reached adolescence.[1]

It would take Du Bois nearly thirty years to unravel the paradoxes in "The Conservation of the Races." If, in his other work, Du Bois was just then beginning to explore the economic and international dynamic of "the problem of the twentieth century," in "Conservation"—as in *The Souls of Black Folk* and later *The Gift of Black Folk*—he wrestled with an entirely different philosophy of history. "Conservation" rested upon a world-historical, or Romantic, interpretation of the role of race in the rise and fall of civilizations. "The history of the world," Du Bois intoned at the Academy gathering where his paper was first read aloud, "is the history, not of individuals, but of groups, not of nations, but of races." Forgetting for a moment the "proto-Marxism" of his doctoral dissertation, *The Suppression of the African Slave Trade,* and leaving aside whatever insights into economics he had gleaned from his brief contact with the German sociologist Max Weber, Du Bois built his pluralist racialism out of Romanticism, Idealism, and the enormous catalog of American texts, lectures, and public debates on the role of race in politics, society, and culture.[2] Speaking to his cultivated audience of black aristocrats and using language that the historian Wilson Moses has characterized as "disgracefully inconsistent," Du Bois called into question "the final word of science," which had divided the world into "two, perhaps three" races marked by color, and instead suggested that there were "eight distinctly differentiated races, in the sense in which History tells us the word must be used." The nonsensical divisions he settled upon (Slavs, Teutons, English, Romance peoples, Negroes, Semites, Hindoos, Mongolians, and "other minor race groups") reflected the pervasive turn-of-the-century problem of classification—the tension between two different schools of thought which emphasized either national narratives or physical differences, world-historical spirit or skin color, as the primary marker of racial difference.[3]

For Du Bois, "The Conservation of the Races" was the first clear expression of a long-lasting Romantic side, nurtured to maturity at Harvard and in Germany and emerging again during the vigorous defense of "the hyphen" mounted by immigrant groups during the Great War and the debates over the National Origins Act. It was this sense of racial destiny, chauvinism, and history that found clear expression in his stupendous pageant, "The Star of Ethiopia," in the Boas-inspired Afrocentrism of *The Negro*, and in the extraordinary racial chauvinism of *The Gift of Black Folk*. Over the same period of time, Du Bois began to dabble in the Marxist tradition and then, tentatively at first, to tincture his profoundly chauvinistic pride in "the Negro" with a thoroughly materialist critique of the white leviathan. From the searing indictments of "the Souls of White Folk" to the grim *Color and Democracy*, Du Bois moved steadily—if never completely—leftward, carving a permanent niche for himself in American political culture. Marxism and Romanticism, the white leviathan and the zeitgeist, anti-imperialism and Afrocentrism became, in Du Bois's long life, radically different perspectives put to the same task by the man burned "black" by the humiliating experiences of American racism. How and why he came to bring together a uniquely potent collection of ideas, concepts, and perspectives is the story of his life.

Du Bois spent the first decade of the twentieth century using his nineteenth-century European education to grapple with the twentieth-century forces of internationalism—socialism, feminism, and white world supremacy. He spent the following three decades fashioning the first and perhaps the most explosive exploration of the world-economic forces behind the history of whiteness and blackness. Somewhere between 1910 and 1930, then, something tipped the balance for Du Bois, encouraging him to move leftward quickly and then—like many other Americans—to speak of race in a way that was decidedly "new." If American economic expansion and the arrival of Caribbean radicalism were decisive, of equal importance in Du Bois's case were the Great Migration and the accompanying acceleration of New Negro protest—key elements of the African-American, and indeed the American, experience. The language of Du Bois's political protest and of New Negro protest more generally came to reflect the changes wrought in racial classification by the migration of "the Negro" northward, by the growing internationalism of American economic culture, and by the tendency toward negrophobia in popular culture. And Du Bois's early attacks on Anglo-Saxonism and the evils of Teutonic overlordship were replaced by a sense that Britain, America, France, Germany, the Firestone

Rubber Company, the U.S. Marines, certain banks in Manhattan, and the United Fruit Company were all part of an economically driven "white world supremacy."

## The Southerner's "Problem"

William Edward Burghardt Du Bois was born and raised in Great Barrington, Massachusetts, a New England hamlet tucked away from the seacoast, far from the deepest southern reaches of the United States. There, as he remembered it in 1940, the color line "was manifest, but not absolutely drawn," with "the racial angle . . . more clearly defined against the Irish than against me." He was quick and smart, and well loved, and these things helped him greatly. Through luck and much hard work, the young Du Bois would gain the trust of a local teacher, and from that trust would spring eventual admission to Fisk and Harvard and graduate work at the University of Berlin. Defying all existing beliefs about education and "the Negro," he would "settle" for a Ph.D. in the "science" of history from Harvard after his funding for work abroad was unceremoniously taken away by Slater Fund magnates uncomfortable with his dogged pursuit of one of the world's most esteemed degrees. By the turn of the century, W. E. B. Du Bois had published a singular work of urban sociology, *The Philadelphia Negro*, as well as a spate of related articles on "the Negro in the North," earning him a reputation as one of the foremost American experts on black folks outside the deep South and a learned expert on "the Negro problem."[4]

As Du Bois well knew, all studies of that "Negro problem" were rooted in southern history. In the New South, the quirks of the *fin-de-siècle* economy—the disastrous depressions that raced like tornadoes over the farming and agricultural regions of the South and West—led directly to widespread social strife, but in contrast to the northeastern cities there was no accompanying influx of "new" immigrants. Farmers and agricultural laborers throughout the South, in what has been termed a Populist movement, orchestrated a political revolution designed to put the less fortunate on equal political footing with wealthy planters and industrialists. "White" working-class anxieties brought on by economic volatility were soothed only when the political landscape shifted quickly against the struggling African-American freedmen and their ambivalent northern benefactors. Southern industrialists, entrepreneurs, and politicos overwhelmed whatever egalitarian sentiments existed in the early Populist movement by lowering the political bar for whites and raising it for "the Negro." A sophisticated, insidiously subtle scheme of legal codes and de facto agreements—segregation, or Jim Crow—was erected throughout the South, securing a stable labor supply for the New South through debt peonage, outright violence, and political disenfranchisement. African-Americans struggled to hold on to the few means of advancement left to them (namely migration and rudimentary education) even as southern political figures sought to bend those same means toward "white" ends. Seemingly overnight, "the Negro" became a "problem" in the South, and a proliferation of negrophobic myths, stories, and assumptions became the bedrock of a resurgent southern distinctiveness.[5]

The supposed gravity of the "Negro problem" in the South and the concomitant need for white solidarity made it politically and economically expedient for "whiteness" in the New South to be comparatively uniform, showing little of the ambiguity that laced northeastern racial discourse. In literature and politics, southerners romanticized the "Old South"—especially the role of African Americans in the antebellum world—and built up a belief that "the Negro" was "the Southerner's problem." When the subject was African Americans in the urban Northeast, popular songs of the 1890s and 1900s—written by whites—emphasized the loneliness and coldness of northern life and celebrated the "yearning" of "Negroes" out of place there to return to the familiar confines of the deep South.[6]

Black protest in the New South was, for several reasons, either hidden behind a public mask of subservience or confined to the barely subversive "uplift" movements of church groups. Predominantly rural, lacking the political and economic strength of immigrant groups in the North, and faced with the ruthless enforcement of social separation, African-American leaders anointed by the powers-that-be in the South urged blacks to "rediscover" thrift and diligence in isolation, paving the way for eventual full citizenship in the always-distant future. Others—especially those in the North or in cities—strongly disagreed. Speaking at the inaugural meeting of the American Negro Academy in Washington, D.C., Alexander Crummell wondered what Booker T. Washington was thinking. "One would suppose," Crummell grumbled, "from the universal demand for the mere industrialism for this race of ours that the Negro had been going daily to dinner parties, eating terrapin and indulging in champagne." But in the 1890s and 1900s the political leadership of black America was tightly controlled by the ameliorative political machine of Booker T. Washington—and not by the angry Crummell or his even angrier protégé Du Bois. A southerner living in the South, Washington was admired by white supremacists for his tact, patience, and willingness to consign his people to a separate, ultimately inferior, existence.[7]

However much Du Bois may later have regretted pouring so much Romantic racial chauvinism into "The Conservation of the Races," in March of 1897, with Alexander Crummell listening, he was tickled with a thoroughly exciting sense of self-satisfaction. Much of "Conservation" was in keeping with Crummell's own recently reconstructed *fin-de-siècle* philosophy of protest (returning to America in the 1870s from years of missionary work in Africa, Crummell shed his earlier devotion to separatism and began to advocate something roughly similar to pluralism). As Du Bois's biographer attests, when a young William Ferris—then years away from his spectacular evocation of "the Negro-Saxon" in *The African Abroad*—rose to question Du Bois's emphasis on the concert of races instead of the contest of individuals, it was the aged Crummell, tall and thin with heavy white hair, who expressed complete satisfaction with "Conservation," ending all debate on the relative merits of that essay. Written for an audience of well-bred, exquisitely educated men, and designed for delivery in an atmosphere choked with genteel elitism, "Conservation" testifies to Du Bois's persistent fascination with the intellectual tools of Victorianism—with Romantic racialism, and with culture, character, and civilization—as well as his devout faith in Alexander Crummell.[8]

That persistent Victorianism was to play an equally important role in Du Bois's most enduring contribution to American literature. In 1903, a few years after that day at the American Negro Academy, Du Bois released *The Souls of Black Folk,* a collection of disparate essays beautifully written and persuasively argued. The chapters in *Souls* originally appeared in a variety of monthly periodicals, though Du Bois "cut, polished, and mounted" them "with a jeweler's precision" for publication in book form.[9] It is tempting to argue that *Souls* shares many of the ambivalences of "The Conservation of the Races" and is a logical outgrowth of that earlier work. Certainly, Du Bois's elegant tribute to Crummell might lead one to that conclusion, as might his cocksure enthusiasm for "the Talented Tenth," a political vanguard composed of the well educated, the very well bred, and the thoroughly bourgeois. The "Volksgeistian" elements of "Conservation" are also ever present, especially in the extended and now famous discussion

of "twoness" and in the chapter entitled "Of the Sorrow Songs," with its extended discussion of "the greatest gift of the Negro people." Additionally,
the notion of "the Negro" as a "seventh son" brings to mind all the ambivalence inherent in the "disgracefully inconsistent" racial classifications
found in "The Conservation of the Races."[10]

One could also argue that the spirit of *Souls* was profoundly different
from that of his earlier work, and that the course of Du Bois's life had been
altered by his participation in the first Pan-African Conference, held in
London in 1900. In late July of 1900, fresh from the imperial splendor of
the Paris Exposition Universelle, Du Bois arrived in London for a series of
meetings organized by the West Indian barrister Henry Sylvester Williams.
The world's "equilibrium," as the Bostonian Brooks Adams would have it,
had not yet left the seat of the British Empire, and, despite the irony of its
all happening in Britannia's bosom, London was home to a wide variety
of international movements. Williams's Pan-African Conference of 1900
thus fit hand in glove with its revolutionary contemporaries, such as the
diasporic racialized Irish nationalism. The early Pan-Africanism, David
Levering Lewis writes, "came with the Zeitgeist, an inevitable derivative
idea . . . exploding into the twentieth century like a stick of dynamite . . .
with the Irish, Afrikaners, Armenians, Serbians and other historic 'races'
already lighting the fuse for the new century." At this first Pan-African
Conference, facing an audience composed of well-educated, "civilized"
men and women of African descent, Du Bois uttered the phrase that would
be forever identified with his name: "The problem of the twentieth century," he intoned, "is the problem of the colour line . . . [if] the black world
is to be exploited and ravished and degraded, the results must be deplor-
able, if not fatal, not simply to them, but to the high ideals of justice, freedom, and culture which a thousand years of Christian civilization have
held before Europe."[11]

When it was time, however, to include the concept of "the color line" in
*Souls,* Du Bois made a few subtle streamlining changes. The "problem of
the color line," he argued in his pointed essay on Reconstruction and the
Freedmen's Bureau, was "the relation of the darker to the lighter races of
men in Africa and Asia, in America and the islands of the Sea."[12] He had
boiled down his lengthy London discussion to a brisk passage of thirty-six
words. Quite simply, the insights into the global dynamics of racism Du
Bois gleaned from contact with Williams and others at the Pan-African
Conference never appeared in *Souls of Black Folk. Souls* became a book
whose focus—however potent—was simply on "the Negro Problem" in the

South. Du Bois had blunted the anger of his global framework and shifted the remaining animus away from Europe's abuses in Africa toward America's abandonment of "the Negro" to the ravages of the New South. Even if the concept of the color line presented in *Souls* seemed to anticipate— however briefly—the crisp, dangerous prose of later Du Boisian protest, his words at the Pan-African Conference (and indeed later at the Universal Races Congress) were quintessentially Victorian and Romantic, and were possessed of the same faith in certain white folks generally and "civilization" particularly.

The emphasis on the southern peculiarity of "the Negro problem" found in *The Souls of Black Folk* reflected Du Bois's prolonged consideration of the political might and economic philosophy of Booker T. Washington. Public discussion of "the Negro Problem" in the United States was then dominated by Washington, the so-called Wizard of Tuskegee, who seemed content to have black folks stay down South. Presiding over a sophisticated and decidedly manipulative political machine from his position as principal of the Tuskegee Institute, Washington played the role of tough party boss in black America while acting as a conciliatory force in white America. Admittedly, Washington's manipulative public persona of "darkie" jokes and rhetorical dissemblance was offset by his secretive schemes to undermine Jim Crow. Few, however, were aware of his efforts to combat the evils of segregation, and fewer still—certainly not Du Bois in 1903— were in a position to usurp his position as overlord of African-American political culture and public distributor of all knowledge about the purported Negro problem in the South.[13]

Speaking at the Atlanta Cotton States Exposition in 1895, with a pencil in hand and with sunlight streaming through windows into his face, Washington suggested to his excited audience that agitation for "social equality" would all but cease if the New South would but have faith in the Negro. "In all things purely social," he waxed pacific, "we can be as separate as the fingers, yet one as the hand in all things essential to mutual progress." Speaking in words that reflected the turn-of-the-century belief that European immigrants were racially different from Old Stock Americans, and that hinted at some laughable attempts to use immigrant labor on southern land, Washington also urged white southerners to look to the Negro for safe, hard-working labor:

> To those of the white race who look to the incoming of those of foreign birth and strange tongue and habits for the prosperity of the South, were

I permitted I would repeat what I say to my own race, "Cast down your bucket where you are." Cast it down among the eight millions of Negroes whose habits you know, whose fidelity and love you have tested in days when to have proved treacherous meant the ruin of your firesides. Cast down your bucket among these people who have, without strikes and labour wars, tilled your fields, cleared your forests, builded your railroads and cities, and brought forth treasures from the bowels of the earth.[14]

Washington astutely recognized that regional variations between "alien menaces" and "the Negro problem" grew stronger with each shipload of immigrants landing at Ellis Island and with each invented "rape" in the New South, and that—for the New South—the Negro could appear less dangerous in certain ways than the New Immigrant. This, writes Wilson Moses, "was Washington's *tour de force,* his suggestion that Protestant English speaking blacks were culturally superior to non-American whites . . . [and] that black people who already had a place in the South were potentially less disruptive than immigrants, and less likely to contaminate society with radical ideas." Conceding nearly every inch of political and social ground gained since emancipation, Washington's speech that sunny day left his white audience cheering wildly for the newly appointed "Negro leader." "The Atlanta Compromise," as it was called, also met with an ambivalent response from the African-American community, reducing one elderly attendee of African descent to tears.[15]

The pivotal concessions of the "Atlanta Compromise" were not the only reason for Du Bois's velvet-gloved rebuke in the *Souls* chapter entitled "Of Mr. Booker T. Washington and Others." If Du Bois took care to paint the ideological differences between himself and Washington as serious enough to warrant the public airing of grievances, he was also careful to avoid mention of the private conflicts between them. Du Bois objected strenuously to Washington's aiding and abetting the dreadful process by which African Americans were stripped of their rights, their land, and their lives in the so-called New South. But his otherwise cordial relations with Washington (relations which continued long past the publication of *Souls*) also reflect the precarious situation in which Du Bois found himself. Any disagreement with Washington's ameliorative methods was tempered by fearful respect for the unprecedented financial power the Wizard, as the handpicked symbolic leader of black America, could command. Despite their growing differences, then, Du Bois and Washington continued to share precious common ground on the education of the masses of African Americans in the United States.[16]

As a Harvard-educated "Negro"—an impossible contradiction in southern terms—Du Bois needed Washington's help to prosper materially, to surround himself with the accoutrements of class and culture. Not surprisingly, then, Washington's coy manipulation of Du Bois in 1900 during the latter's attempt to secure the position of superintendent of schools in Washington, D.C., was the moment at which Du Bois began to sour on the Wizard. Having assured Du Bois that he was the first choice for the job, Washington withdrew his written support and then, after urging Du Bois to have faith, cast his vote publicly for another man. From that point onward, Du Bois was increasingly sensitive to Washington's political abuses, and his criticisms of the Tuskegee headmaster's "wholesale hushing of all criticism and the crushing out of men who dared criticize" escalated, eventually, into open warfare. And yet "Of Mr. Booker T. Washington" also contains countless references to the "invaluable service" of the Wizard, reflecting the persistence of Du Bois's difficult sleight of hand—subject to constant surveillance by "boss" Washington, Du Bois needed to convince the master of Tuskegee to watch his left hand and not his right, to pay attention to his respectful public disagreements and not his growing private agitation at the manipulation of his professional life.[17]

For all its focus on the southernness of "the Negro problem," and for all its ambivalence toward the Wizard of Tuskegee, *Souls* was a remarkable response to Washington's apparent capitulation to the needs and desires of the Progressive negrophobes—the Vardamans and Tillmans—of the South. With Washington, the New South, and negrophobia as his targets, Du Bois drew upon his own experiences in the South—his summer excursions away from Fisk as a schoolteacher and his work at Atlanta University—to offer a grave rebuke of the politics of compromise. With Washington's Tuskegee in cotton country, with so many lynchings every year in the New South, and with so many negrophobes professing their grim faith in the coming degeneration of the Negro and the supposed propensity toward violence, theft, and rape among black men, Du Bois painted a new portrait of the South's most downtrodden residents. But Du Bois, striving to make a living and a difference in Atlanta—"one of the meanest places in the United States"—was too immersed in the baleful malevolence of Dixie to compare North and South profitably, or to discuss the Negro problem as anything other than a southern problem.[18]

## Ambivalence and Revolution

The first hints of a leftward shift in Du Bois's political thought can be detected after *Souls,* first in "The Souls of White Folk," and then in Du Bois's awkward biography, *John Brown.* After mentioning to the editor Ellis Paxson Oberholtzer that he might write a biography of Frederick Douglass for the American Crisis Biography series (and subsequently discovering that his nemesis Booker T. Washington had chosen to do the same), Du Bois settled upon Nat Turner as a possible subject. Oberholtzer parried by suggesting Brown, and Du Bois somewhat reluctantly agreed. With several other biographies of John Brown then recently published—and with Oswald Garrison Villard's book in the works—Du Bois wove together the life of Brown in a decidedly original interpretive framework, especially in his concluding discussion of the "legacy" of a man many of Du Bois's contemporaries believed to be insane.[19]

Bringing his life of Brown to an end with a sweeping condemnation of the spirit of Social Darwinism and the "hegemony of the white races," Du Bois lashed out at "the movement" behind the enthusiastic passion for "holy white blood":

> It is still to-day a living, virile, potent force and motive, the most subtle and dangerous enemy of world peace and the dream of human brotherhood. It has a whole vocabulary of its own: the strong races, superior peoples, race preservation, the struggle for survival and a variety of terms meaning the right of white men of any kind to beat blacks into submission, make them surrender their wealth and the use of their women and submit to dictation without murmur, for the sake of being swept off the fairest portions of the earth or held there in perpetual serfdom or guardianship.

Here, in the concluding passages of *John Brown,* was evidence that the vigorous turn-of-the-century tradition of anti-imperialism had taken root in Du Bois's protest. He was as yet unable to escape the problem of classification—he castigated "the white races" throughout. But there were also hints of his later criticisms of absolute whiteness, especially in his portrait of a concerted world movement of white folks, "fencing in America, Australia, and South Africa and declaring that no dark race shall occupy the land which they themselves are unable to use." And when Japan defeated Russia in 1904—though Russia had always been cursed with a "dingy" white-ness—Du Bois rejoiced that the "magic of the word 'white' is . . . broken."[20]

There was, then, more to the "legacy" of *John Brown*—and to Du Bois's changing outlook on the world—than the genteel, racialized anti-imperial-ism of the Bostonian Charles Francis Adams Jr. or Stanford University President David Starr Jordan. For Adams, heir to the antislavery activism of his grandfather, John Quincy Adams, anti-imperialism was the moral imperative of Progressive forward-thinking Anglo-Saxonism. For Jordan, anti-imperialism was of a piece with racial preservation, and with the per-vasive fear that white folks in tropic zones could lose themselves in tropical neurasthenia. But in Du Bois's deepening anger at empire, in his repeated discussion of the costs to "social progress and spiritual strength" of "pro-curing coolie labor, the ruling of India, the exploitation of Africa, the prob-lem of the unemployed, and the curbing of corporations," there was an air of international socialism, and of the far left wing of Progressivism.[21]

Somewhere between *Souls* and *John Brown*, then, Du Bois had shed some of the Romanticism in his conception of history and world politics, picking up on the lingua franca of Progressivism—the "scientific" concep-tion of the world as a mechanical and economic organism. Together with settlement houses, meat-packing exposés, and government trust-busting, Progressivism led many to view the world in economic terms, with races as classes, adding new meaning to Frederick Jackson Turner's dictum that "the age of machinery, of the factory system, is also the age of socialistic in-quiry."[22] And as popular culture probed the depths of the American com-mitment to the world the robber barons made, as discussions of social life took on decidedly economic and moralistic twists, a growing number of Americans applied this perspective to global questions of labor, political economy, and race. Du Bois, inspired by the idealism of Progressivism and an armchair international socialist by temperament, had, by 1909, begun to pepper his own prose with worldly, moralistic conclusions that were de-cidedly opposed to those offered by the right wing of Progressivism.

Despite the heat of the fiery epilogue to *John Brown*, however, the final pages of that biography reflected no permanent earth-shaking transforma-tion of Du Bois's thinking about the role of race in world affairs. If the so-cialist in Du Bois was increasingly critical of the role of empire in stripping Africa bare and keeping the Negro fixed in the capitalist and colonial order of things, the Romantic racial chauvinist in him was, more or less, still in control. Indeed, Du Bois's budding Afrocentrism continued to mature, leading him increasingly to put Africa and Africans at the center of a racial history of the world, rather than at the periphery of a world economic system. Reminiscing on the eve of the Second World War, Du Bois fixed the moment of his Afrocentrist awakening to a late spring day in 1906: "Franz Boas came to Atlanta University where I was teaching and said to a graduating class: You need not be ashamed of your African past; and then he recounted the history of the black kingdoms south of the Sahara for a thousand years. I was too astonished to speak. All this I had never heard."[23] For a moment, at least as Du Bois told it, the universe had conspired to throw together two of the most radical propagandists of the early twentieth century: Du Bois, the self-appointed champion of "the Negro," and Boas, whose pioneering anthropology was beginning to shake up the certainties of racially informed ethnology.

Boas's work was to supply two important ingredients to Du Bois's burgeoning Afrocentrism. As many have noted, Boas's efforts helped to change the political calculus of science when it came to matters of social equality and racial aptitude. Boas, as Lee D. Baker has argued, was extremely influential both at Columbia University, where he presided over a group of young anthropologists who were busy "advancing the notion of cultural relativity and refuting ideas regarding racial inferiority," and among the NAACP leadership. Perhaps just as important, he offered the suggestion that "at a time when the European was still satisfied with rude stone tools, the African had invented or adopted the art of smelting iron." Here, at last, Du Bois had powerful proof with which to counter the chauvinisms of Western civilization. The presumption of technological superiority was so central to European—or "white"—world dominion that the very idea that the Negro could be responsible for, in Boas's words, "a giant's stride forward in the development of human culture" was, to Du Bois's ear, like a firebell in the night. The smelting of iron quickly became a leitmotif of Du Boisian Afrocentrism, as did the conclusions drawn from the rediscovery of "the Negro" by the new anthropology of Boas and others. Backed by the "new science" of Boas, Du Bois could finally include people of African descent as actors in history, and, indeed, as technological innovators equally responsible for the advancements of civilization—not the passive prehistoric beings of the German philosopher Hegel. It was an insight that would emerge publicly in Du Bois's most chimerical work of Afrocentrism, *The Negro,* and throughout his life, always complicating the unorthodox Marxism that would be his other ideological legacy to the struggle for human rights.[24]

The personal dimensions of Du Bois's ambivalent step leftward before the Great War are tragic proof of David Levering Lewis's conclusion that the life story of this precocious, Harvard-educated, Europhile African American born just outside Boston is truly the "biography of a race." Personal slights against Du Bois and his chosen professional activities left the Atlanta University professor angrier, less trustful of white folks, and less likely to argue vociferously for the recognition of the rights and privileges of "civilized Negroes" alone. If the failure of the Slater Fund to fully underwrite his pursuit of a doctorate from the University of Berlin rankled, his tussle with the American Historical Association over the capitalization of the "n" in "Negro" when it came time to publish an early essay must have further dampened his enthusiasm for his fellows in academe. The callous dismissal by the Sons of the American Revolution of Du Bois's claim to have a lengthy "Old Stock" pedigree must likewise have suggested to him that the "one-drop rule" was deeply perverse both in conception and in application. And even if Du Bois had never been subject to the personal intimidation and violence endemic to the South, he reacted to exceptionally brutal incidents as if he had been struck and forever changed by lightning. He recalled an incident from 1899:

> I remember when it first, as it were, startled me to my feet: a poor Negro in central Georgia, Sam Hose, had killed his landlord's wife. I wrote out a careful and reasoned statement concerning the evident facts and started down to the Atlanta *Constitution* office, carrying in my pocket a letter of introduction to Joel Chandler Harris. I did not get there. On the way news met me: Sam Hose had been lynched, and they said that his knuckles were on exhibition at a grocery store farther down on Mitchell Street . . . I turned back to the University. I began to turn aside from my work.

Marked by a lifetime of painful incidents, Du Bois grew increasingly callused as slight followed slight, riot followed riot, and lynching followed lynching in America. And in the 1910 essay "The Souls of White Folk," his vitriol toward those "in whose minds the paleness of their bodily skins is fraught with tremendous and eternal significance" reveals "a profound hardening of Du Bois's expectations of white people."[25]

Du Bois's coldness toward white America and his growing criticism of whiteness can be traced to the growing malevolence of American race relations and the awful explosion of hate in the New South and the Northeast. In August and September of 1906, Atlanta, Du Bois's home and the capital of the New South, exploded with rage and hate. Fed by excessive newspaper reports about the aggressions of "the Negro," a horde of white folks swept through Atlanta, exacting from every African American they found a brutal vengeance for supposed transgressions of the South's unwritten but strictly enforced code of behavior. Almost exactly two years later, in Springfield, Illinois, once home to the great emancipator, Abraham Lincoln, another transgression—as always, the supposed rape of a white woman—sparked an equally brutal rampage against the growing African-American population in that northern city.

Atlanta and Springfield would loom large in Du Bois's mind. At the time of the Atlanta riot, he had been across state lines in Alabama, conducting sociological research. Hurrying home to his wife and family, he sat on the steps of his home with a shotgun in hand, expecting at any moment to see the inhuman faces of the white rioters. "Bewildered are we," he wrote on the train back to Atlanta, "and passion tossed, mad with the madness of a mobbed and mocked and murdered people." Coming as it did merely weeks after the momentous first meeting of the Niagara Movement at Harper's Ferry, the site of John Brown's fateful struggle with slavery, the Atlanta riot must have driven home—as nothing else could—the urgency of Du Bois's cause. More important, the madness in Springfield—complete with angry cries of "Lincoln freed you, we'll show you where you belong"—hinted that the great national movement of black people into cities had struck its first sparks off the cold hearts of "the white races" in the North. Both Atlanta and Springfield had seen an influx of African Americans, and both had struggled, materially and psychologically, with the complexities engendered by the arrival of "the Negro." If Atlanta hit Du Bois hard personally, however, the riot at Springfield reflected a fact that would change his understanding of race problems: the "riot that devastated Springfield signaled that the race problem was no longer regional—a raw and bloody drama played out behind a magnolia curtain—but national."[26]

Surveying the wreckage of African-American life, Du Bois concluded that there was much work to be done. "My career as a scientist," he would later write, "was to be swallowed up in my role as master of propaganda." That role began with the financially hamstrung and racially exclusive Niagara Movement, then continued with the better-funded, interracial National Association for the Advancement of Colored People. Never has an organization so perfectly captured the ambivalences and the promises of an era as did the NAACP. Its genesis can be traced to William English Walling, a southerner, a socialist, and a descendant of slaveholders. Shocked and disgusted by the Springfield riot, and motivated in part by Progressive idealism, Walling began communicating with others of liberal Progressive leanings. Drawn from almost every popular reform movement, signers of the "Call" and eventual participants in the NAACP would include Franz Boas, John Dewey, Florence Kelley, Lillian Wald, Du Bois, Oswald Garrison Villard, and Jane Addams, and would represent the woman movement, anti-imperialism, socialism, the settlement house movement, neo-abolitionism, academe, and the Jewish community. Du Bois, whose animosity toward the pontificating Villard grew out of the latter's scathing review of *John Brown*, was, after some wrangling, appointed director of publicity and research and editor of *The Crisis: A Record of the Darker Races,* a monthly magazine with Villard's name on the masthead next to Du Bois's. The feisty professor from Atlanta University who moved North to Manhattan in 1910 was cursed with serious doubts about white folks and a growing anger toward the Wizard. Later he remembered that his "activities [with the NAACP were] to be so held in check that the Association would not develop as a center of attack upon Tuskegee."[27]

One of Du Bois's most profound contributions to African-American life was *The Crisis,* a small monthly devoted to exposing the hypocrisy of racism and the evils of riots and lynching. "The span of my life from 1910 to 1934," he would later write, "is chiefly the story of *The Crisis* under my editorship."[28] With a vision that must have surprised the elitist, condescending Villard, Du Bois's *Crisis* immediately became the mouthpiece of the more aggressive set of neo-abolitionists. From the first, however, *The Crisis* was more than a clearinghouse for liberal progressive consideration of the Negro problem, and more than a forum for Franz Boas, Villard, Jane Addams, and others. Including a wealth of information about people of African descent around the world—and the surprisingly similar forces arrayed against their progress and uplift—*The Crisis* brought anti-imperialism, world politics, and antiracism together as no American periodical had ever done before.

Readers who picked up *The Crisis*—and during the 1910s a growing number were African American—could find up-to-date information about the segregationist trend in Natal, South Africa, following the "Black Peril," or about Brazil, where many supposed (incorrectly) that there was no such thing as a "race problem," or even about the ill-fated rebellion of the Partido Independiente de Color in Cuba. "The Union of South Africa,"

Du Bois began angrily, "in imitation of . . . the southern section [of the United States, has] decreed that a white skin is always to be the *sine qua non* to the realities expressed by the high sounding phrases about 'life, liberty, and the pursuit of happiness.'" Editing *The Crisis* with an acute sensitivity to race questions around the world and with little fear of public reprisal, Du Bois acted as midwife at the birth of a "Black Atlantic" culture. Illuminating the connections between race problems at home and abroad, *The Crisis,* together with its postwar competition, *The Negro World, The Messenger,* and *The Crusader,* crafted the shared sense of time, space, and culture that would help reshape the boundaries of race and race-consciousness after the coming war. "Color consciousness," Du Bois remarked wryly, without commenting on his own partial responsibility for the fact, "is getting to be all pervasive."[29]

And yet, for all the evils that Du Bois had witnessed and experienced, and for all the inspiration he derived from the Niagara Movement, the NAACP, and *The Crisis,* there was, as before, a studied ambivalence in his discussion of races and race problems. When, in October of 1911, McClurg

W. E. B. Du Bois, ca. 1910, seated regally at his desk in the offices of *The Crisis.*

and Company brought out the first novel by W. E. B. Du Bois, romantically entitled *The Quest of the Silver Fleece,* many readers no doubt agreed with the impression of McClurg's reader, the activist Fannie Hale Gardiner, who pitched the book as neither "seditious or revolutionary." Though *Quest* was a pointed literary exposé of the banal pretensions of Washington politics and the evil machinations of white southerners—rich and poor, but mostly rich—to control the fate and fortunes of "the Negro," there was little else in the work to suggest that Du Bois was just then embarking upon a new phase in his career of radical activism. Recent scholars have noted that the novel was of a piece with the spirit of the realist works of Frank Norris and Upton Sinclair, even if the focus on African Americans was unique ("the muckrakers," Herbert Aptheker reminds us, "tended to ignore the oppression of Black people, while writing reams about bad meat"). What little socialist spirit one finds in *Quest* was "randomly presented and undeveloped, like Du Bois's own real-life advocacy of the political philosophy during this time."[30] Certainly there was nothing in *Quest* to rival the zest of two contemporaneous essays by Du Bois—nothing in Bles and Zora's travails to match the forceful concluding pages of *John Brown,* where an inchoate racialized socialism anticipated so much of Du Bois's future protest. And *Quest* lacked the stirring sweep of vision and genius for words found in the *Crisis* editor's angry and magnificent "The Souls of White Folk."

But the conventionality of *The Quest of the Silver Fleece* was perhaps most apparent in the author's choice of setting for the novel. *Quest* begins in the South and, after a short change of scene, ends in the South. In so doing, the novel reveals itself as a response not just to the growing popularity of Thomas Dixon's work but also to the enormous body of literature on "the Negro" as "the Southerner's Problem." The compromise that healed the wounds of the Civil War and Reconstruction not only involved the abandonment of African Americans to the whims of the New South but also relied on the continued faith that "the Negro problem" was indeed a southern one. Those principles being agreed upon, white southerners were thereafter allowed to hold forth as the undisputed experts on "the Negro" when it came time to debate the matter. Du Bois, the author of pioneering work on black Philadelphia and New York, does little to refute this troubling cliché, mentioning only briefly in *Quest* those "five hundred thousand or more black voters in . . . Northern states."[31] If Bles and Zora, the protagonists of the novel, venture to the supposedly progressive climate of the nation's capital, the move there and the subsequent harsh lessons they learn serve only to emphasize the importance of being in the South when it comes to "the race question." Bles and Zora return somewhat chastened and markedly older to the land of cotton, white supremacy, and aristocracy, hoping to change forever the nature of the Negro problem and assuming that the problem is in fact confined to the South. In *Quest*, Du Bois, having spent several years in pursuit of social justice in the deep South and at Atlanta University, eschewed his developing quasi-socialist convictions and succumbed to one of the more powerful southern myths of the age of regional rapprochement.

Much like his sensitivity to race problems around the world, Du Bois's professed anti-imperialism came and went. For three days in late July of 1911, with *The Quest of the Silver Fleece* in press, Du Bois traveled to London for the First Universal Races Congress. Du Bois, then recently named the editor of the fledgling *Crisis* and a leading advocate of immediate civil rights for the "American Negro," attended the Congress as a correspondent and was elected co-secretary of the American delegation. The Races Congress, Du Bois hoped, would provide an excellent forum in which to rebut the claims made by Booker T. Washington during his tour of England in 1910. To the great consternation of Du Bois and the struggling National Association for the Advancement of Colored People, Washington's ameliorative approach to race problems had won great acclaim in Britain. The *Crisis* editor subsequently embarked on a series of lectures in England designed to steal support from the Tuskegee machine. The divisive political thrust of Du Bois's trip to England was, however, undermined by the congenial ethos surrounding the Races Congress. A unity of purpose, it seemed, had vitiated any chance of public acrimony over "the Negro problem" in America. Indeed, after a cordial discussion with Du Bois in London, Washington's man on the spot, R. R. Moton, concluded that Du Bois's participation in the event marked no real threat to the Tuskegee Wizard's reputation or influence.[32]

Later, remembering the friendly spirit of the event and the immense body of social scientific work presented, Du Bois described the Races Congress as "a meeting of widely separated men, as a reunion of East and West, as a glance across the color line or as a sort of World Grievance Committee." Without regard for the hints of war in Europe, Du Bois marked the first Universal Races Congress as an epoch-shattering event of profound significance for those "fifty different races" representing "fifty countries" that participated. "When fifty races look each other in the eye, face to face," he wrote, "there rises a new conception of humanity and its problems . . . in the continual meeting of strangers comes gradual illumination." Gathered together in the hallowed halls of the Imperial Institute, the several thousand representatives of "fifty different races"—some from India and Africa but most representing the various imperial powers—spoke earnestly of the need for greater benevolence, faith, and, perhaps more important, patience in the "burden" of uplift and civilizing. Curiously, Du Bois barely noticed the overwhelming celebration of empire present at the Congress, and he shared none of his fellow NAACP member Mary White Ovington's disgust at the absence of anti-imperialist agitation.[33]

The evasion of critical discourse on empire was partly a logical result of the "liberal internationalism" of the Universal Races Congress, an internationalism "rooted in the ethical concern to transcend national divisions . . . in the promotion of a world order that could secure the perpetuation of peace"—and, one might add, the continued profitability of imperialism. The early stirrings of anticolonialism were present at the Races Congress— as they had been at the Pan-African Conference—in more than a few papers and in the tangible connections made between colonial activists during the event. In the comparative context of the Races Congress, the Egyptian national and strident Pan-Africanist Dusé Mohamed Ali and the South African activist John Tengo Jabavu, together with other nationalist leaders from India, Egypt, and Haiti, forged ideological ties in support of nascent anticolonialism and in direct opposition to the general thrust of the Congress. Such connections, however, were masked by the incorporative "liberal" atmosphere of the Congress—a subtly coercive and consensual liberalism which manifested itself in the prominent roles accorded to radical figures like Du Bois, Mohamed Ali, and the young Oxford-educated lawyer Mohandas Gandhi, and in the direct participation of such notable progressive thinkers as Felix Adler, John Hobson, and Gustav Spiller. In Du Bois's case, his belief that cosmopolitan Europe was bereft of the provincial racial hostilities of the United States, together with his ego-inflating role at the Congress, his faith in social science, and a series of sublimely romantic evenings with a mysterious woman in London, led him to speak of the Universal Races Congress lovingly for the rest of his life.[34]

Du Bois's experiences at the Races Congress, and the qualities of his first novel, *The Quest of the Silver Fleece,* reveal that an important ambivalence marked his thoughts on race before the Great War. Du Bois's castigation of imperialism, like that of many of his contemporaries, rested upon an understanding of empire as competition between European nations—between the white races. After fifteen terrible years in the deep South and one Pan-African Congress, his understanding of race had changed only slightly. To be sure, there were bursts of profound insight into the worldwide making of whiteness and blackness. And in his editorship of *The Crisis* Du Bois had begun to forge a variety of popular connections with black folks around the world. But despite his fame for pronouncing the importance of "the color line" in America, Du Bois continued to emphasize the inherent southernness of "the Negro Problem," and his division of the world into "fifty races" at the Universal Races Congress reflects the use of an older logic of words and things and a lingering ambivalence about the Marxist tradition and the new race-consciousness.

The Great War in Europe encouraged Du Bois, much as it did Madison Grant and Lothrop Stoddard, to emphasize color over national character and whiteness and blackness over every other possible marker of race. For Du Bois, the war illuminated the connections between the Darwinian struggle in Europe and the overlordship of Africa. He argued from the outset that it "is not merely national jealousy, or the so-called 'race' rivalry of Slav, Teuton and Latin, that is the larger cause of this war . . . [but instead] the wild quest for Imperial expansion among colored races between Germany, England and France primarily." Du Bois's article "The African Roots of the War" emphasized the irony of the conflagration—that the suicide of Nordic Europe should be over Africa, or that "it is directly in [the] outer circle of races, and not in the European household, that the real causes of present European fighting are to be found."[35]

What was it, precisely, that the white world was thought to see in Africa? Wealth, Du Bois answered in "African Roots," the once and future wealth of white folks. Desire for this untapped wealth of the "dark continent," he suggested, had sparked a rushed "investment" in "color prejudice" and race-consciousness in Europe and America. But in celebrating the virtues of Europe over Africa in the nineteenth century, Western civilization had sown the seeds of war around the world—once all of Africa had been claimed, the grim competition for the remaining land, wealth, and labor would intensify. Here, in this brief essay of 1915, lay the heart of much of Du Bois's future criticism: peace between whites, or at least between white labor and white capital, was achieved through both a widespread investment in color and a psychological wage of absolute whiteness, in turn underwritten by the deliberate, explicit exploitation of people of color around the world. It was an argument of remarkable insight, used most powerfully in the concluding passages of *Black Reconstruction:* "Immediately in Africa," Du Bois wrote there, "a black back runs red with the blood of the lash; in India, a brown girl is raped; in China, a coolie starves; in Alabama, seven darkies are more than lynched; while in London, the white limbs of a prostitute are hung with jewels and silk."[36]

Far more than the Great War itself, the steady stream of African Americans into the urban North—driven by the war and the consequent cessation of European immigration—would prick Du Bois's racial sensibilities and inflame whiteness and blackness in the North. From the first indications that the steady trickle of black folks northward might become a torrent, Nordics and New Negroes commented upon the revolutionary quality and unforeseeable results of the coming migration, especially in the context of the New Negro Movement. "The intricate social and political problems," one writer wisely suggested, "occasioned by the presence of two dissimilar races in the United States have heretofore been deemed purely sectional matters . . . the Negro race was found almost entirely within the Southern states, and it was always assumed that it would probably always remain there. Now suddenly the race, moved by some widespread impulse, begins of its own volition a migration northward which may alter the entire aspect of the racial question in America, and possibly swell into one of those mighty floods which . . . changes history." Du Bois, sensing the political possibilities of a large voting bloc of African Americans in the North, and moved by the worsening violence of the South, leapt to encourage those who could afford to move to do so quickly: "The only effective protest that the Negroes *en masse* can make against lynching and disfranchisement is through leaving the devilish country where these things take place." In addition to the postwar lunacy about immigration and the Red Scare and the nervous anxiety about the fate of Western culture and civilization, any explanation for Du Bois's increasing agitation at the growth of the white leviathan must include the first waves of this unprecedented demographic shift, the migration of African Americans northward during and after the war.[37]

Almost immediately upon their emancipation from slavery, African Americans had celebrated their freedom by the simple act of movement. At first, the revolutionary freedom of movement was practiced on a small scale—leaving, for instance, the farm or plantation of one southern family for another with slightly higher wages, or perhaps with a greater guarantee of personal safety. What followed were short bursts of movement to the more open possibilities of the Midwest and the gold of the Far West. Freedmen and women also left the isolated rural spaces of the southern countryside and began settling in New South cities. Later, as the New South sought to restrict the ability of black folks to leave the medievalism of Dixie—or, as others put it, to wander dangerously unattached through the South—the drift to the North became more pronounced. By 1917 Du Bois could claim that for the first time since the end of the Atlantic slave trade and the abolition of slavery "a larger proportion of our colored population [lives] in states other than those in which they were born."[38]

Two years into the Great War, severe crop failures, the varied and increasing rigors of life under Jim Crow, and the lure of higher-paying work encouraged hundreds of thousands of African Americans to flee Dixie and head North. "From one-quarter to one-half a million dark workers," as Du Bois put it, "arose and poured themselves into the North." Between 1910 and 1920 Chicago's black population more than doubled to 109,458. Other northern centers experienced a similar rise. The demographic shift in Manhattan was, in comparison with those in Detroit, Cleveland, and Chicago, relatively small, but Manhattan's black population did increase by eighty percent between 1910 and 1920, as over 315,000 African Americans migrated to the Northeast and Mid-Atlantic states alone. In addition to migrants from the American South, a rapid influx of Caribbean immigrants contributed both strife and excitement to emerging black communities. In New York City, migrants from Jamaica, Haiti, Santo Domingo, and elsewhere settled in Harlem, the heterogeneous community above Central Park where rents had skyrocketed and white renters had nearly vanished.[39]

Once they were settled in the North, the sense of relative safety (real or imagined) from the medieval violence of the South afforded New Negroes some precious room in which to argue assertively for civil rights. Well-heeled "aristocrats of color" might scoff at the prospects of the mass of uneducated African Americans pouring into the cities of the North, but, for better or worse, they found that few whites in the Northeast were willing to privilege class, or to distinguish them from the new arrivals. Seeing only a deep shared blackness, white folks, with their fists and stones, their fears and hatreds, knew no difference between rich and poor, educated and illiterate. And when violence, hatred, and negrophobia refused to recognize the importance of class, collective organizational protest resulted. Sparked by overwhelming unease at the so-called decline of Western civilization, and with headquarters in Manhattan, or Chicago, or Philadelphia, a wide range of protest groups led by the NAACP (now famous for its national protests against *Birth of a Nation*) harnessed the power of communal despair, anger, and assertiveness, and began focusing it. Some forms of protest were both public and provocative, such as the Universal Negro Improvement Association's massive open-air convention of the summer of 1921; other changes were subtler but had profound consequences—Du Bois's *Crisis*, anticipating the anger and vitriol of *The Negro World*, *The Messenger*, and *The Crusader*, began publishing incendiary photographs of black men with guns during the Great War. With most African Americans exhibiting little sympathy for the war effort—Du Bois's great *faux pas* "Close Ranks" notwithstanding—the New Negro Movement, born of the migration, helped change wartime apathy into postwar dissent.[40]

The arrival and transformation of "the Negro" in the urban North also helped to forge the cognitive connections of absolute whiteness. While the Great Migration was an important catalyst for the New Negro Movement, the reinvigoration of northern negrophobia in the 1920s and 1930s suggests that a related by-product of the Great Migration may have been the psychological impact of an altogether "out of place" black presence in the North. It was, in part, the after-effects of this symbolic and real penetration of "the Negro" into the secure Nordic world of urban northeastern America that encouraged Madison Grant (among others) to reorganize his thoughts on "race" in accordance with what he termed the "Southern way," and to "sympathize with the firm resolve of the handful of white men in South Africa."[41]

Similar fearful sentiments inspired New Immigrants and Old Stock Americans alike to beat, pummel, and generally abuse the new arrivals in urban centers around the country for every minor transgression of the unwritten laws of social intercourse. In Tulsa and Knoxville, rumors that black men had either assaulted or engaged in consensual sex with white women sparked riots and the near-total destruction of burgeoning African-American communities. In Chicago, the stoning of a teenage boy innocently swimming with friends just off a "white" beach, and talk that an Italian woman had been killed in retaliation, ignited smoldering racial hatreds. So bad was it in Chicago that, as the sociologists St. Clair Drake and Horace Cayton revealed, between 1917 and 1921 fifty-eight homemade bombs were thrown into communities composed of newly arrived Negroes. Violence, it seemed, was contagious. In the stifling heat of mid-July, in Washington, D.C., a city in which only a scattered few migrants had settled, white soldiers marched through African-American neighborhoods in a striking imitation of the Atlanta riot of 1906. In Chicago and Washington—as in Houston—"colored people," writes Constance McLaughlin Green, "convinced that the time for meekness had passed, fought back." Given the postwar association of race with class and racial protest with Bolshevism, New Negro agitation also brought federal supervision of the African-American leadership class and a swift curtailment to many organizational activities, including a deep suspicion of the NAACP.[42]

For Du Bois, no one incident captured the complex dynamics accompanying "the prevailing drift of migrating Negroes" like the riot that shook East St. Louis in July of 1917. Arriving in East St. Louis, African-American laborers found themselves pitted against New Immigrants for jobs, homes, and wages. "Black men poured in," wrote Du Bois, "and red anger flamed in the hearts of the white workers."[43] With labor tensions already high, and with meat-packing plants hiring ever increasing numbers of black workers in place of high-paid immigrant labor, it was perhaps inevitable that a whitening tide of violence would soon sweep over the city. Local labor leaders protested that the "influx of undesirable negroes" posed a "growing menace" to the life and happiness of the city's white immigrant workers, and that "drastic action" alone could stem the tide of black folks. "Here were black men, guilty not only of bidding for jobs which white men could have held . . . but also guilty of being black! It was at this blackness that the unions pointed the accusing finger." On July 2 the desired "drastic action" commenced, first with carloads of "white 'joy riders'" firing slugs into African-American homes, and then with wholesale slaughter. When it ended, dozens of African Americans were dead—the streets were "wet with blood"—and entire neighborhoods had been reduced to rubble.[44]

As East St. Louis burned, Du Bois raced to the site of the riot, collected a solid week's worth of evidence, and then put together a grim, photo-filled commentary on the inhuman violence. Castigating labor leaders for inciting the riot, Du Bois published a facsimile of the labor leader Edward F. Mason's dangerously provocative memo to delegates of the Central Trades and Labor Union. Punctuating his angry commentary with a dash of nativism, Du Bois said: "It is not that foreigners . . . Czechs, Slovaks, Lithuanians . . . are ousting Americans of any color or hue, but [that] the 'Southern Negro,' the most American product there is, is being used 'to the detriment of . . . white citizens.'" The stench of death in East St. Louis would linger in Du Bois's mind for some time. And when his exposé of the riot was later revised as "Of Work and Wealth" in *Darkwater,* he fabricated a heroic and ultimately tragic tale of the resistance of black folks, revealing in the process the very different forces behind the assimilation of white immigrants and the African-American quest for social equality.[45]

With New Negro magazines drawing attention to the links between the Negro problem in America and European imperialism around the world, the African-American reaction to the riot took on a global character. At the Silent Protest March organized by the NAACP in response to what the *Washington Bee* termed "The Unspeakable Horrors Attending the Massacre of Innocent, Unoffending Members of Their Race by a Mob of White Savages," a shared, global blackness was evident; "The native born, the for-

The Silent Protest Parade on July 28, 1917—one of the first mass demonstrations in Manhattan featuring African Americans.

eign born, united by ties of blood and color, all owing allegiance to the Mother of races, will parade silently with the flags of America, England, Haiti, and Liberia."[46]

The proliferation of northern race riots in Chicago, East St. Louis, Springfield, and elsewhere, the brief national resurgence of the second Ku Klux Klan, and the patrician nativists' increasing fear of African Americans reflect an unanticipated consequence of the Great Migration: the increasing negrophobia and general obsession with "the Negro" in New York and elsewhere. Whites and blacks—or Nordics and Negroes—were becoming prominent in each other's minds and in the urban geography of the North. While political commentators in black America preached the glorious freedom of the North, most migrants found only communal isolation and a slightly more subtle brand of discrimination. Not surprisingly, patterns of residential segregation that had been developing since the 1890s—since the very first arrival of African Americans—crystallized after the war, after the riots, and after the Great Migration. Part of the process behind the reinvention of whiteness and blackness, in other words, was the trend toward residential segregation in the urban North, fed in part by the Great Migration and the widespread public fear of black folks.[47]

But bloody riots, lynchings, and the bitterness of war could not quite shake Du Bois's faith in an idealistic understanding of Anglo-American liberalism, especially when counseling Afro-America about patriotism and war. When it came time to pick a side in the war, Du Bois was, almost from the first, firmly on the side of the Allies, partly because he believed that the British and French were relatively benevolent masters compared to the imperial despotism of Germany and Belgium. There was, of course, more to Du Bois's surprising wartime patriotism than a pragmatic assessment of versions of empire. "Close Ranks"—the editorial in which Du Bois advocated support for the Allied war effort—was a surprising about-face for Du Bois, standing at odds with nearly all of his wartime criticism of American racism and white supremacy. "Let us, while this war lasts," he intoned therein, "forget our special grievances and close our ranks shoulder to shoulder with our white fellow citizens and the allied nations that are fighting for democracy."[48]

Negative reaction to Du Bois's illusory hope that comradeship-in-arms would breed citizenship for all was swift and severe, partly because few aside from Du Bois were so fooled by Wilsonian rhetoric and partly because Du Bois himself had been offered a captaincy in the army just prior to the publication of "Close Ranks." Friends and allies chided Du Bois for his naiveté. "I believe," offered his Niagara Movement comrade Byron Gunner, "that we should do just the reverse of what you advise. Now . . . is the most opportune time for us to push and keep our special grievances to the fore." Careful not to give the impression that he had been lured away from his post as guardian of African-American civil rights, Du Bois insisted that "Close Ranks" had come first and the offer of a captaincy second, and that the editorial was "entirely consistent" with his "well-known attitude."[49] And yet the seductive charms of an officer's appointment—much like the heady excitement of Crummell's praise and the saccharine flattery of the Universal Races Congress—had blinded Du Bois, stroking his Victorian nerve in just the right way. And there is substantial evidence that "Close Ranks," as the historian Mark Ellis puts it, "was a *quid pro quo,* and that the editorial and the captaincy were firmly linked."[50]

If the road from liberal internationalism to ardent anticolonialism was marked with alluring detours for Du Bois, the shift from Romantic racialism to the new race-consciousness was just as attenuated. When he was nearly fifty years old, Du Bois's lifelong quest for social justice intersected the Great War just as his critical faculties reached the height of their power. Tempered not just by age and experience but also by Bolshevism, the Great Migration, the decline of the West, and the bone-chilling racism of 1917–1919, Du Bois increasingly drew connections among "Negro problems" around the world years before most of the New Negro radicals did, recognizing—however ambivalently—that the Marxist tradition had something to offer African-American protest. In doing so, Du Bois shed much of the clumsy imprecision of Romantic racialism and helped to move the lines of racial classification from "the fifty races of the world" to five: black, brown, red, yellow, and white. In an America where experience itself was constructed in economic or mechanical terms, and in a world where the connections that bound hundreds of millions of people together were tightening, the new race-consciousness was part of the new order of things. In the aftermath of war, Du Bois, his synapses firing and his editorial pen a blur, inscribed that new language of racial difference into American political culture.

## The Magic of the Word "Black"

During and immediately after the Great War, the political capital Du Bois had amassed during the great debate with Booker T. Washington was stolen away by a younger, purportedly more dangerous group of West Indian

and African-American radicals. Inspired by Bolshevism and Irish nationalism, these "New Negroes" castigated the NAACP in general and Du Bois in
particular for their refined gentility and cozy friendships with white America, as well as for their presumed favoritism of light-skinned "mulattos."
The challenge of this New Negro Movement, together with the postwar response from the African-American leadership class, made the period between 1919 and 1929, from Versailles to the Great Depression, one of the
most creative and fertile periods of "black" protest in U.S. history. Indeed,
the conflict between "New" and "Old" Negroes—however fictive the differences actually were—changed the course of African-American life, if
only because of its focus on and redefinition of American foreign policy as
a cornerstone of what was then called "white world supremacy." In the
middle of it all was Du Bois, increasingly embittered about the prospects
for real social justice and struggling to retain his pride of place as the most
important—and therefore the most dangerous—"Negro" in America. If
"Close Ranks," the editorial in which he urged African-American support
for the war effort, was Du Bois's worst miscalculation, the anger and fire of
his postwar life in the 1920s were part of an ingenious, if incomplete, recovery.

Though less than twenty years separated them, *Darkwater* and *The Souls
of Black Folk* were worlds apart. The literary scholar Eric Sundquist has
noted some crucial similarities between these works, including a critical framework that is "inevitably diasporic in its horizons." Like *Souls,*
Sundquist notes, *Darkwater* (1920) was a collection of "fugitive pieces" reworked for collective publication; unlike *Souls,* however, *Darkwater* drew
strength not from the nadir of American race relations but instead from
the increasingly interconnected and "global" qualities of white world supremacy. In *Darkwater,* Sundquist argues, "Du Bois intended to create,
across a full spectrum of topics, a foundation for black America's Pan-African cultural mythos, repeating the strategy of *The Souls of Black Folk* now
on a global scale." The essays in *Darkwater* (which included earlier works
like "The Souls of White Folk," a reworked version of "The African Roots
of the War," and "Of Work and Wealth" on East St. Louis) overflowed with
anger and determination, and with insight into what Du Bois aptly termed
"the discovery of personal whiteness among the world's peoples."[51]

*Darkwater* was also the opening salvo of Du Bois's postwar political
reinvention and thus anticipated many of the battles to come in the struggle over the leadership of "the Negro" in the United States. The strident
controlled rage therein marked the public demise (or repression) of the

dreamy-eyed Du Bois of the Universal Races Congress, of the American Negro Academy, and of "Close Ranks." In *Darkwater,* published just months before Lothrop Stoddard's earth-shaking anti-Bolshevist blockbuster, *The Rising Tide of Color against White World Supremacy,* Du Bois stated that the "European world is using black and brown men for all the uses which men know," and named himself as a member of the oppressed, shouting, "I am black!" The book's title—*Darkwater*—perfectly reflected postwar debates about "rising tides" and "the Yellow Peril," connecting Jim Crow to jingoism and to Stoddard's desperate attempt to "salvage a shipwrecked world" by forging race and class together. Indeed, the threat of a war of the races (or classes) lingered in the pages of the most powerful essay in *Darkwater,* the republished "Souls of White Folk": "As wild and awful as [the Great War] was, it is nothing to compare with that fight for freedom which black and brown and yellow men must and will make . . . The Dark World is going to submit to its present treatment just as long as it must and not one moment longer." Those terrified authors bewailing the "crisis" of the West—like Stoddard—lent a degree of backhanded support to Du Bois's assertion that the "darker world" was rising, as well as to similar pronouncements from Marcus Garvey, Cyril Briggs, Hubert Harrison, and others. George Luther Cady, secretary of the American Missionary Association, reviewed *The Rising Tide of Color* alongside *Darkwater,* and wondered if it wasn't "significant" that "Prof. Du Bois, representing the black race, and Lathrap [*sic*] Stoddard, representing the white race, should emerge from the study of this [Negro] problem with a sword in hand?"[52]

To a certain extent, *Darkwater* did encourage a public reappraisal of Du Bois. His actions in the aftermath of the war—the heated words of *Darkwater,* his angry editorials on Red Scare race-baiting, race riots, and the general abuse of African peoples around the world—were viewed as increasingly dangerous by New England "Nordics" and southern segregationists alike. Responding to the charge by one reader that *Darkwater* might incite a race war, Du Bois hinted angrily that some wars were justifiable.[53] Lothrop Stoddard, given a few months to respond to *Darkwater,* dismissed people of African descent as incapable of self-governance and named Du Bois personally as a threat to the stability of the republic and to the supremacy of "the white race." Congressmen, editorialists, and armchair eugenicists agreed, pointing to Du Bois as a great danger and urging a curtailment of the publication of *The Crisis* and greater surveillance of the magazine's firebrand editor.

In the African-American community the response to *Darkwater* was somewhat more varied, hinting at Du Bois's coming war with the vanguard of New Negroes. If conservative African-American publications took careful note of Du Bois's vented spleen, the *Crusader*, the leftward-leaning mouthpiece of the African Blood Brotherhood, dismissed the book as "weak" and unscientific, and wished that Du Bois had not been so cavalier in purporting to speak for, and not to, "the Negro." "Like some god standing high over the world," concluded a review generally dripping with sarcasm, "he has looked down and spoken for the Negro multitude." "The new negro," Eric Walrond suggested, "feels that Mr. Du Bois is to [*sic*] far above the masses to comprehend their desires and aspirations . . . [and that] 'Darkwater' . . . reveals the soul of a man who is sorry and ashamed he is not white."[54]

These critiques of *Darkwater* signaled the arrival of a new, supposedly more aggressive cadre of African-American and Afro-Caribbean leaders. Filling their incendiary rhetoric with striking Bolshevisms and references to the Irish, these "New Negro" radicals offered a strong challenge to the NAACP, the National Urban League, and other Progressive protest groups. Before the Red Scare, Du Bois, Crummell, the American Negro Academy, and the NAACP had wrapped their chauvinistic rhetoric in the swaddling clothes of elitism, "invent[ing]," as Judith Stein once put it, "a view of the race to support a politics to address the elite discrimination they faced." But the communal legacy of the wartime veneration of Jim Crow, the Great Migration, and Red Scare negrophobia (the "Black Scare," as Robert Hill terms it) was the explosive emergence of the New Negro Movement and an accompanying sense of shared blackness—of race as class. "The movement [north]," concluded Abram Harris, in words that might just as aptly have described the New Negro Movement, "must not be considered as exclusively racial."[55] In short, if the Great Migration inspired the prophets of the new global whiteness, it also encouraged a similarly ardent celebration of global blackness in Afro-America. Suspended between Victorian elitism and the Marxist tradition, New Negroes—much like the postwar Du Bois—spoke of "the race" in words that were, on the surface, all about the proletarianization of people of African descent around the world (even if, deep down, both Garvey and Du Bois, for instance, retained a certain fondness for pomp and glamour). The consequences for Du Bois were important. When Booker T. Washington had been Du Bois's nemesis, the black Brahmin could easily position himself as the more radical advocate of social justice even as he pursued a moderate, elitist agenda. But with

Washington dead, and with the "class of 1917" stirring up trouble in Harlem, Du Bois was suddenly one of the "old crowd Negroes."

Emboldened by Harlem's new Afro-Caribbean community—and by intraracial tensions—the advocates of a New Negro "manhood" movement also drew strength from the increasing importance of black folks as a "mudsill" in American political and popular culture. Prior to the mid-1920s, even during the postwar Black Scare, northeastern political discourse remained ambivalent about which racial threat was more dangerous: "the Negro" or "the alien menace." The crucial juncture was reached in the 1920s after the abrupt curtailment of European immigration, and after the arrival of African Americans in the Northeast. Fears of the Negro were exacerbated by the acceleration of black migration (the flooding of the Mississippi in 1927 was responsible for a renewed dispersion of African Americans northward that lasted for several years), strengthening the later incarnations of the New Negro Movement and easing the transformation of nativism into negrophobia. Lothrop Stoddard's *Re-Forging America*—a work that captures this transformation better than any other—urged that the after-effects of the Great Migration be understood as America's most pressing racial quandary, and hoped that the ever intertwining forces of race-consciousness (Nordicism and the New Negro Movement) offered a solution to this problem: a permanent social separation of the races that he named "bi-racialism."[56]

New Negroes met this national trend toward negrophobia head on. "Just . . . about four years ago," Marcus Garvey mused in a speech in 1921, "a few of us thought that we could do something on our own account." Laced with celebrations of the future imperial glory of "the Negro race," and with a decidedly materialist approach to racial betterment, Garvey's vision of black protest captured the imagination of African Americans everywhere. Universal Negro Improvement Association branches sprang up in New Orleans, Chicago, Harlem, and Los Angeles. Thousands of dollars poured into UNIA coffers for Garvey's half-baked Black Star Line scheme, money that would be spent unwisely on several worn-out rusting hulks—tired ships that were entirely inadequate for the grand global steamship line planned by a man who styled himself, after the Irish leader Eamon De Valera, "the Provisional President of Africa." With his disparaging characterization of the "hereditary leadership" of African America as without "one bit of hope," Garvey offered the UNIA as a new and dangerous, and therefore very potent, force for social justice, reflecting the new sense of activism among the world's "Four Million Negroes." "We have," he reminded one audience, "a National Association for the Advancement of Colored People, we have a National Equal Rights League, we have many organizations in this country. Do you hear the Government saying anything about them? Not a word, but the Universal Negro Improvement Association is feared so much . . . We want you to have all the courage possible in this world. A race of cowards never conquered . . . Don't be a cringing sycophant today as you were yesterday."[57]

As the editor of *The Crisis,* and as the most prominent African-American spokesman for racial justice in the United States, Du Bois was destined to clash with Garvey for control of both the direction of black protest and the flow of black dollars. In many ways, the elder statesman of Afro-America was a ripe target for the Jamaica-born Garvey. Proud of his light skin and mixed ancestry, Du Bois had sometimes come close to what can only be called mulatto chauvinism, writing even in *Darkwater* of his "flood of Negro blood, a strain of French, a bit of Dutch, but, thank God! No 'Anglo-Saxon.'" The growth of a vibrant Caribbean community in New York, coupled with Garvey's oft-expressed love for the "pure black race" and his disdain for "the curse of many colors within the Negro race," set the stage for an extended debate on Afro-America's most jealously guarded secret: the politics of skin color.[58] In the age of Jim Crow, the African-American encounter with whiteness was most powerfully expressed in the importance assigned to skin color, facial features, and "good breeding." Personal fortunes, the potential for community leadership, and the all-important considerations of marriage owed much to the sometimes subtle and always imprecise differences between "coal black," "nut brown," and "high yaller," differences that resonated in both "white" and "black" America. For most Americans, in short, "good" skin tone and strong European features marked fate, destiny, luck, and the capacity for citizenship and civilization, on the very body of "the Negro"—though not all agreed that lighter was better. Du Bois, of course, was prone to confuse skin color with social class, or caramel-colored skin with upright manhood and prim, custodial womanhood.[59]

The Jamaican Claude McKay, reviewing the wildly popular Broadway musical *Shuffle Along,* put it succinctly: "As whites have their blonde and brunette, so do the blacks have their chocolate, chocolate-to-the-bone, brown, low-brown, teasing-brown, high-brown, yellow, high-yellow, and so on." "You can't blame light Negroes for being prejudiced against dark ones," Wallace Thurman later cautioned. The larger symbolic surround of American culture was built and maintained by white men of pristine Anglo-Saxon and Protestant origin, and placed the highest value on those things which fell all too clearly within the pale. "White is the symbol of everything that is pure and good," Thurman continued. "Ivory soap is advertised as being ninety-nine and some fraction per cent pure, and Ivory soap is white. Moreover, virtue and virginity are always represented as being clothed in white garments. Then, too, the God we, or rather most Negroes worship is a patriarchal white man seated on a white throne, in a spotless white heaven, radiant with white streets and white-appareled angels eating white honey and drinking white milk." If mainstream culture taught all Americans that whiteness was righteousness, white Americans themselves repeated the same lesson, with a great deal more explicitness, in countless face-to-face encounters. In a racist country the success of the lighter skinned could not exist without the sanction—explicit or not, conscious or not—of the white world. "Mulattoes," Truman further opined, "have always been accorded more consideration by white people than their darker brethren. They were made to feel superior even during slave days . . . made to feel proud . . . that they were bastards."[60]

But for Garvey and other recently arrived dark-skinned West Indian émigrés, the "curse of many colors"—a tragic curse rooted in the slave past—needed to be exorcised and replaced with a deep, abiding respect for the purest blackness. Disgusted with Du Bois, and increasingly at odds with the NAACP, Garvey branded Du Bois a "lazy dependant mulatto," a "monstrosity," or an "unfortunate mulatto, who bewails every day the drop of Negro blood in his veins, being sorry that he is not Dutch or French." "Dr. Du Bois," concluded Garvey's ally Wheeler Sheppard, "dare not deny . . . [that] no matter how much bleaching powders, 'Sure-Cure for Blackness,' [American Negroes] may use in their hopeless physical transformation; how much hair tonic 'Kink-no-More' they may apply to their hair; how much white blood they can rightfully lay claim to; how blooded related in kith and kin; how well they may appear in action and outward physical appearance in point with the opposite Race . . . the echo from the same old historical answer comes straight back home again, 'The United States of America is and ever will be a White Man's Country.'"[61] In an explosive *Crisis* editorial, "A Lunatic or a Traitor," Du Bois labeled Garvey a "wretch." Later, in a very rare display of nativism, he dismissed Garvey's criticisms as part of a "West Indian conception of the color line" and wrongly suggested that "when the rank and file of ignorant West-Indian negroes were going wild over Garvey, the American negroes sat cool and calm." In response, Garvey growled that this over-bred "one third Dutchman" deserved a "good horse whipping." When Du Bois accidentally found himself confronted with Garvey in a crowded elevator in New York City, Wendell Dabney believed that he saw Du Bois's nostrils quiver with disgust.[62]

Gone were the judiciously phrased, thinly veiled, and genteel accusations of the prewar era: the rise of the New Negro and the general disparagement of Du Bois had turned African-American political culture into an old-fashioned barroom brawl. In the heat and bluster of the early 1920s, the lucid *Darkwater* was simply not enough, prompting Du Bois to further restrain his deeply felt blue-vein enthusiasms and compose the most thoroughly chauvinistic passages in *The Gift of Black Folk*, and to fight back, tooth and nail, against his detractors. Soon there was a steady stream of invective in *The Crisis* and *The Messenger* directed at Garvey. Garvey, Robert Bagnall wrote, was a "Jamaican Negro of unmixed stock, squat, stocky, fat and sleek, with protruding jaws and heavy jowls, small bright pig-like eyes and rather bull-dog-like face." Bagnall's words—and the lengthy tradition of African-American nativism—carried even more weight in the midst of the contemporary debate about immigrants and Americanization.[63] Garvey's own less than adroit exploitation of skin-color politics was even more directly evident in his assertion that Cyril Briggs, a disgruntled former ally and founder of the African Blood Brotherhood, was a "WHITE MAN—NEGRO FOR CONVENIENCE," whose organization was devoted to "catch[ing] Negroes, no doubt." After a long court battle—Briggs, like Garvey a recent West Indian immigrant, had sued for libel—Garvey was forced to retract the charges against his lighter-skinned enemy.[64]

In this heated context, Du Bois found himself caught up in the assault against the UNIA launched from NAACP headquarters. After an appointment as Minister Plenipotentiary to Liberia and just a few short months after he made an official visit to that country, there were accusations that he had persuaded the Liberian consul-general to forbid entry to "any person or persons associated with the Garvey Movement in the United States." A letter containing documentation of charges against the UNIA worthy of investigation, signed by seven of Garvey's enemies in the Afro-American civil rights community (but not by Du Bois), was forwarded to the attorney general of the United States. A tireless Walter White of the NAACP shamelessly curried support from a variety of New Negro leaders. And the African-American leadership class found an unusual partner in the Department of Justice, which ruthlessly investigated and infiltrated the UNIA, ironically suspecting Garvey of Bolshevism but convicting him of capitalist excess in mail fraud.[65]

It would take more than the conviction of Garvey to shore up Du Bois's crumbling reputation in the African-American community—an organization, or a rallying point, was necessary. In the intertwined battles for racial justice and for the leadership of the race, Du Bois's postwar Pan-Africanism was a cleverly advertised "phase of war."[66] An earlier Pan-African Conference, attended by the likes of Edward Blyden, Henry Sylvester Williams, and Bishop Henry Turner, had aroused some attention, but by the end of the war Williams, Blyden, Turner, and most of the other leaders present at that conference had died. Du Bois, increasingly challenged by Garvey and others, seized the opportunity presented by the Peace Conference and, after months of hard work and with the support of the NAACP, left for Paris aboard the *Orizaba*. The Pan-African Congress itself, held in February of 1919, was packed with NAACP figures of note, including William English Walling and Joel Spingarn, who mingled, argued, and sympathized with Blaise Diagne of Senegal and like-minded leaders from South Africa, Kenya, Liberia, the French and Belgian Congos, and elsewhere.

For the next ten years, Pan-African Congresses were held throughout Europe—in Brussels, Paris, and London—stimulating anticolonialism in Africa and the Caribbean. Du Bois, reveling in his undisputed leadership role and always a bit Victorian, proudly announced to the American public that those present at the congresses "were undoubtedly an intelligenzia," and privately described the Pan-African movement as an attempt to organize "many millions of people of Negro blood varying from men of modern education in America and West Africa to the barbarians and savages of Africa." If Pan-Africanism "signified the militant, anticapitalist, solidarity of the darker world," it was also part of the broader transformation of American racial discourse. The liberal mulatto chauvinism of the old Du Bois had been replaced—though not entirely—by the unorthodox Marxism of the new postwar prophet of transnational blackness.[67]

Du Bois's sweeping and surprisingly safe *The Gift of Black Folk* (first published in 1924) was, to a certain extent, meant to counter his radical departure. Taking aim at the collective forces of "Americanization," an um-

brella term he used to refer to advocates of immigration restriction, eugenics, and Jim Crow, *The Gift of Black Folk* was the purest expression of Du
Bois's long-lasting pluralism. Hastily conceived as part of a larger Knights
of Columbus response to the severe restriction of immigration under the
National Origins Act, *Gift* argued eloquently that the "Negro's" contribution to the making of America had been both different from and more important than that of any other racial group. Modern democracy, Du Bois
suggested, was a product of "the persistent struggle of black men" for social
justice in America, as were American literature, humor, and music. "Above
and beyond all," he averred, "is the peculiar spiritual quality which the Negro has injected into American life and civilization . . . a certain spiritual
joyousness; a sensuous, tropical love of life . . . a slow and dreamful conception of the universe, a drawling and slurring of speech, and intense sen-
sitiveness to spiritual values."[68]

*The Gift of Black Folk* would satisfy the deepest needs of middle-brow
white liberals and immigrant pluralists, and captured Du Bois's heroic attempt to find a place for black Americans in the larger context of American
life and culture—a decidedly moderate agenda not quite laced with the
global dangers of Bolshevism and the new race-consciousness. It was, however, a book that spoke to many different audiences. Certainly, *Gift* was decidedly "progressive" in its implicit sympathy for the public demonstrations against "National Origins" and in its ardent pluralism, but it could
also be read as an extended epistle on racial chauvinism—on the myriad virtues of blackness. Indeed, in many ways, by offering its readers a
comfortable sense that black folks were naturally different, *The Gift of
Black Folk* was a fitting complement to the unflinching descriptions of the
worldwide process of whitening found in "The Souls of White Folk" and
*Darkwater.* Despite the foregrounded vision of harmonious interaction,
then, a general enthusiasm for blackness—and indeed for the manifest virtues of "the Negro"—could be read in several different ways.

Pushed leftward by the rhetorical Bolshevisms of his New Negro antago-
nists, Du Bois increasingly spoke of the conflict of races as color-coded
class conflict. Even before the war, Du Bois had one-upped Lenin, drawing
sweeping, powerful conclusions not simply about empire and industrialism but also about the nature of the relationship between race, class, and
"the increasingly intricate, world-embracing industrial machine that . . .
civilization has built." In organizing the Pan-African Congresses of the
1920s, Du Bois was among the first to "reach out"—imaginatively, spiritually, materially, and politically—to Africa. And when he drafted the mani-

festo of the Second Pan-African Congress, with both Haiti and Africa on
his mind, he spoke of liberation from the "industrial machine," and the
need to "judge men as men and not as material and labor." "If we are coming to recognize that the great modern problem is to correct maladjustment in the distribution of wealth," he argued, "it must be remembered
that the basis of maladjustment is the outrageously unjust distribution of
world income between the dominant and suppressed peoples; in the rape
of the land and raw material, and monopoly of technique and culture. And
in this crime white labor is particeps criminis with white capital." To argue
that white labor and capital were complicitous in the exploitation of people of color around the world, to invoke class so readily, was to go against
the grain of American culture after the Red Scare.[69]

New Negro protest against colonialism, imperialism, and ruthless economic exploitation found its *cause célèbre* in the avaricious abuse of Haiti,
which the United States had occupied in 1915. With its incendiary connections to race war, the French Revolution, and Toussaint L'Ouverture,
Haiti loomed large in the minds of New Negroes and Nordics alike after
the occupation, especially after a large number of people from the Caribbean emigrated to the United States during the 1910s and 1920s. Lothrop
Stoddard wrote his doctoral dissertation on the "Black Jacobins" of Saint-
Domingue, emphasizing the murderous rage of the darker-skinned masses
and the treachery of the island's mulatto population. The arrival of a few
politically radical Caribbean blacks in Harlem—Garvey, Briggs, Harrison
—inflamed memories of L'Ouverture. The stylish and widely publicized
New Negro Movement of the 1920s further strengthened the symbolic
connection between Haiti, Africa, and "the Negro problem" in America.
Despite the purportedly humanitarian gestures of the American military
expedition to Haiti, postwar New Negro radicals were quick to criticize the
Wilson administration, Secretary of the Navy Josephus Daniels, and the
sinister forces of "American capital" lurking behind the scenes. A deeper
cognitive connection had been forged as a result of this nakedly exploitative occupation, which witnessed the exporting of Jim Crow and white
southern soldiers to the Caribbean home of black revolution. When Jake,
the "transnational" protagonist of Claude McKay's *Home to Harlem*, comes
to understand the evils of American imperialism in Haiti, he is transformed—he is, in words reminiscent of Stoddard's color-coded map, "a
boy who stands with the map of the world in colors before him, and feels
the wonder of the world."[70]

Led by the rejuvenated patriarch of African-American dissent, the National Association for the Advancement of Colored People—more than any other group outside the early UNIA—was in the vanguard of New Negro protest against the American occupation. The NAACP executive Herbert Seligman and field secretary James Weldon Johnson journeyed to Haiti on an anti-imperialist fact-finding tour. Johnson later published his critical findings in *The Nation*. A fact-finding group led by Emily Greene Balch of the Women's International League for Peace and Freedom concluded that American businesses had imposed near-total control of the Haitian economy. Johnson and Seligman and *The Nation*, Du Bois later suggested, had exposed "the seizure of a nation by the National City Bank of Wall Street." Much like the American South, Africa, and the Caribbean, the NAACP averred, Haiti suffered under the heel of white world supremacy: the racial and economic dynamic was perpetually uneven, and the same everywhere. "The United States," Du Bois said bitterly, "is at war with Haiti." Directing his scorn against what he now termed "the American Congo," Du Bois drew startling parallels between the evils of Belgian administration in the Congo and the authoritarian rule of Jim Crow in the New South. In doing so, he sounded very much like Garvey himself, or like Hubert Harrison, or Cyril Briggs, or A. Philip Randolph—members of the "younger generation" of New Negroes whose antiracist protests were accompanied by heavily gendered anticolonial messages and who repeatedly raised the specter of a worldwide manly revolt of "the darker masses" against their degenerating white "overlords." Eugenically inspired militant anti-imperialism (accented by ruthless fratricidal impulses) had become a central tenet of New Negro politics.[71]

In the midst of this extended leftward lurch of black politics, certain white supremacists—Lothrop Stoddard, for one—engaged in a surprisingly civilized dialogue with their counterparts in Harlem. After the Great War, radicals and conservatives, New Negroes and Nordic voguers had a lot in common when it came to speaking, thinking, and symbolizing the idea of racial difference. New Negro advocates of the new race-consciousness—Garvey, Harrison, Briggs—directed their barbs not at "old-fashioned" Anglo-Saxonism but, instead, at proponents of a worldwide Nordic vogue. The patrician eugenicist Madison Grant and the *World's Work* correspondent Lothrop Stoddard were often singled out for criticism or, perhaps more interestingly, for praise in New Negro magazines.[72] Du Bois, for instance, enjoyed the constant censure of the terror-stricken Stoddard, and that censure helped to secure for him a renewed prominence as a virile and active New Negro leader. Like Du Bois, Hubert H. Harrison found much to admire in reviewing Stoddard's *Rising Tide of Color*. Lauding Stoddard's use of science as "organized daily knowledge and common sense," Harrison urged his readers to purchase the book, writing that it "should be widely read by intelligent men of color from Tokio to Tallahassee." Harrison was so enamored of Stoddard's work that he struck up a chatty correspondence with the busy journalist, sending him chapter outlines for a book on Islam and reminding the "blond overlord" that "naturally, since I am a Negro, my sympathies are not at all with you: that which you fear I naturally hope for."[73]

Harrison's admiration of Stoddard was roughly analogous to the curious relationship between Marcus Garvey and Earnest Sevier Cox. Cox, an aristocratic Virginian, a self-styled negrophobe, and a southern protégé of Madison Grant, had traveled to "white colonies" around the world before the war, an experience he later recounted in his autobiographical *Black Belt Around the World*. After serving as an aide to the arch-segregationist James K. Vardaman, Cox founded the "White America" society and began work on his first critical treatment of the American "race problem," putting it in a global context. His anthropological survey of race problems in the colonies, Cox believed, had given him a unique insight into the striking sameness of race problems around the world. In 1924, with Garvey's legal troubles growing, Madison Grant clipped out a report of one of Garvey's speeches on black repatriation to Africa and sent it to Cox, urging him to "get in touch with Garvey."[74] When Cox did so, the "Provisional President of Africa" responded with eager overtures of friendship and insisted that the UNIA and the Ku Klux Klan, which Cox was presumed to represent, shared social visions. "A black man who advocates racial integrity," Cox would later write, "cannot be opposed by a white man who advocates racial integrity . . . They are drawn to each other, for they fight in a common cause." The two men shared a thirst for "race purity," and both headed movements which were explicitly about reconstructing manhood around an electrified vision of racial classification in modern America.[75]

Within a matter of months after their initial contact, Cox had spoken at two separate UNIA meetings and Garvey had written to Cox in support of Virginia's Racial Integrity Law (written, in part, by Madison Grant)—a law prohibiting racial intermarriage, and which thus took Garvey's ideas of race purity to their logical conclusion, expunging the very idea of "the mulatto" from Virginia's legal system. Race purity and a general disparage-

ment of the idea of the mulatto—key aspects of the new race-consciousness—were at the heart of the relationship between Cox and Garvey: "For
once," Garvey asked of his public, "will we agree with the American white
man, that one drop of Negro blood makes a man a Negro?" As proof of his
devotion to the aristocratic Cox—who worked diligently for Garvey's early
release from prison—Garvey printed a full-page advertisement for Cox's
*White America* in the back of his own *Philosophy and Opinions*. Writing
from prison, and sending encouraging letters to Cox about *White America*,
Garvey commented upon his own "unchangeable" opposition to Du Bois's
"mad dreams and purpose," and suggested that the mulatto Du Bois, unlike the pure black Garvey, was "too tricky" to properly understand Cox's
work on behalf of "the Negro problem."[76]

For Du Bois, indeed for many African Americans, the relationship
between Garvey and Cox was far too cozy and comfortable. The jailed
Garvey's public enthusiasm for Cox and the Ku Klux Klan was to be his
final misstep in the freshly laid minefield of African-American politics. Du
Bois, for one, suggested grim parallels between Garvey and "the Grand Cy-
clops of the Ku Klux Klan," noting that "they were indeed birds of a feather,
believing in titles, flummery, and mumbo-jumbo, and handling much
gullible money." *The Messenger,* never a friend to Garvey, headlined that
the UNIA president-general had become the "MESSENGER BOY OF THE
WHITE KU KLUX KLEAGLE," and orchestrated the "Garvey Must Go!"
campaign. Eager for the coming decline of "Garveyism," the Darwinian
competitors for a mass constituency of African Americans clambered to
deliver the death-blow to the UNIA.[77]

Much more so than Cox, Lothrop Stoddard came to embody the Nordic
side of the new race-consciousness, becoming a shadowy reflection of the
world views and racial chauvinisms of the New Negro Movement. Frederick Lewis Allen would later recall that the racial tensions of the early 1920s
were "not alleviated by the gospel of white supremacy preached by Lothrop
Stoddard, whose *Rising Tide of Color* proclaimed that the dark-skinned
races constituted a worse threat to western civilization than the Germans
or Bolsheviks." By the late 1920s Stoddard was perhaps the most prominent white supremacist in the United States. A journalist and an author
of immensely popular and influential works on race and world politics,
Stoddard was the perfect foil for New Negroes who yearned to be seen as
dangerous. With his trembling pronouncements of danger around the
world, Stoddard's fears that "the rising tide of color" would—through the

stupidity of benevolent imperialism—master European technology and re-alize a class-consciousness seemed, to Garvey, Harrison, and others, to lay out a blueprint for the political ambitions of the "400,000,000 Negroes of the World." The shriller Stoddard's cries for a renewed race-consciousness became, the more fervently New Negro admirers lauded his work, their sole regret being that Stoddard seemed to pay far more attention to the dangers posed by "the yellow peril." "The coming together of big nations everywhere," Garvey yelled triumphantly in a speech against the disarma-ment of the "darker world" (especially Japan) supposedly under consider-ation at the Washington Naval Conference, "is but an attempt to . . . keep down the 'rising tide of color.'" Stoddard, in turn, cited Garvey and Harri-

Lothrop Stoddard, ca. 1940.

son as laudable examples of "race-consciousness" and dismissed Du Bois as a northern mulatto whose integrationist radicalism hinted at those peculiar mental failings found in mixed-race offspring.[78]

"Here is Garvey," Du Bois said incredulously, smarting from the constant accusations of mulatto degeneration, "yelling to life, from the black side, a race consciousness which leaps to meet Madison Grant and Lothrop Stoddard and other worshippers of the great white race." Du Bois's cynicism notwithstanding, Stoddard, Nordicism, and white world supremacy had become, by the 1920s, thoroughly intertwined with the New Negro Movement, changing the nature of race in the process. Local libraries, newspapers, and political organizations began scrutinizing Stoddard's writings, clipping articles from the daily papers, and cheering whenever a member of "the race" struck down in print the man many African Americans equated with the white leviathan itself.

If Du Bois, in direct contrast to Garvey and Harrison, professed nothing but scorn for the most ardent Nordic enthusiasts, he nevertheless did pay attention to Stoddard's body of writings. While Garvey endlessly cited Stoddard's *Rising Tide of Color* in the pages of the *Negro World,* and Harrison favorably reviewed the book and struck up a chatty friendship with its author, Du Bois attacked Stoddard immediately, even relentlessly, rebutting his arch critique of the modernization of "backward" people in the appropriated metaphors and vitriolic content of *Darkwater.* Asked about Stoddard's belief that "Negroes" had no ability to govern themselves, Du Bois replied: "Lothrop Stoddard has no standing as a sociologist . . . [he] is simply a popular writer who has some vogue now."[79] Stoddard's much-publicized tour of Tuskegee (he was a guest of R. R. Moton) and his hankering for the separatist leadership styles of Booker T. Washington and Marcus Garvey no doubt added fuel to the fire.

When Stoddard and Du Bois met one night at a debate on "the race problem," Du Bois's anger was evident. "Suppose you say," he suggested grimly, "despite anything that the Darker races . . . may ask, we are going to sit tight and keep them where they belong. Then the question is, can you do it?" "Who in the hell," he added, "said we wanted to marry your daughters?" Du Bois's cool and deliberate consideration of an anticipated war of the races between Nordic "supermen" and "the darker peoples" was, in comparison with the ameliorative voices of the NAACP, the National Urban League, and the onetime author of "Close Ranks," revolutionary.[80]

Up against a determined cadre of youthful revolutionaries, soapbox orators, and charlatans, Du Bois emerged victorious from the fratricide of the early 1920s partly because he alone effectively—and frequently—engaged Stoddard in public dialogue. During the 1920s the two mismatched champions of contradictory causes came together repeatedly in scholarly debate. In late July of 1925 Du Bois was asked by Will Durant, director of the Labor Temple School, to debate "The Problem of Race" with Stoddard, Madison Grant, Robert Lowie, and Sidney Gulick. Grant, who later confided in Stoddard that "it is a shameful thing that [debate with black folk] has to be done at all . . . to have educated such Negroes as Locke and Du Boise [sic] was a crime," quickly backed out of the debate.[81] But Stoddard's speech, "Is the White Race Doomed?" went on as planned, as did Du Bois's, entitled "The Future of the Negro Race." When, less than a year later, Stoddard debated Alain Locke in the pages of *The Forum*, Du Bois provided a short response. And following the debate with Locke, Du Bois and Stoddard scheduled their own radio debate. "Everyone . . . agrees that it was a corker," said E. C. Aswell of *The Forum*.[82] The *coup de grâce* was the debate held by the Chicago Forum Council in the North Hall of the Coliseum, where Du Bois presented his well-rehearsed rebuttal to Stoddard's theory of the "magic Nordic germ plasm" in front of a mixed audience with a large number of African Americans quite vocal in their hostility to Stoddard's "Negative" stance on the question, "Should the Negro Be Encouraged to Seek Cultural Equality?"[83]

That exchange in the Chicago Coliseum was tremendously revealing. Hoping to keep race-consciousness in the public mind after the passage of the National Origins Act and the cessation of European immigration, Lothrop Stoddard helped to remake Du Bois even as Du Bois made Stoddard the leading popular advocate of Nordicism. They could never agree, of course, about "the Negro problem": the unrelenting racial bloodshed around the country and the apparent permanence of Jim Crow made such an agreement impossible. But despite their quite contradictory solutions to the now national "Negro problem," and despite the omnipresent evils of American racism, Stoddard and Du Bois had found common ground in aristocratic pretensions. As erudite Harvard men of New England, as proponents of race-consciousness, as journalists interested in world politics, and as somewhat closeted Victorians in a modern world, the angry *Crisis* editor and the Nordic contributor to *World's Work* and the *Saturday Evening Post* shared a willingness to debate each other publicly and with moderate civility—a willingness rooted in elitism and mutual respect.

Du Bois and Stoddard also shared an aristocrat's faith in the power of birth and heredity: in eugenics. As a valued member of the board of directors of the American Birth Control League, Lothrop Stoddard, when sitting in the audience at the Sixth International Neo-Malthusian and Birth Control Conference at the Hotel McAlpin in Manhattan, must have agreed when he heard Du Bois's written statement (requested in advance by Margaret Sanger) read aloud at the conference. What the world needed, Du Bois had written, was "the regulation of birth by reason and common sense instead of by chance and ignorance." Stoddard himself could hardly have disagreed. "Among human races and groups," Du Bois would later argue, in words that might well have come directly from Stoddard or Madison Grant, "as among vegetables, quality, and not mere quantity really counts."[84]

As men, and as the most supremely evolved representatives of their races, Stoddard and Du Bois believed that they shared obligations of privilege and social responsibility. Upon hearing that Du Bois was to be his opposite number in the 1929 radio debate arranged by *The Forum,* Stoddard expressed great pleasure and asked E. C. Aswell to tell Du Bois on his behalf "that he looks forward to this opportunity to make your acquaintance." The two great advocates of Nordic supremacy and justice for the Negro cordially exchanged papers prior to their radio debate, and the experience was satisfying enough that Stoddard agreed to the debate before the Community Forum in Chicago, where he was far less likely to win over his audience (Du Bois privately ventured that Stoddard might fail to appear as scheduled).[85] As the debate began, Fred Moore, director of the Chicago Forum, reminded his audience that "every man and woman here this afternoon [should] have high respect for Dr. Stoddard's courage in coming here to face this issue, to speak his opinions, and to put before you . . . an unpopular point of view." Even the Chicago *Defender*—with the two-inch banner headline "Du Bois Shatters Stoddard's Cultural Theories"—admitted in small print that the "applause was equally divided between the two speakers." A large integrated crowd, the *Defender* reported, had gathered on a Sunday afternoon "to hear two men, both celebrated scholars and writers, different in the color of their skin, but equal in intellectual ability, discuss the question." Stoddard was so impressed with Du Bois that day—and so struck by his fiery intelligence during their numerous confrontations in the late 1920s—that he would retain a lifelong respect for the older *Crisis* editor.[86]

On the eve of the Great Depression, Du Bois continued to move toward a decidedly unorthodox Marxism. No one piece of New Negro propaganda captured his radical rebirth in the 1920s quite like his second novel and great contribution to the burgeoning Harlem Renaissance, *Dark Princess,* first published in 1928. In *The Quest of the Sliver Fleece* Du Bois had chosen prototypically southern characters (Bles and Zora) as his protagonists, and like the prewar Du Bois, those protagonists were dreamy and almost fatally optimistic. In contrast, Matthew Towns, the well-traveled Pullman porter of *Dark Princess,* is—much like Du Bois himself—denied social advancement strictly because of his race, and is soon full of hate for the white leviathan and thoroughly disillusioned about the prospects for political change in the United States. Conspiring with the Princess Kautilya (the "dark princess" of the title), Matthew eventually concludes that the hope of "the Negro" in America lies with "the new dark will to self-assertion." "China," Du Bois insisted through the novel, "must achieve united and independent nationhood. Japan must stop aping the West and North and throw her lot definitively with the East and South. Egypt must stop looking north for prestige and tourists' tips and look south toward the black Sudan, Uganda, Kenya, and South Africa for new economic synthesis of the tropics." Contrasting the futility of Matthew's early work as a Chicago alderman with the romantic optimism and certain future of his later work as a revolutionary in the war against "the Pale Masters of today," Du Bois offered an argument about the nature of African-American protest and suggested that "the political machine" was hardly a potent force for social justice. A global perspective alone, he argued, could shed light on the world economic forces that imprisoned "the Negro" in poverty and hopelessness.[87]

*Dark Princess* captured Du Bois's own transformation from ardent Victorian spokesman for "the Negro" in the South to worldwide anti-imperial agitator, from a man possessed of a youthful blind faith in civilization to a pragmatic and far-seeing idealist in the Marxist tradition. The revolution, for Du Bois, had come during and after the Great War, with the arrival of hundreds of thousands of African Americans in the urban North and the cataclysmic social transformations that attended the simple migration of common folk in search of better lives. The unprecedented Great Migration and the virtual end of European immigration altered the demographic and racial calculus of northeastern life, grinding down Du Bois's faith in pluralism, civilization, and white folks. Angry protest soon followed. If *The*

*Souls of Black Folk* offered an analysis of the supposed peculiar race problems of the New South, *Darkwater* and *Dark Princess* put "the Negro problem" in a powerfully global context. In "Close Ranks" and at the Universal Races Congress, Du Bois had believed that there were real and tangible differences between Anglo-American and German colonial policies; in *The Quest of the Silver Fleece,* he had presented "the Negro problem" as a problem of the South. *Dark Princess,* Du Bois's signal contribution to the literary revival, would argue that "the Negro problem" had become a global dilemma, and that the "white leviathan was the same vast, remorseless machine in Berlin as in New York."[88]

## Depression

The collapse of the white leviathan would change little for black folks. Though few white Americans noticed, the Great Depression brought only misery for African Americans. After they hamstrung the New Negro Movement and the Harlem Renaissance, and even while they exacerbated the anxieties of the Nordic vogue, the social forces behind the plummeting economy of the United States might have swept away the great liberal myths of individualism, pluck, and success that had softened, or hidden, the clashes between economic groups, allowing for a real and honest discussion of class, caste, and race in America. To be sure, as the bread lines grew longer, as labor strife turned increasingly violent, and as the Depression stretched into an eternity, there were signs that a very public exploration of deepening social divisions would explode across American political culture. But, suggests Lawrence Levine, the "remarkable thing about the American people before reform did come was not their action but their inaction, not their demands but their passivity, not their revolutionary spirit but their traditionalism." As always, "the Negro" was largely excluded from that warm and cozy "traditionalism." When faced with awful circumstances, white Americans clung to one another and to the nation with manic ferocity.[89]

For most African Americans the Depression brought increasing misery—more evictions and fewer jobs in the New South, more violent lynchings, and an infuriating avalanche of popular stereotypes in film, radio, and literature. The mechanization of agriculture displaced growing numbers of black sharecroppers and farmers, leaving them rootless and hungry. The New Deal, moreover, offered little, if any, relief—on a local level, few programs were immune from southern prejudices. Indeed, but for a few well-intentioned and strategically placed white liberals, the nationwide recovery programs instituted by Roosevelt and others would have skipped over "the Negro" entirely. As economic help for struggling black families dwindled to nothing, Works Progress Administration efforts to preserve black folk traditions, to recover the voices of former slaves, or to sponsor various murals merely borrowed the same, tired stereotype—the Du Boisian notion that black folks were inherently artistic, or gifted with an innate ability to express their pain and suffering in art, literature, song, and drama.[90]

The radical edge of American political culture during the ameliorative Popular Front era did occasionally merge with the African-American struggle for social equality, especially between 1929 and 1934. During these dark days of the early Depression, the tragedy of Scottsboro (where nine young boys were jailed and nearly lynched on trumped-up charges) was offset by the heroism of the Communist Party of the United States and its Industrial Labor Defense (ILD) attorneys. In the deepest South of Alabama, the CPUSA attempted to do what no one thought possible: to organize black sharecroppers in the face of violent repression and the constant threat of prison, gunfire, and death. For a few remarkable years, the CPUSA was the most aggressive advocate of civil rights for "the Negro," and many African Americans in the deep South and the urban North accepted the help of the Party and celebrated the leftward thrust of American culture, albeit with some rather creative adaptations.[91]

But if the general drift of American culture during the Depression was leftward, the dominant voices in upper-crust African-American political culture—Walter White, James Weldon Johnson, A. Philip Randolph—were, by and large, staunchly anticommunist. Indeed, the NAACP and the CPUSA viciously competed to defend the legal rights of "the Negro" in the American South. When the nine African-American boys and young men were arrested at Scottsboro for the alleged (and completely fabricated) rape of two white women on a freight train, the NAACP had balked at financing a legal defense for accused rapists, allowing the ILD to take the case and to revel in the publicity that came with it. "For better or worse," writes the historian Dan T. Carter of the early 1930s, "the politics of the nation had shifted to the left; the National Association for the Advancement of Colored People had not." Walter White, the NAACP's self-styled administrative superman, never forgot the lesson of "losing" the

Scottsboro case to the ILD. The resultant disputes between the NAACP and the Communist Party continued even through the Popular Front, when the NAACP leadership class uncomfortably forged fragile connections with the Old Left, and as the CPUSA attempted to transform itself into a respectable protest organization. When the Popular Front alliance collapsed during the Second World War, the NAACP practically leapt into the forefront of Red Scare antiradicalism, functioning as "the left wing of McCarthyism," and countering the subversive threats of black radicalism and economic revolution with its own supposedly moderate agenda of judicial and legislative reform.[92]

Despite the seeming possibilities of the Depression and the New Deal, however, reform always came at a glacial pace and was inevitably conceived and implemented with the color line—the adamantine hardness of the line between whiteness and blackness and between whites and blacks—firmly in place. The conflict between the NAACP and the CPUSA over the Scottsboro case revealed the limitations of both groups in the face of growing despair, suffering, and anxiety—a point made by Du Bois in his 1931 essay "The Negro and Communism." However subversive the NAACP's program might be, Du Bois argued, it hardly addressed all the pressing questions of the Depression. "The platform of the NAACP," he offered carefully, "is no complete program of social reform . . . [but] a pragmatic union of certain definite problems." "As America appeared to unravel," David Levering Lewis notes, "the [NAACP's] general staff gave only perfunctory attention to the deepening economic hardship assailing the great majority of black people—electing to pursue litigation and lobbying rather than to focus on economic strategies." Having written of the NAACP's deficiencies, Du Bois then dismissed the Communist Party's efforts in Alabama, if only because of the disjunction between CPUSA rhetoric and the negrophobia of the "white worker" in America. If the Communist Party branded the NAACP as a tool of American capitalism, Du Bois said, it only proved that "American Communists are neither wise nor intelligent." "The persons killing blacks in Northern Alabama and demanding blood sacrifice are the white workers—sharecroppers, trade unionists and artisans," he contended; "capitalists [in contrast] are against mob-law and violence and would listen to reason in the long run because industrial peace increases their profits."[93]

In the bewildering context of collective gloom and racial violence, the NAACP's disheartening fascination with obscure legalisms had encouraged Du Bois to lunge leftward yet again. His deepening radicalism was most potently expressed in his continued criticism of American foreign policy and in his desire for a "union of color"—an "effective brotherhood" of "the colored world." Domestic politics, however, was a slightly different issue. Having used the new race-consciousness to reinvent himself in the 1920s, and having outlasted his battered New Negro opponents, Du Bois soon found himself proposing a radical version of Lothrop Stoddard's biracialism in the 1930s, finding in racial separatism the pragmatic solution to the supposedly intractable "race problem" in America. "Biracialism," Stoddard had written during his debate with Alain Locke, in words that must have resonated with the elitist Du Bois, "is not discrimination; it is separation. Biracialism does not imply relative 'superiority' or 'inferiority'; it is based on the self evident fact of difference. Those Negroes who believe in their race should not object on principle to an arrangement which would permit the American Negro to remain himself and develop his special aptitudes . . . biracialism is not caste . . . [it] draws one vertical line through society, from top to bottom, and then allows individuals to rise as high as their talents will take them, on their side of the line."[94]

By 1934, when he resigned from the editorship of *The Crisis* and from the NAACP over issues of political philosophy and personal temperament, Du Bois was advocating a position very close to that of Stoddard, albeit from the weaker side of the political dynamic. "There should never be an opposition to segregation pure and simple unless that segregation does involve discrimination," he argued in one of his final *Crisis* editorials, entitled "Segregation." "It is the race-conscious black man cooperating together in his own institutions and movements who will eventually emancipate the colored race."[95] "Race-consciousness" and racism, he had concluded, were entirely different things, and given the seeming permanence of the latter, there was nothing inherently wrong with the former. And if Du Bois—if African America—was to be perpetually denied the Jeffersonian "natural right" of social advancement in accordance with one's own inborn abilities and gifts, then democracy in the United States was a sham and was hardly worth pursuing.

This voluntary segregation of Afro-America, Du Bois had come to believe, was the surest route to economic and material advancement—to the mastery of American capitalism. If economic development had spurred the integration of the labor force, it had also witnessed the racialization of that same body of laborers, with white labor gaining skilled positions of technological prestige and black folks confined to far less important posts. What was needed, Du Bois suggested, was access to those "key positions" guiding "the industrial machine." "The Negro," Du Bois suggested, "must settle beyond cavil the question of his economic efficiency as a worker, a manager and controller of capital." The argument put forth in "Segregation" was, then, quite different from the tired program of Booker T. Washington, the old enemy who had once waxed rhapsodic about old-fashioned industrial education and out-dated artisanal capitalism. Nor was it entirely consistent with more orthodox Marxism. If Washington had offered "the Negro" as the solution to America's pressing need for cheap, unskilled labor, Du Bois hoped for a replication of the entire capitalist system from "captains of industry" to shoeshine boys. What the Negro needed was a presence in highly skilled fields—"in manufacturing, in the telephone, telegraph and radio business."[96]

The long-term outcome of such developments, Du Bois hoped, would be positive. A direct appropriation and complete command of the technology of capitalism by black folks might eventually convince men like Stoddard that their presumptions about "the Negro" were wrongheaded, and might force the future integration of the United States. Given the immediate context of the Depression and Jim Crow, however, there was little hope that these investments would pay dividends anytime soon. And even more sadly, the psychological scars produced in Afro-America by prolonged contact with the cold, inhuman stereotypes of "the Negro" turned the idea of separate development—or bi-racialism—into an act of humanitarian self-preservation. "If the economic and cultural salvation of the American Negro calls for an increase in segregation and prejudice," Du Bois wrote, "then that must come." Race-consciousness in economics, in education, and in all phases of social life offered a possible solution to the awful quandary of life in Jim Crow America, although it might also spark a race war, or a "great physical segregation of the world along the color line." In racial difference, Du Bois had found group salvation.[97]

For generations, as Du Bois had noted earlier, African Americans had believed that "we were going to escape into the mass of Americans in the same way that the Irish and Scandinavians and even the Italians were beginning to disappear." The youthful Du Bois of the Universal Races Congress, and of the early NAACP, had possessed the same blind faith in the supposed advance of a "spiritual and psychic amalgamation with the American people." But the older Du Bois of the 1930s was less optimistic about the chance of assimilation, more distrustful of white folks, and more aware of the critical role of "the Negro" in facilitating the whitening of other immigrant groups. Time and time again, the hopes of "the Negro" for equal citizenship had been dashed on the rocky shoals of American racism. All that remained, he suggested bitterly, was for "colored America" to dissolve the "class lines within the Negro race"—to withdraw from the American experiment and unite for the greater good of the darker world. "American Negroes," he concluded, "will be beaten into submission and degradation if they merely wait unorganized to find some place voluntarily given them in the new reconstruction of the economic world. They must themselves force their race into the new economic set-up and bring with them the millions of West Indians and Africans by peaceful organization for normative action or else drift into greater poverty, greater crime, greater helplessness until there is no resort but the last red alternative of revolt, revenge, and war."[98]

Du Bois still believed "in the ultimate uniting of mankind and in a united American nation," but his earlier exuberance about the future integration of the United States had been significantly tempered by thirty years of lynchings, race riots, and tightening Jim Crow restrictions. He had hoped that the modern world would bring "the disappearance of 'race' from our vocabulary," but instead found cause only for "increased segregation and perhaps migration." Integration, he argued, "is an ideal and is to be realized only by such intensified class and race consciousness as will bring irresistible force rather than mere humanitarian appeals to bear on the motives and actions of men."[99] Now angrily advocating the isolation of Negroes from Nordic America—a physical separation of white and black folks to mirror the growing distance between whiteness and blackness—and consorting with much younger (and now suitably deferential) advocates of Negro radicalism, Du Bois was at odds with his own youthful faith in civilization and white folks, and with the ruthless bureaucratic integrationism of Walter White and the NAACP. "Segregation," Du Bois's inflammatory *Crisis* editorial, had put a Stoddardesque spin on the resolutions of the NAACP's 1933 Amenia Conference, suggesting that cultural nationalism—and, above all, human survival—was best pursued through economic, social, and cultural separation. Some countries, it seemed, were simply too racist to allow for both integration and uplift, or striving, or self-improvement. Here, then, was an insight sixty years in the making—an insight that Du Bois would spend the final thirty years of his life exploring, first in Cold War America and then, pointedly, in Kwame Nkrumah's Ghana, the heart of the soon-to-be-awakened dark continent. A pluralistic world of whites and blacks—a world defined by race-as-color, a world where white people cold-heartedly abused or studiously ignored black people—demanded a nearly total separation of the two groups.

But the autobiographical essay "Miscegenation," submitted in 1935 to the editor of the *Encyclopedia Sexualis,* reveals a decidedly personal ambivalence about Du Bois's new racial philosophy. The idea of race, the essay began, was useless—after all, no two scientists agreed on any principles of classification. Still, when all things were considered, skin color seemed to be the most useful marker of division. Going on to discuss transgressions of the color line between white and black, Du Bois argued that the sexual offspring produced in interracial relationships were not sterile, nervous, and chattering weaklings—mulattos, he averred, showed "an especially high fecundity" and a deeply civilized appreciation for the finer things in life. Amalgamation or separation thus posed two possible eugenic solutions to "the Negro problem," and Du Bois offered himself as proof that miscegenation could remedy intellectual inequality between the worst sort of peoples and the best sort. Asking for "careful and unbiased scientific inquiry," he also wondered "how fast and under what condition this amalgamation ought to take place, and equally . . . if separate racial growth over a considerable time may achieve better results than quick amalgamation":

> If a poor and ignorant group amalgamates with a larger and more intelligent group, quickly and thoughtlessly, the results may easily be harmful. There will be prostitution and disease, much social disorganization, and the inevitable loss of many human values by both groups . . . On the other hand, if by encouraging mutual respect and even-handed social justice, the two races can possibly readjust their social levels until they attain essential equality in well-being and intelligence; then either amalgamation will take place gradually and quietly by mutual consent or by equally peaceful methods the groups will seek separate dwelling places, either in the same or in different lands.[100]

The end of Jim Crow, then, was simply the first step toward equality, to be followed by a eugenic process of "amalgamation" that would level the genetic playing field, rendering all racial categories useless and leading to a truly human world. Or perhaps, as Du Bois must have realized with lasting sadness, whites and blacks would grow further apart in life, in love, and in culture, perpetuating a sense of separateness and social apartheid and fostering the institutional discrimination that survived Jim Crow. Of these two alternatives, amalgamation must have seemed far more hopeful and humanitarian and also much less likely to succeed. "We have tried democracy and failed," he would tell a group of Columbia University students in 1936, "but we must keep trying."[101]

# 4

# The Hypnotic Division
# of America

One man, happening to glance my way, seemed curious. He kept
looking as though trying to size me up. Evidently he was scrutinizing my body only, assuming that he was thereby taking my
measure. No doubt of it, he was equating my body with myself.
What a queer sensation it gave me to be taken for my body when I
was so starkly aware that I was a being.

—JEAN TOOMER, "FROM EXILE INTO BEING" (ca. 1946)

I am an invisible man . . . That invisibility to which I refer occurs
because of a peculiar disposition of the eyes of those with whom I
come into contact. A matter of the construction of the *inner* eyes,
those eyes with which they look through their physical eyes upon
reality. I am not complaining, nor am I protesting either. It is
sometimes advantageous to be unseen . . . Or again, you often
doubt if you really exist. You wonder if you aren't simply a phan-
tom in other people's minds.

—RALPH ELLISON, *INVISIBLE MAN* (1952)

"In the year 1923," Jean Toomer wrote, "I came to the end of my rope . . . I
found myself in a pocket from which I could not move . . . No breaks came.
No help. All was closed and sealed tight."[1] Composing his autobiographies during the Great Depression, Toomer might have looked back upon
that year with fond memories—after all, he had just then published *Cane,*
hailed by contemporaries as the first modernist novel of the Harlem Renaissance. The problem, for Toomer, was that the culture of the 1920s
yearned for a novel like *Cane* to be written by someone clearly and definitively "black." Reviewers of *Cane,* hoping to find in "the Negro" a cure for
the soul-dead, postwar world, saw in Toomer's work racial qualities from
which the author himself soon recoiled. With *Cane's* critical reception, the

emergent hegemony of "race" and racial thinking in American culture—
which brought a new hardness and breadth to the concepts of whiteness
and blackness—imprisoned Jean Toomer. Looking back on 1923, Toomer
suggested that a new zeal for whiteness and blackness had silenced all those
(including him) who had struggled to find a position "above" either classification. The new pluralistic Americans of mixed "bloods," he wrote, "have
been so compelled and are now accustomed to use the dominant, which is
to them alien, language" of blackness and whiteness, "that they can find no
words with which even to talk of themselves."[2]

Jean Toomer's personal struggle against what he termed "the hypnotic
division of Americans into black and white" was a microcosm of a broader
cultural transformation of profound significance.[3] During the 1920s the
lines of racial classification were redrawn with a heightened emphasis on
race-as-color. Driven by the Great War, the Great Migration, the foreclosure of European immigration, and the emergence of a national popular
culture obsessed with "the Negro," many Americans—and most especially
those in the northeastern United States—replaced their old-fashioned
nativist distaste for European immigrants with a negrophobic concern
about black folks strikingly reminiscent of the Jim Crow South. The end
result of this transformation was a pattern of racial classification termed
"bi-racialism," a pattern that encouraged Americans to focus exclusively on
skin color, and almost completely on whiteness and blackness. It was this
new sense of race that obscured many of the ambiguities in turn-of-the-
century racial classification and divided the world's peoples into the simple
categories of white, brown, yellow, and black—pegging Jean Toomer as a
"Negro."

Toomer's travails in the 1920s illuminate then-popular understandings
of blackness and masculinity with a particular efficacy. The enthrallment
with the orderly, well-tooled, and athletic male body that pervades
Toomer's personal writings, for instance, reveals his own deep homoeroticism and also the painful connections and even more painful
disjunctions between blackness and maleness in Progressive America.
Toomer's extensive autobiographical work, much like his obsessive and
private exercise campaign, was as much a reflection of the new meaning of
race as it was a testament to one troubled individual's attempt at self-
building. And his inability to see that his own radical proto-pluralism was
bound closely to the language of race reflected a certain blindness to the
dangers of bi-racialism and to the connections between physical culture,

the modern American obsession with technological sophistication and efficiency, and the emergent national "discovery" of "the Negro."

When *Cane* was rediscovered in the 1960s, Toomer was both praised as a pioneer in the black literary tradition and bemoaned as a traitor to "the race." His evasion of blackness was at first ignored and then confused with "passing" and, even more incorrectly, with a "yearning for racelessness."[4] More recent commentators have suggested that the "dominant discourse of race in American culture" was at the root of Toomer's distress. "The belief in unified, coherent 'black' and 'white' American 'racial' identities," argues George Hutchinson in an essay on Toomer's troubles in the 1920s, "depends . . . upon the sacrifice of the identity that is both 'black' *and* 'white.'"[5] The social forces responsible for the vogue of Harlem were, therefore, behind the psychological dilemma Jean Toomer faced after the publication of *Cane,* the beautiful novel so "peculiar," so identifiably "Negro," that its author, despite his vociferous claims to the contrary, was assumed to be black. The advent of bi-racialism was a revolution of sorts. Toomer recognized it as such, and then sought to undermine it by offering his own racialized American nationalism as an alternative. As that revolution in racial thinking unfolded between the two world wars, the pace of the reclassification of American culture picked up, and it became increasingly impossible for Toomer's contemporaries to understand his attempts at racial self-fashioning.

### From an Unclassified World

"Toomer's first two decades," notes the literary scholar Henry Louis Gates Jr., "read like the diary of a transient." Toomer was the son of Nina Pinchback, the privileged daughter of the Reconstruction political wildcat Pinckney Benton Stewart Pinchback, and Nathan Toomer, a dandy and drifter of questionable means and motives, whom Nina had married in 1894 against her father's wishes. She named her son Nathan Pinchback Toomer—honoring the vagabond husband who would soon abandon them both. Raising the child alone was a task beyond her abilities. She was forced to leave her rented home in Washington, D.C., and return to her father's residence in that same city. "Nina," commented Jean Toomer's biographers, "stubborn and high-spirited though she was, was simply not raised to struggle against the world to support herself and her child." Not surprisingly, the first contest between strong-willed daughter and imperious father developed around the infant's name, which was soon officially changed to Eugene Pinchback Toomer, but which remained in unofficial dispute for some time. The tug of war over the naming of Jean Toomer, which gave young Jean a lifelong love of the "individualization of names," was complicated by Nina's continued movement in the 1900s—from Washington, D.C., to New Rochelle, New York, to Brooklyn. With his mother's death in 1909, young Jean went back to Washington, D.C., but the pattern of personal rootlessness had been set.[6]

Toomer's irascible grandfather, with whom he lived through the late 1910s, was a former Reconstruction governor of Louisiana and an inveterate gambler, playboy, and socialite, the privileged son of a white planter and a freedwoman. As Pinchback's political fortunes, tied as they were to the fate of Reconstruction, declined over the late nineteenth century, he settled in Washington, D.C., to claim whatever benefits he could from government largesse. The nation's capital had become a haven for African Americans because of the hundreds of federal patronage positions made available to "the Negro" in the late nineteenth century. But by the early twentieth century the substantial African-American community in Washington found itself confronted by increasing residential segregation and political misfortune.[7] By Jean's teenage years, the aging Pinchback, less and less able to capitalize on the dwindling patronage of the Republican party, moved his extended family out of their exclusive residence in a "mixed" community and into a well-heeled "Negro" neighborhood on Florida Avenue. Having attended "white" schools in his childhood, Jean—for the first time in his life—was surrounded by people of African descent in his new school.

Upper-class Victorian African-American life in the nation's capital has been beautifully described by the historian Willard Gatewood as "the genteel performance." As the nineteenth century waned, a group of cultured African Americans, some of whom were light skinned, developed the exclusive neighborhoods and attempted to replicate the parlors and gentlemen's clubs of high Victorianism. These cultured men and women of color in Washington and elsewhere widened the social and cultural gap between themselves and the unlettered black masses through physical separation, developing tiny communities apart from "Negro" neighborhoods. With his social prominence in one such community and his remarkable personal history, P. B. S. Pinchback's light skin, character, and luck marked him as a member of the elect. And like many light-skinned mulattos, Pinchback emphasized the diversity of "bloods" coursing through his veins in order to highlight the political good fortune and intellectual "gifts" bestowed upon him by heredity—going so far as to pass for white on occasion and being tickled when he was mistaken for Andrew Carnegie.[8]

When writing of Washington during the 1930s, Toomer would focus solely on this thin upper-crust culture and emphasize the racial complexity and light skin of the inhabitants of this rare world. "These people," he argued autobiographically, "were Americans of mixed blood." As Toomer remembered it, he had grown up in a geographical, racial, and phenotypical "space" situated between the "white" and "colored" worlds. Living in his grandfather's increasingly anachronistic world, raised to have faith in Pinchback's aristocratic mulatto chauvinism, Toomer believed that the lives of light-skinned mulattos were socially, culturally, and epistemologically distant from those "Negro" communities structured by the "one-drop rule." Indeed, adamantly cutting against the grain of American racial thought, Jean Toomer came to identify his own destiny with that of the mythical province of blue-veiners and "high-yellow" Washingtonians. And when Toomer sat down to write his autobiography in the mid-1930s, his vision of *fin-de-siècle* Washington focused on the terrible transformation which he believed had undermined the uniqueness of that wonderful creolized culture:

> Looking back on it, here was the germ of a group of unlabelled, unclassed, nonstratifiable, traditionless and yet cultured people who in many ways could have been free to identify themselves with the needs of the nation as a whole. Racially they were of white and dark bloods, Negro and Indian, sufficiently blended through several generations to show the beginnings of a new racial type. If there is anything in racial heredity with respect to predispositioning prejudices and preferences, these people could not have been for the colored against the white, or for the white against the colored: they would have to be for both. Socially, though they were classified as colored, they had contacts in both groups, and were without any marked race-consciousness one way or another . . . Their descendants—namely those who were of my age then—have gone into the white group or else have fastened in the colored group: in either case they have contracted the now prevalent consciousness of race and of class which their parents were free of.

Many of the major themes of Toomer's racial thought are present in this remarkable passage: the emphasis on blood mixture, the sense that "race-consciousness" had destroyed the paradise of this "new racial type," and the hubris which would motivate him to castigate the younger generation of creole Washington, D.C., as racially conformist and to describe himself as the "first" member of the hybrid American race.[9]

Despite the absence of significant labor conflict between European immigrants and African Americans—the traditional catalyst for the whitening process—the peaceful neighborhoods of Toomer's privileged youth were not spared the startling reversal of fortunes suffered by African Americans in the wake of Reconstruction, the rise of southern Redeemers, and regional reconciliation. The centrifugal energies of the late 1890s— pushing "black" further and further away from "white"—eventually transformed the social status of Washington's "aristocrats of color." The local press had previously recognized some social and cultural divisions within the black community, and cultured blacks and mulattos had celebrated the physical, social, and "racial" distance between themselves and the mass of blacks. With the return to power of Southern Democrats and the end of the politics of "the bloody shirt," as well as the push toward nationalization in communications, economics, and consumer culture, any emphasis on the stratification of "colored" Washington was unfashionable. "Genteel" African Americans—no matter how light skinned or well mannered—increasingly found their only possible outlet in the leadership and uplift of "the race."

In the midst of this political transformation, Jean Toomer began to carve out an interpretation of himself as unique and different. Leaving his grandfather's carefully structured world of "genteel performances" for college, Toomer struggled to develop a coherent identity as anything other than a "Negro." In his autobiographies, this adventure in self-definition takes place before young Toomer—"his skin," like that of Faulkner's Joe Christmas, "a level dead parchment color"—leaves for the University of Wisconsin, and is described as a prescient and ultimately heroic attempt to explain his unclassifiable nature. "I had heard of the color line," Toomer writes airily. "I foresaw that not only in college but in my general future life I might run into some unpleasant situations. How would I meet them? What would I say?"[10] Given Toomer's peripatetic life, and given his grandfather's social prominence, it is highly unlikely that he managed to escape the perils of classification until college, and his rather egotistical autobiography uniformly paints the young Jean Toomer of the early 1900s in the Promethean shades of gray favored by the older Jean Toomer. But if the young Jean Toomer living in his grandfather's shadow wasn't the acutely

sensitive chameleon of the post-*Cane* years, it is still almost certain that between his mother's death in 1909 and the end of the Great War Jean
Toomer began to wonder just who and what he was. Renaming himself after Victor Hugo's Jean Valjean and Romain Rolland's Jean-Christophe,
Toomer chose two "alienated" figures "misused by society" and revealed in
the process a penchant for shrouding his own racial self-discovery in melo-
drama.[11]

Unsure about his choice of college and career path, Toomer decided to
refer to himself as an "American, unqualified." This decision owed much to
an ambitious and extracurricular self-improvement campaign that continued while he was in Chicago, at his grandfather's stately residence in Washington, D.C., and in New York. Mesmerized by the literature on American nationalism—he marked his mother's death with a note on Herbert
Croly's hopelessly optimistic discussion of American individualism, *The
Promise of American Life*—Toomer was quickly under the spell of socialism, with its evolutionary message of national rebirth. The impact of socialism on Toomer would be profound, if somewhat unusual. In 1916,
hearing of Darwin, Lamarck, and Ernst Haeckel for the first time during a
lecture on socialism given by Arthur Lewis in Chicago, Toomer was dumb-
struck: "It was as if a blade of steel had pierced my heart." The scientific
revolution preached by socialists gave direction to Toomer's agonizing
struggle for self-definition, and helped him to understand the national implications of his emergence as a "new type." What was most important to
Toomer, however, was not the economic philosophy of socialism but rather
the cultural mentality behind it—the rush and excitement of radically applied science. Inspired by "the ideas of socialism and evolution," and increasingly interested in writing, Toomer began during the 1910s to compose "The First American," the poetic manifesto that would eventually be
published as "The Blue Meridian" nearly twenty years later.[12]

In other ways, Toomer's dalliance with socialism was even more directly
responsible for his development as a writer and as a cultural commentator.
The literary critics Charles Scruggs and Lee VanDemarr have revealed the
depth of Toomer's commitment to the ideal of socialism as expressed
in the work of Randolph Bourne, Waldo Frank, and "Young America."
Toomer, Scruggs and VanDemarr argue, was deeply angered at the race riots of 1919—especially the one in Washington, D.C.—and was committed
enough to American radicalism that he produced three articles for the socialist *New York Call*. "All over the country," Toomer remembered, "my

generation was growing up within a terrific pod, restless, ruthless, up-rooted, upheaving . . . to face and experience the post-war dislocation, to face and experience the issues between capital and labor, nationalism, ra-cialism, the boom years, [and] the narrow passage of the world depres-sion." By 1920, inspired by the cultural ferment surrounding Frank's *Our America*—the "little magazines," the near-perfect synthesis of radicalism and avant-garde sensibilities in Greenwich Village—Toomer believed that the literary "world-city" of Manhattan offered unparalleled opportunities for a "new type" of American. The revolution in sensibilities engendered by war, immigration, and economic stress had helped form Jean Toomer's nationalist racial chauvinism, which would in turn inspire the piecemeal construction of *Cane*.[13]

By the early 1920s, moved by possibilities of postwar pluralism and Afri-can-American protest, Toomer found himself surrounded by the vanguard of those responsible for the "discovery of the Negro by creative America." The tumult of the postwar era had laid the foundation for Toomer's re-markable self-invention. Unfortunately, the postwar fascination with "the Negro" in American political culture—what Toomer called "a certain type of discovery"—reflected in the race riots, Red Scare surveillance, and gen-eral negrophobia had also paved the way for Toomer's reclassification. Describing the "Negro emergent," Toomer noted the New Negro's fond-ness for blackness, for the "beauty, uglincss, passion, poverty, rhythm, and color" of African-American life in Harlem. The racial pride and activ-ism of postwar New Negroes were not, in and of themselves, inherently dangerous; but, as Toomer recognized, the magical qualities of blackness could only be understood in relation to the Nordic vogue. "More rapidly than [the Negro] emerges towards it," he suggested, "the white world of America takes steps towards him. The Negro is being studied in relation to the general economic problems. The problems of population. He chal-lenges attention from those who are sincere in their democracy. His social and educational aspects are being investigated and aided. Psychoanalysis has interesting data concerning him. Articles about him are appearing with increasing frequency in the leading magazines and newspapers. Books are coming out, and publishers are receptive of Negro material. Clubs, socie-ties, forums wish to hear about the Negro."[14]

If, then, the explosion of postwar racist violence was, as Scruggs and VanDemarr suggest, the historical background for Toomer's composition of *Cane*, the national popular interest in blackness and whiteness provided an equally disturbing context for the reception of that brief prose-poem. In the midst of his own self-discovery, Jean Toomer came up against the forces unleashed by the Great War—up against the new race-consciousness. More than any other single event, the advent of the New Negro Movement and the accompanying titanic struggle waged within the "New Negro" community for control over the course and direction of African-American protest was what sealed Toomer's fate.

## Cane

There was something very different about the nature of race relations after the Great War. "In the good old days," mused Harlem's streetcorner philosopher, the West Indian émigré Hubert H. Harrison, "white people derived their knowledge of what Negroes were doing from those Negroes who were nearest to them, generally their own selected exponents of Negro activity or of their white point of view . . . Today the white world is vaguely, but disquietingly, aware that Negroes are awake, different, and perplexingly uncertain."[15] Harrison had put his finger on the defining characteristic of the New Negro Movement: a profound awakening of the racial sensibility in the United States that he elsewhere termed the "New Race Consciousness." In the aftermath of the Great War, many Americans saw black folks as a rising proletariat held in check only by brutal violence and institutional control. In Manhattan, the symbolic center of the emergent postcolonial America, an ardent and national negrophobia was countered by the New Negro Manhood Movement, a movement which laced its chauvinistic rhetoric of uplift and civilization with highly provocative Bolshevisms.

If the New Negro Manhood Movement of Marcus Garvey, the Universal Negro Improvement Association, Harrison, and Cyril Briggs was a powerful response to the exploitation of the "darker world" by the white leviathan, the Harlem Renaissance—also known as the New Negro Renaissance—combined the clever Bolshevisms of radical New Negroes with a nod to "high culture" and modernist primitivism. Indeed, reacting to the popularity of the Garvey movement and to the postwar race riots, the genteel and polished set of the African-American leadership class attempted to steal the Universal Negro Improvement Association's thunder and to harvest the sympathy of the lyrical left and neo-abolitionism in support of African-American arts and letters. This New Negro Renaissance, directed by

Walter White, James Weldon Johnson, Jessie Fauset, and Charles S. Johnson—all highly educated officials in the NAACP or the National Urban League—put "Negro art" in the service of the civil rights struggle, and in the process catered to those fragile postwar white bodies hungry for the presumed freedom and vitality of "the Negro." A melange of leaders, their authority underwritten by the early stages of black migration northward during the war, thus gamely submitted a host of "New Negro" artists for white consumption, trumpeted the virtues of the unique aesthetic "gifts" of "the Negro," and named Harlem the cultural capital of black America.[16]

White consumption of the New Negro was every bit as important as black production. At every step, the politically liberating potential of the pluralistic New Negro Movement was aided, abetted, and ultimately undermined by the heightened Freudianism of popular culture and the concomitant rise of "primitivism," which celebrated "pure" races as a panacea for a neurasthenic, overcivilized Western culture. "Freud's relevance to the black moderns," Ann Douglas writes, "might have been less than to the white ones, but his quasi-anthropological equation of the 'primitive mind' and the 'savage' with the unconscious and the id helped to shape the New Negro's creative possibilities." The avant-garde white press and Village literati, bemoaning industrialization and thirsting for the "primitive" and the "vital," had been conditioned by writers like Sherwood Anderson and Gertrude Stein to be familiar with the therapeutic potential of Africa and Africans. The larger public, encouraged to see in "the Negro" a prehistoric past, experienced a similar thirst for the primitive that could easily be slaked by an urban safari through Harlem's nightclubs, or by a visit to any of the amusement parks, movie palaces, and Broadway shows that drew large crowds to see white men in blackface, or an increasing number of African Americans, acting "Negro." The younger generation of New Negro artists—Langston Hughes, Wallace Thurman, Zora Neale Hurston—soon joined in, laughingly offering "the eternal tom tom beating in the Negro soul" as the antidote to the soul-sapping "weariness in a white world, a world of subway trains, and work, work, work." The flip side of anti-Bolshevist negrophobia, in short, was the sense that black folks were also the living embodiments of human passion, physicality, and emotion—a sensibility that Lothrop Stoddard termed "the lure of the primitive."[17]

There was something special about the "Rhythm of Harlem." Fleeing Jim Crow and running toward opportunity, black folks pushed and struggled their way into Harlem, carved out a world of improbable opportunity, and promptly became the subject of national fixation. In the process, Harlem was soon something of a euphemism—for better or worse—for the dark, lush wonders of Africa. Harlem, suggested the NAACP everyman James Weldon Johnson, "is experiencing a constant growth of group consciousness and community feeling. Harlem is, therefore, in many respects, typically Negro. It has many unique characteristics. It has movement, color, gayety, singing, dancing, boisterous laughter and loud talk." The fixing of race and place—and of the New Negro in Harlem—did, however, have some rather disturbing elements, as African Americans soon realized that finding homes anywhere other than in Harlem, or even opening businesses, was increasingly difficult. "The same people," commented the physician-cum-novelist Rudolph Fisher, "whose spokesmen" guarded against an African-American "invasion" of the exclusive theaters and housing markets of Broadway and Manhattan, "flood Harlem night after night and literally crowd me off the dancing floor."[18]

Many in the African-American vanguard believed that the "creative discovery" of "the Negro" was part of a grander postcolonial pluralism, or the replacement of a supposedly parochial tradition of arts and letters with an emergent American nationalism that would incorporate a wide variety of racial "gifts" and expressions. The New Negro, argued the philosopher Alain Locke, "must be seen in the perspective of a New World, and especially of a New America . . . America seeking a new spiritual expansion and artistic maturity, trying to found an American literature, a national art, and national music implies a Negro-American culture seeking the same satisfactions and objectives." And, almost invariably, those New Negroes who, in the immediate aftermath of the war, advocated pluralism concluded that "the Negro," like "the Celt" in Britain, possessed a peculiar facility for artistic expression. "The great gift of the Negro to the world," wrote Du Bois hopefully, "is going to be a gift to Art." Such an interpretation looked to the theater, and to drama, for evidence of the gift of the Negro: black folks, it was argued, had a real "racial aptitude for the theatre."[19] Irish antecedents were also important. "Without pretense to their political significance," wrote Locke, "Harlem has the same role to play for the New Negro as Dublin has had for the New Ireland." Locke also hoped that modernist representations of the Negro would have "a poetic and symbolic manner that will remind us of Synge and the Irish Folk Theatre." Floyd Dell, reviewing James Weldon Johnson's collection of folk verse, *God's Trombones,* urged Johnson to "attune his ear to the peculiar grace" natural to the Negro, and to "study" that innate "Negro" grace "just as Synge studied it in the speech of the fishermen and tinkers and peasants of the Aran Islands."[20]

The crucial differences between the Irish Renaissance and the New Negro Renaissance came down to timing. As the Irish struggled for independence, it looked to many as if the marshaling of folk art by a small cadre of carefully selected New Negro artists would similarly liberate American culture from the rusting shackles of parochial Anglo-Saxon Victorianism. The Irish analogy, however, was soon entirely useless, for whatever political capital might have been gained from claiming the Irish renaissance as a precursor (much as Garvey had claimed the rebels of 1916) was lost once the "Irish question" had been resolved and the Irish in America had been brought into the pale of absolute whiteness. On the surface of it all, New Negro artists and patrons may have spoken of "the Negro" in the same pluralistic idiom that Daniel Cohalan once used to further the Irish cause, but the cultural innovators of the New Negro Renaissance—much like the radicals of the Black Scare before them—could not but notice the increasingly undeniable whiteness of the Irish in America. Analogies to "the Irish Renaissance" of Yeats, Synge, and Lady Gregory vanished by the mid-1920s, as "the Negro" quickly replaced "the Celt" in national popular culture. The "discovery of the Negro"—whether in avant-garde literature or race riots, in national popular obsessions or Negrophobic fears—would thereafter be as much about the magic of whiteness as it was about the magic of the word "black."

Into an anxious, soul-starved world obsessed with the arrival of "the Negro" in the North, Jean Toomer dropped *Cane,* a prose poem so perfectly "Negro" by the logic of the 1920s that it immediately garnered wrongheaded praise from all the right people. Those who read it found something in the lyrical speech and sensualized lifestyles of the black South for which they had long been searching: a sense of authenticity or accuracy about race in America. Still, there was far more to *Cane* than a modern rendering of the throbbing vitality of "Negro life." Indeed, in a series of powerful—and sometimes mystifying—vignettes, *Cane* mapped the troubling moral landscape of southerners. "Miscegenation," note Scruggs and VanDemarr, "is the thing in *Cane* not *named* but always there." Filled with vivid, sensual characters of African origin, many of them women, *Cane* also drew upon the easy and popular connections between "the Negro," femininity, and sexuality. But again the work defied common expectations, for there was a provocative hint of difference, or peculiarity, about the male relationships in *Cane,* suggesting that Toomer was aware of—and sympathetic to—the ambiguous world of same-sex relationships that would later be described by the historian George Chauncey.[21] The unprecedented depth of feeling in *Cane,* best reflected in its descriptions of human relationships, was also unique. With depictions of African Americans as "beasts" abounding, to write, as Toomer did, of the darker world in America as "jazzed, strident, modern," as infinitely human and bewilderingly complex, was a terribly subversive act. Toomer himself once asserted that *Cane* was "Negro . . . only in the *boldness* of its expression." But in a world where the Great War had cast serious doubts on the continued progress of civilization in Europe, and where the ruthless pace of corporate consolidation and economic expansion was dulling the brightness of life, that very boldness would be precisely what attracted primitivist attention to the novel.[22]

*Cane* also arrived at bookstores in a rapidly changing legal context in which light-skinned people of African descent were increasingly named as "black" and not as "mulatto." For much of the nineteenth and early twentieth centuries, "mulatto" had been a separate census category, reflecting the strange liminal position of the generally light-skinned and well-heeled upper crust of darker America. "Mixed bloods," wrote Charles S. Johnson, "they are suspended between two races—mulattoes, quadroons, musters, mustafinas, cabres, griffies, zambis, quatravis, tresalvis, coyotes, saltaras, albarassadores, cambusos—neither white nor black." But from 1920 onward, the United States Census contained no "mulatto" category, and one could only choose between the calcifying borders of whiteness and blackness. The flourishing culture of mixed-race Americans—the world of P. B. S. Pinchback and Jean Toomer, and of the private W. E. B. Du Bois—was "vanishing." Lamenting the decline of these exotic mixed-race "ghosts," the editor of the National Urban League's *Opportunity* magazine concluded that the quickening segregation of American life was leading some to ally themselves with the masses of Afro-America and others to "pass" as white folks: "Men who, by and by, ask for the Negro, will be told—'there they go, clad in white men's skins." In this context, it was becoming ever more difficult to understand certain kinds of literary expression—and especially a novel as "perfectly Negro" as *Cane*—as anything other than quintessentially "black" or "Negro." It was also harder and harder for Jean Toomer to be understood as anything other than a "Negro" writer.[23]

With whiteness and blackness spinning apart, Jean Toomer's racial faith rested upon an older logic of race than that of the aesthetic Negrotarians, Nordic voguers, and New Negroes. Bringing together a wide variety of ideas about race, Toomer described himself as the embodiment of the pluralist project, and as the final product of human evolution. "It is possible," he wrote, "that there are Negro and Indian bloods in my descent along with English, Spanish, Welsh, Scotch, French, Dutch, and German." He alone had the ability to consciously manipulate the particular race traits that all hybrid Americans possessed: "The only time I think [like a] Negro is when I want a particular emotion which is associated with this name." As the "first American" raised in an environment which left him "unlabelled" and capable of defining his own "race," Toomer stridently concluded that he was capable of doing what no one else could—orchestrating himself into a functional symphony of race traits, tapping into his own genius for whatever "racial" needs he might encounter in life and personifying evolutionary millennialism. In so doing, he fashioned a coherent political ideology out of the bits and pieces of late-nineteenth-century science and philosophy he had absorbed over the course of his life, and then applied that ideology to protest the increasing polarization, or reclassification, of American society. *Cane,* then, was meant only as a reflection of his peculiar "Negro" talents, which constituted just a small part of his pluralistic potential.[24]

Toomer's celebration of the various "bloods" and "stocks" that coursed through his veins and enabled his own excessively embodied American citizenship owed more to the classical Victorian science of heredity, especially neo-Lamarckianism, than to the postwar allegiance to Mendel. Neo-Lamarckianism was closely connected to discourses of civilization and millennialism, and averred—contra Mendelian genetics—that behaviors and personality traits acquired by one generation could be passed on to the next (the classic example was that of the giraffe which stretched its neck reaching for a branch and then passed its "acquired" long neck to its offspring). Despondent and vertiginous, flitting from one college to another, or from one style of life to another, Toomer first articulated individual racial chauvinism after his encounter with socialism and with the works of Ernst Haeckel, Lester Frank Ward, and George Bernard Shaw—all of whom expounded different variations of neo-Lamarckianism. For Toomer, one of the more alluring features of this quintessentially Victorian understanding of heredity was its tendency to envision human evolution as progress toward an ideal—what the historian Gail Bederman has called a

"Darwinist version of Protestant millennialism." Toomer's postwar proto-pluralism, then, was really a heady blend of mainstream pluralism, neo-Lamarckianism, and mulatto chauvinism, bodies of ideas which allowed him to ground in science his claim that he represented a "new" type of American—new and decidedly superior.[25]

Toomer's postwar reinterpretation of Darwinist millennialism cut against the grain of the dominant discourse on race—the bi-racialism of the new race-consciousness. The smart set of American letters thus invariably commented upon the racial qualities of the extended prose poem. "The book *is* the South," wrote Waldo Frank in the foreword to *Cane*, venturing even further to label the author of the work a "poet in prose" who was "wise enough to drink humbly at this great spring of his land." In attempting to explain the absence of "false notes" in an idiosyncratic work of fiction dealing mostly with black life in the South, the reviewer for the *Dial* credited the young author's finely tuned "negro ear." "Other writers have tried, with less happiness, to handle the material of the South," summed up the literary critic Paul Rosenfeld, invoking the widespread belief that "the Negro" was inherently musical, "but Toomer comes to unlimber a soul, and give of it dance and music." The black press likewise became enamored of *Cane* and claimed its author as one of their own. "In . . . the author of *Cane*," hummed William Stanley Braithwaite, "we come upon the very first artist of the race." In expressing his "Negro gifts" in *Cane*, Jean Toomer had, it seemed, unwittingly declared his own absolute blackness.[26]

The New Negro aesthetic that dictated the reception of *Cane* was part of the pluralist nationalism predicated on the belief that racial differences were a functional necessity in the modern American polity. The devout white-on-black pluralism of the early Harlem Renaissance drew much of its political heat from the emergent national obsession with the global "Negro problem." In doing so, however, it slowly recast the idea of cultural pluralism to fit the new idiom of race, making the Renaissance more interested in synchronizing white and black cultures than in harmonizing the world-historical destinies of the Anglo-Saxon, Irish, Italian, and Negro races. Indeed, many pitted the New Negro Renaissance not against "antihyphenate hysteria" (as the wartime and postwar pluralists Kallen, Bourne, Cohalan, and Frank had done) but, instead, against all the talk of a "rising tide of color"—an indication that something profound had transpired. If anticolonial protest had shifted its focus from Anglo-Saxondom to white world supremacy, the New Negro Renaissance had followed suit, making the politics of art a matter of harmonizing distinct white and black cultures and little else. "In terms of the race question as a world problem," suggested Alain Locke, "the Negro mind has leapt . . . upon the parapets of prejudice and extended its horizons . . . persecution is making the Negro international. As a world phenomenon this wider race consciousness is a different thing from the much asserted rising tide of color. Its inevitable causes are not of our making . . . [and] the consequences are not necessarily damaging to the best interests of civilization."[27]

What was the New Negro Renaissance, then, but an ingenious response to the dystopian global racism of Stoddard and Grant? A response which shed the grimness and grit (and much of the unorthodox Marxism) of postwar New Negro radicalism in favor of a more ameliorative vision of cultural harmony? That precious cognitive connection between Negro problems and "shadows" around the world united many with differing views on the politics of art, helping to make whiteness and blackness—and not the fragmented whiteness of Romantic racialism and Irish-American nationalism—the key organizing concepts of the Renaissance. The concert of fifty races had become a duet of white and black.

The collective force of New Negro minds "reaching out" toward the "darker peoples of the world," and of Nordic minds shocked awake by the Great Migration, had refashioned the bounds of race. As New Negro radicalism was diffused into the literary renaissance of the 1920s, W. E. B. Du Bois, for one, kept hammering home the new race-consciousness. Alain Locke's edited collection, *The New Negro,* has generally been seen as an epochal or inaugural text of the so-called Harlem Renaissance. In keeping with Locke's faith in the idea of art for art's sake, that collection includes nothing from the socialists Asa Randolph and Chandler Owen, and certainly nothing from Marcus Garvey or Hubert Harrison. But it does end with a powerful essay by Du Bois, one previously published under the title "Worlds of Color." Retitled "The Negro Mind Reaches Out," that essay connected the new radicalism among African Americans with the "darker peoples of the world." "Led by American Negroes," wrote Du Bois, "the Negroes of the world are reaching out hands towards each other to know, to sympathize, to inquire." And a wide variety of New Negroes gave literary expression to the new race-consciousness, with examples as different as Du Bois's grim *Dark Princess* and George Schuyler's sardonic and pseudonymous "Black Empire" and "Black Internationale" stories.[28]

When, basking in the afterglow of the publication of *Cane,* Jean Toomer mused upon his next likely topic, he spoke of writing a novel of world-historical ambition and scope, a work steeped in this same new race-consciousness. He wrote to Frank:

> I'm not quite ripe enough for a novel. But brother, one is coming! As I now vaguely see and feel it, it is tremendous. This whole brown and black world heaving up against it, here and there mixing with the white world. But the mixture being insufficient to absorb the heaving, it but accelerates and fires it. This upward heaving is to be symbolic of the proletariat or world upheaval. To be likewise symbolic of the subconscious penetration of the conscious mind. Great guns, brother! Whenever I get a real glimpse of the thing, a terrific emotion sweeps me.

In his occasional moments of supreme confidence, then, even Jean Toomer appropriated elements of the new race-consciousness as literary fodder without fear of being misunderstood.[29] Forsaking the Romantic pluralism of Frank for the color-coded pluralism of Locke, Johnson, and Du Bois, Toomer—at least in this particular letter—did sometimes fail to recognize the difference between the wartime pluralism of "the white races" and the postwar pluralism embedded in the new race-consciousness. Indeed, mixing pop psychology with a global sense of race-as-color, he even anticipated Du Bois's dystopian *Dark Princess* by several years, seeming—if only momentarily—remarkably unperturbed by *Cane's* reception as a "Negro" text.

Not surprisingly, Toomer's interest in the literary potential of the new race-consciousness was quickly extinguished by the torrent of praise for the young "Negro artist" who had written *Cane.* The white fascination with the presumed vitality of black culture and New Negro chauvinism led many to champion Toomer's work—and Toomer himself—as "authentically Negro," an assumption his racial philosophy was meant to contest. Thus his early enthusiasm for *Cane* soon gave way to wariness. When his publisher Horace Liveright asked Toomer if he could "feature Negro" in advertisements for *Cane,* the young writer, while allowing Liveright to do so, refused to "feature" that "racial factor" of himself more than he had already done: "I have sufficiently featured Negro in *Cane.* Whatever statements I give [as advertisements] will inevitably come from a synthetic human and art point of view; not from a racial one." Writing to Frank, Toomer suggested that while the world described in *Cane* was indeed "Negro . . . in the boldness of its expression," the same could not be said for the novel itself, which was purely "American." Frank's foreword to *Cane,*

Toomer felt, had failed to clarify his racial position, leaving the public to define him as it saw fit. "Even before last Fall," he wrote sadly to Frank, "I am certain that you saw race and color as surfaces. Perhaps your mind still retained a few inhibiting wraiths." But so complete had the sea change been—so quick and complete had the move toward bi-racialism been—that few could understand Toomer and fewer still (certainly not flighty Waldo Frank) were listening.[30]

Having stepped into the public spotlight, Toomer had come up against

Winold Reiss's portrait of a whimsical Jean Toomer (1925).

the same "one drop rule" with which white supremacy hoped to control black folk, and with which Garvey and other New Negroes hoped to unite black America. He had not been raised to think of himself as "black," or as a "Negro," and he had devoted a great deal of time to organizing his symbolic universe of racialized proto-pluralism. And so, soon after the publication of *Cane*, Jean Toomer—a rising star—removed himself from the cast of New Negro artists. That growing thirst for "the Negro" in Harlem had become anathema to this light-skinned young man of mixed ancestry born and raised in an atmosphere of mulatto chauvinism, who instead chose to seek release in a Whitmanesque transcendence of white and black. As he put it in a stern letter to the *New Freeman*, where an editor had been "misinformed" that Toomer was a great "Negro writer": "I am chiefly concerned with . . . a position above the hypnotic division of Americans into white and black."[31] Toomer's affiliation with Harlem's intelligentsia had always been less important to him than his Greenwich Village ties. And when more and more people began talking about Toomer as the heir apparent to Charles Chesnutt—another "great Negro writer"—he abruptly walked away from the young artists and racial chauvinism of Harlem and threw himself into mysticism, bohemian cultural pluralism, and physical exercise.

## Man and Superman

After *Cane*, Jean Toomer's attempts at racial self-fashioning became more and more frantic and increasingly complicated. Devoting himself to the utopian Gurdjieff movement and to the composition of his autobiographies, Toomer tried to rewrite his own personal history, emphasizing the heroic possibilities of body building and his righteous indignation against the lure of whiteness and blackness. Written during the late 1920s and the 1930s, the repetitive autobiographies describe Jean Toomer as the embodiment of American modernity, or as the living incarnation of the modernist zeitgeist of technocracy, Art Deco, Taylorism, and precisionism. And yet such a self-interpretation raised profound contradictions, most particularly highlighting the odd disjunction between Toomer's desire for a sense of belonging—found in his fascination with the fascist aesthetics of physical culture—and his lonely fight against the racial structures of whiteness and blackness. Indeed, Toomer's long-term interest in the body politic *and* the politicized body suggests a striking sameness in all phases of his life, connecting his youth with his authorship of *Cane* and his interest in Gurdjieffism.[32]

Toomer's constant assertion of a decidedly new, nationalistic racial pluralism was complemented by a strangely reverent homage to the virtues of manly exercise, proper diet, and character building. He was prone to gaze at himself in the mirror and given to expressing a deep love for physical exertion shared with other men, and race and gender were intertwined most thoroughly in his private thoughts. "I liked drilling," he once recalled. "The precision of it won my immediate enthusiasm . . . There were order, command and response, coordination, a clean definite expert character about the whole thing. And it was masculine, as much or more of a man's world than handling a boat upon the open waters. The movement delighted and satisfied some deep thing in me . . . I love structures. I would rather march than hike. I would rather be a private in a company than a leader of a mob." This love of collective physical exertion contrasts with his continued celebration of his own unique racial genius—his own lonely position in the vanguard of a slowly emerging "American race." Longing to belong, but disgusted with what he called the "psychological enslavement" to whiteness and blackness, Toomer offered manliness and manly sport as a space where race mattered less than muscle, and where (to paraphrase) he might be a private in a company composed of men.[33]

It was not to be. The conception of manliness was quite thoroughly racialized at its bedrock. As Alice Walker has noted, Toomer should have seen, felt, and heard the ever-present sting of racism in all aspects of his life, including the sacred space of athletics and exercise. "He does not find it odd," Walker wrote sadly, "that when his schoolmates mistake him for an Indian they brutalize him so severely on the football field that he is forced to call time out for good."[34]

Manliness was hardly the panacea for which Toomer had long hoped. Black men were assumed to be unable to control their sexual urges, and the brutal lynching of hundreds of African Americans was thus excused by the imagined threat posed by black men to white women. The huge catalog of highly sexualized representations of "the Negro" as a "dangerous beast" was expanded upon after the war with the proliferation of images of black men with guns, widespread rumors that black soldiers had attacked white women in France and Germany, and the modernist fascination with the supposedly primitive qualities of African Americans. And the advent of a truly national consumer culture spread stereotypical representations of "the Negro" throughout the United States.[35] This postwar interest in race-consciousness was evidenced in the celebration of whiteness and blackness, or Nordicism and New Negrodom, in movies, literature, advertisements, and song. Whether one was a negrophobe or a Negrotarian, a northerner or a southerner, the line between black and white, or between manly and unmanly, seemed especially well-defined on the eve of the publication of *Cane*. The grim labor strife and class tensions of the Great War and its aftermath were buried beneath an avalanche of pop culture ephemera which argued that, regardless of social status, religion, or national origins, the markers of citizenship—whiteness and manliness—were within the reach of anyone, provided he or she worked hard and fixated upon the difference of "the Negro."

No wonder, then, that things got worse for Jean Toomer after *Cane*. For the postwar literary vanguard, writing about the supposedly primitive—and thus potent—sexuality of "the Negro" was the ultimate act of revolution in the war against the stale conventions of the "genteel tradition." Some in this small vanguard envisioned the triumph of "modernism" as a headlong flight into sexual liberation and, perhaps, the breaking of American culture's most vexing social taboo—the prohibition against interracial sex. For others, American modernism simply brought with it a sublime sense of whiteness founded on the belief that black folks were living evidence of the long-gone human past, sexual beings unable to control their urges and desires. In either case, black men were especially apt to be portrayed as sexual and physical dynamos, or as "beautiful pillar[s] of black strutting muscle topped with a tremendous display of the whitest teeth on earth."[36] The connection between blackness and sexuality was not merely a product of Manhattan's literary avant-garde, or an imagined nightmare of patrician negrophobes. The proper sexual relationship of the races was a hotly debated topic up and down the East Coast in the 1920s, engendering heightened police surveillance in Harlem, a popular obsession with "the Negro" as a sexual icon, and an increasingly sophisticated body of laws and codes designed to regulate the meanings of the term "race relations."[37]

Popular interest in race and sexuality in the North matured during the Great War and intensified throughout the decade that followed, encouraged, in part, by the insatiable appetite of the press for scandal. On March 4, 1916, for instance, a young Presbyterian minister, the Reverend Ferrer F. Martyn, was arrested in New York at "a negro tenement at No. 223 West 132nd Street on the charge of violating the Mann White Slave law." Ferrer

Martyn, the daily gossip columnists chattered in Manhattan, was the troubled son of the well-respected "Rev. Dr. Charles Martyn" of Noroton, Connecticut. The elder Martyn had once been the pastor of the Old Pilgrim Church in St. Louis, Missouri. With the arrival of thousands of African Americans in that growing city, and the subsequent evolution of his flock from white to black, Charles Martyn had left St. Louis; his son, Ferrer Martyn, had not. Unwilling to leave St. Louis, Martyn transformed himself to suit the needs of his flock, abruptly changing both his denomination and "his identity from that of a white clergyman with distinguished relatives to that of a negro living in a negro colony and consorting with negroes."

Crime soon followed him everywhere: "When he abandoned the Dr. Jekyll side of his character and assumed the Mr. Hyde side, his descent was swift." There were two years in Sing Sing for the theft of "a white girl's diamond ring on board a Coney Island excursion steamboat." There were also, according to the newspapers, brief "periods of reformation": "He married a most estimable young woman who knew nothing of his consorting with negroes." However, these moments of redemption were followed by at least one dangerously close encounter with bigamy (the untimely arrival of the first wife spoiled the coming marriage to the second) and an abrupt flight back to St. Louis without either his white wife or his white fiancée and "in the company of a negress from the home of his father in Noroton." Martyn's saga came to a close when, having abandoned the "negress" and returned to New York as the new pastor of the First Negro Baptist Church, he took up with a fifteen-year-old parishioner named Vera Douglas and moved to "the Harlem negro colony under the name of Hobson." There he was arrested. Stories like Martyn's—or the scandalous Rhinelander divorce case that pitted a young aristocrat against his wife's curious heritage, or the rumored mixed ancestry of President Warren G. Harding, or even Toomer's own interracial marriage—whetted the public's appetite for more of the same while helping to make the line between whiteness and blackness all the more firm.[38]

Toomer's attempt to escape imprisonment by blackness and hypersexuality thus came at a most inopportune moment, and rested upon the improbable appropriation of some of the new modern consumer culture's more fantastic elements. In those unpublished autobiographies, Toomer consistently tied together his deliberate racial self-fashioning with the "physical culture" world of Bernarr Macfadden and others. Macfadden had

produced a veritable mountain of advertisements, pulp fiction, and magazines which championed physical fitness as the road to spiritual well-being
in a mass society. "Make the body splendid," he crowed, "[and] your mind
supreme; for then you become your real self, you possess all your attainable
powers . . . [and] possess a capital that cannot be financially measured." If
blackness was a permanent mark of inferiority and unmanliness, Toomer's
deliberate attempt to lift himself out of blackness through exercise and diet
was nevertheless part of this reconstructed American patriarchy—part of
the refurbished American belief that the gritty, hard work of the self-
made man could change everything. As Toomer himself put it, "the desire
for body improvement is the physical division of the desire for self-improvement." An exhausting exercise regimen and a healthy diet, Toomer
believed, would give him much-needed control over his body and his sexuality, allowing him to will into existence his new "consciousness" as a
member of the "American race." If he could not rid himself of his black
blood, then he would—against all odds—control it.[39]

The nefarious connection between a vaguely defined "business culture"
and "racial crystallization" that Toomer despised was thus to be combated
through the achievement of physical perfection, which would then give
Toomer that "unmeasureable"—or unclassifiable—quality for which he
longed. Remembering his life in Washington, D.C., Toomer described a
private atmosphere swirling with copies of *Physical Culture Magazine*. He
set up gymnastic equipment in his room, purchased a "lung testing machine," subscribed to "Farmer Burns's correspondence course of wrestling"
and brought other boys to his room to test his strength, and enjoyed numerous breakfasts of "Tyler's macerated wheat." "All of this," he recalled,
"had taken place within the privacy of my own room . . . I had built up a
certain strength of will over my body. I could make it do things."[40] It was
this "strength of will," he believed, that enabled him to emerge as "the first
self conscious member of the American race," or to command his "Negro
gifts" as one might command a muscle, repressing them one moment and
releasing them the next.

Remembering his youthful attempts at physical perfection and bodily
control from the vantage of the 1930s, in his new history of himself
Toomer emphasized the modern consumer culture's conflation of "personal efficiency" with youth—in this case with the embodiment of "Young
America." But there was more to Toomer's thirst for physical perfection
than a middle-aged longing for boyish good health and vigor. Indeed, the

act of crafting a new manly physique to harness the potential of the "new American race" was of a piece with Toomer's devout neo-Lamarckianism and Darwinist millennialism. And the popularity of physical culture, as Michael Budd has shown, was rooted in the modern world's mastery of technology and nature, and was thus quite sympathetic to the *fin-de-siècle* eugenics movement. There was, then, something decidedly eugenic and at the same time terribly original about Toomer's determined efforts at body sculpture and self-control—especially given Budd's claims that the "genetic elitism of eugenics was never reconciled with physical culture's persistent utopian promises of bodily empowerment for all."[41] Given Toomer's interest in circumventing restrictive racial classifications and his own peculiar racial chauvinism, it may have been that same "persistent utopianism" that inspired him to a lifetime of dogged exercise. Thus, for Jean Toomer—in contrast, for instance, to the eugenicist Madison Grant—building a better American meant creating the perfect body for the new and emergent perfect race, and not the careful supervision of the purity of some patently aristocratic and uniformly white Pharaonic class.[42]

Nowhere were the problems of blackness and manliness more evident than in Toomer's troubled relationships with men and women. Raised in his grandfather's home, Toomer often seemed an impossible combination of Victorian morality and modern aesthetics. When puberty arrived, Toomer, steeped in Victorian prudery, suspected that he had lost control of himself: "Suddenly, I had a body on my hands that I could not handle." And with puberty came troubling desires and breathless yearnings for the stuff of adolescence. "Sex was the worst," Toomer recalled, "I wanted to take a girl . . . day after day, night after night, the fire burned me in short circuit." He was seized with desire for sex—though his pride and character insisted that it be sex with a girl he "liked and respected." Suffering from an enervating bodily weakness, he concluded that "the sex act was linked with . . . an access of manliness . . . I explained my weakened condition as due to the fact that I had never touched a girl." Here was a conundrum—control of the physical body and its sexual urges was the hallmark of Victorianism (and whiteness), but the directives of Toomer's ardent Victorianism conflicted with his belief that sex—and only sex—could give him "access to manliness."[43] A thinly veiled, youthful homoeroticism posed similarly demanding questions. His insights into the nature of manliness came to Toomer—as he remembered it—in the midst of an intense relationship with "Ken," a physically attractive boy from the neighborhood who, "from the first, seemed unlike the others," and with whom young Jean may have had a sexual experience that was both somewhat satisfying (their relationship was to be long-lasting) and eternally troubling.[44]

"It's a dangerous thing," Waldo Frank wrote to Toomer upon the publication of *Cane*, "to have god in one's brain, a dynamo in one's flesh, a volcano in one's loins." Such a sentiment—Frank's idea of a witty commentary on Toomer's lifelong predicament—perfectly captures the cultural dynamic Jean Toomer faced in his struggle to be heard. As a young man, Toomer, in a typically Victorian outburst, scolded his Washington contemporaries for their "loosening of character," for their obsession with "physical vulgarity." "Some of them," he remembered later, "believed that I was not only queer but crazy." Given his biographers' suggestion that Toomer was bipolar, and given the lingering homoerotic qualities of *Cane* and of his friendships with Hart Crane and Waldo Frank, one should conclude, then, that he may have fallen somewhere outside the Victorian norm.[45] What is more important and equally fascinating is how closely the rest of Toomer's life followed the pattern set in his late teens and early twenties: easy, earnest sexual relationships with many of the women in his life were complemented (and somewhat compromised) by intimate and personally frustrating friendships with men. There was a paradox to the pattern that he seems never to have understood. Needing a string of successful relationships with women to demonstrate (to himself and others) his manliness, Toomer complicated his drive to elide blackness, to escape the representation of "the Negro" as unwitting dupe to his sexual desires. Any and all expressions of sexuality—same sex or otherwise—played into the damnable stereotype of the oversexed "Negro."

A lonely, introspective child, raised in a Victorian household by an aloof, chameleon-like grandfather, the young Jean Toomer must have suffered considerable private adolescent agonies. To be raised in a household that prided itself on mulatto chauvinism, or racial ambiguity, and to come of age as a young man of mixed ancestry with contradictory desires in what was arguably one of the more brutal periods in race relations, would have marked anyone. But for someone with Toomer's obsessive and increasingly anachronistic interest in being neither white nor black, for someone prone to bipolar behavior, the combination of "Negro blood," a drive to recover manliness, and a barely suppressed homoeroticism set the stage for a lifetime of mental anguish, broken relationships, and social isolation. For more reasons than one, Toomer, quite simply, could *never* escape the contradictions of blackness and manliness.

Toomer's inability to communicate his bodily transcendence of blackness and whiteness was most dramatically exposed upon the occasion of his marriage to a fellow novelist and Gurdjieffian, Margery Latimer. Toomer and Latimer had met at the Portage "experiment," a gathering of Gurdjieffians outside Chicago in the summer of 1931. Marriage soon followed. After Toomer granted an interview to a local reporter in 1932, a grim comedy of errors ensued, and eventually the Hearst newspaper chain picked up the story and played the race card: a white woman had married a "Negro poet." The hysterical exposés of the Portage commune eventually led Toomer to publish a piece entitled "Just Americans" in *Time* magazine emphasizing his views on racial amalgamation. "Americans probably do not realize it," Toomer pontificated for the *Time* reporter, "but there are no racial barriers anymore, because there are so many Americans with strains of Negro, Indian, and Oriental blood."[46] Such sentiments were anathema to the very idea of bi-racialism, the social system of racial difference then presiding over American political culture. In his private writings, Toomer reacted quite bitterly to his classification as a "Negro" in press reports of his marriage. "The newspapers," he wrote, "had no racial evidence or justification for labeling me a Negro." "Is a man," he continued despairingly, "what he is called?"[47]

Time and time again, whenever bi-racialism threatened to "label" him a "Negro," Toomer returned to a consideration of his body—paradoxically the site of his most determined resistance and the source of his perennial misclassification. In addition to facilitating his command over various racial "gifts," Toomer's carefully cultivated Machine Age tastes were intimately connected to his own rather autobiographical understanding of the place of *Cane* in American culture. The Progressive Era's signal contribution to American life was a thirst for technocracy, scientific engineering, and—above all—efficiency and streamlining. These aspects of American politics and economics emerged in literature and art in a wide variety of contradictory expressions, from Art Deco to "streamlining" to the poems of William Carlos Williams.[48] Unlike the ambivalent Victorian advocates of the "genteel tradition," many of the self-consciously "modern" writers of the postwar world embraced the cool efficiency of the machine as a template for art. Toomer was no different. "The aesthetic of the machine," he mused in a letter to Lola Ridge, "the artistic acceptance of what is undeniably dominant in our age, the artist creatively adopting himself to angular, to dynamic, to mass forms, the artist creating from the stuff he has at hand—these things have life and vitality and vision in them. They punch. They stimulate. I like them. They are clean and fine and healthy."[49]

*Cane*, Toomer believed, was not part of the clean precision of the machine age, but was nevertheless understood to be a sorrowful complement to the encroachments of the modern industrial world. The "aesthetic of the machine" needed to undergo a "process of spiritualization" to burn away certain crudities: "My own contribution will curiously blend the rhythm of the peasantry with the rhythm of machines. A syncopation, a slow jazz, a sharp intense motion, subtilized, fused to a terse lyricism." In *Cane* Toomer captured some intangible essence of "the Negro," offering it both as evidence of the power of "mechanization" to assimilate even the most different, or peculiar, of races, and as foreshadowing of his own emergence as a "new American." He cautioned Waldo Frank:

> There is one thing about the Negro in America which most thoughtful persons seem to ignore; the Negro is in solution, in the process of solution. As an entity the race is loosing its body, and its soul is approaching a common soul . . . if anything comes up now, pure Negro, it will be a swan-song. Don't let us fool ourselves, brother: the Negro of the folk-song has all but passed away: the Negro of the emotional church is fading. A hundred years from now, these Negroes, if they exist at all will live in art. And I believe a vague sense of this fact is the driving force behind the arts movements directed toward them today. (Likewise the Indian.) America needs these elements. They are passing. Let us grab and hold them while there is still time . . . The supreme fact of mechanical civilization is that you become a part of it, or get sloughed off (under) . . . A few generations from now, the Negro will still be dark, and a portion of his psychology will spring from this fact, but in all else he will be a conformist to the general outlines of American civilization, or of American chaos.[50]

Ironically, Toomer never recognized the role of the Great Migration in changing—for the worse—the racial landscape that surrounded him. Instead, he offered the migration of black folks as the catalyst for the end of the concept of "the Negro." At the root of the "swan-song" of "the Negro," he argued, was the Great Migration, which he described as "the trend . . . towards the small town and then towards the city—and industry and commerce and machines." The arrival of "the Negro" in the North, he believed, would ultimately lead to the end of anything that might be identified as peculiarly "Negro," and so *Cane* was as much a work of ethnographic preservation as it was a literary creation. And as racial folklore, *Cane* was also of a piece with the widespread nationalist obsession with the collection and publication of folk materials around the world—in Ireland, Russia, the American South, and elsewhere—and, of course, it was also a crucial part of Toomer's pluralist project, the most direct outward expression of his "Negro gifts." "The folk spirit," Toomer mourned, "was walking in to die on the modern desert." The primitive, vital, natural experiences of American life and culture were "swiftly disappearing, swiftly being industrialized and urbanized by machines, motor cars, phonographs, movies."[51]

The erasure of the primitive, the vital, and the racially natural was not, however, necessarily a bad thing—not necessarily something to resist or fight against. In the end, the metaphors of mechanization, efficiency, and streamlining would, Toomer suggested, lay the groundwork for the emergence of "the new American." Even the institutional underpinnings of Jim Crow could not halt the mechanization of American life and the accession of "the American race": "Segregation and laws may retard this solution [of the Negro]. But in the end, segregation will either give way, or it will kill. Natural preservations do not come from unnatural laws." If *Cane* was the swan song of an authentic, idealized "Negro" folk culture, its publication, Toomer later came to believe, also marked the swan song of his own troubling blackness. "*Cane*," as one historian put it, "marked the beginning of the end of Toomer the black man." "The problems of life were not respecters of colors or racial groups," Toomer wrote, "[and those] who sought to cure themselves by a return to more primitive conditions were either romantics or escapists."[52]

In short, writing about black folks, celebrating the primitive virtues of "the Negro," or cultivating a black aesthetic more generally would do nothing to solve the larger problems of the world—the problems of class disparity and of disillusionment. What was needed, Toomer argued, was a carefully constructed scientific program of "breeding on the basis of biological fitness" to achieve racial fusion. Eugenics, in other words, with regard only for class, not race. Having captured the folk-essence of "the Negro" in *Cane*, Toomer moved on to the consideration of those larger problems in his work with Gurdjieff, in his studies of human psychology, and—most important—in his extensive autobiographical writings: "I . . .

would be a builder of the world." "*Cane*," he would later write, "was a swan-song. It was a song of an end. And why no one has seen and felt that, why people have expected me to write a second and a third and a fourth book like *Cane,* is one of the queer misunderstandings of my life."[53]

In sum, Toomer's autobiographical angst was, by and large, a reflection of his visceral reaction to the publication and reception of *Cane.* Expressing "great disappointment" that Toomer had failed to capitalize on his "great gift," W. E. B. Du Bois wrote to Toomer in 1931: "Haven't you got some article or poem lying around?" With the wrong-headed reception of *Cane* in mind, Toomer had little interest in sending off a poem to *The Crisis* or having parts of his first novel excerpted in an anthology of New Negro literature. "It would seem," he averred, "that the new negro is much more negro and much less American than was the old negro of fifty years ago."[54] Stuck between the opposing forces of the new race-consciousness, Jean Toomer had become a human tragedy. He wrote bitterly:

> There are Nordics who feel and think that not only their own souls but the very spirit of America would be violate should any save those of their own stock exercise decisive influence in this country. They aim towards an inviolate aristocracy, are sympathetic towards a western modification of the caste system, and see all virtue to be menaced by the rising tide of Southern and darker peoples . . . Some Negroes contend particularly for legal and social equality . . . Some are opposed to the whole capitalistic order of things, and are opposed to capitalists whatever the color of their skin. Others are mainly interested in educating the Negro industrially and academically under existing conditions. Still others are primarily concerned with the Negro's career in art, and are engaged in building up what might be called a black aesthetic. Still others would be willing to leave America to the white man and themselves go elsewhere.

"The new type" of American, he wrote despairingly, could never emerge so long as Nordics and New Negroes—"hard little undigestable wads"—were "'foreigners,' 'strangers,' [and] 'menaces' to each other." Even Toomer's utopian eugenics, it seemed, had limits. It had become almost impossible to speak or symbolize "race" without using the language of bi-racialism—of the new race-consciousness.[55]

Writing his autobiographies, Toomer had composed a history of himself in which physical perfection and racial ambiguity went hand in hand. Working to control his body and its supposedly inherited racial "gifts" and sexual urges, Toomer resisted the new patterns of classification with more than words; the demons of *Cane*—the "jazzed" sensuality of the novel—needed to be physically exorcised. And in this nadir of African-American life, blackness was commonly and scientifically understood to imply hypersexuality and a related lack of self-discipline; blackness was the negation of white manliness. The laws of nature, prophets of the new gospel of race argued in the aftermath of the Great War, allowed for a relatively unambiguous genetic understanding of racial destiny, leading many others to doubt the power of experience and reform—or "nurture"—to bridge the presumed gap between the heritage of "aliens" and "Negroes" and the demands of citizenship. New Negroes—of any variety—disagreed, but in responding to Nordic chauvinists, they, too, spread whiteness and blackness all over the debate about race and citizenship. In the privacy of his home, far away from this world, Toomer, faced with sexual urges he attributed to his "Negro" blood, and believing himself to embody the pluralist potential of America, attempted to control his rebellious body through rigorous exercise and a carefully cultivated masculine ethos. The more machine-like and perfect his body became—streamlining his long, tan limbs—the more Toomer came to believe that he could "will" himself into being as the "first self-conscious member of the American race."

It was not, however, a story with a happy ending. In 1923 a twenty-nine-year-old man who had for years wanted desperately to be an author published his first book. If his life before *Cane* had been private, almost cloistered, Toomer's life after *Cane* was a living nightmare. Writing *Cane* marked him publicly as a "Negro" and as something less than the masculine ideal he had set for himself. Coming of age in an America dominated, as he put it, by "the now more crystallized and articulate" champions of blackness and whiteness, he had sought release from the bounds of race in physical perfection. In doing so, however, he found himself in a dilemma that he was never able to resolve. Few cared for his "new type" of American, and, contrary to his claims, gender, sexuality, and race could not be separated: to be manly was, simply put, to claim a racial identity. After *Cane*, feeling discouraged, hurt, and angry, Toomer struggled to set his life down on paper, composing draft after draft of repetitive autobiographies, many of which did not get past the year of *Cane's* publication. With each successive draft, Toomer came up against that infuriating "dominant . . . language" of race and struggled to "find . . . words with which to talk" of himself.[56] The demons of *Cane*, in short, could not be exorcised.

# Epilogue

The Negro has to be defined according to social usage, and his African ancestry and physical characteristics are fixed to his person much more ineffaceably than the yellow star is fixed to the Jew during the Nazi regime in Germany.

—GUNNAR MYRDAL, *AN AMERICAN DILEMMA* (1944)

Torn away from their nineteenth-century moorings, Jean Toomer, Daniel Cohalan, W. E. B. Du Bois, and Madison Grant struggled to find a safe harbor in the tempest-tossed sea of dread racial conflicts and difficult questions of identity. For each of them, and for the larger American community, the shrinking dimensions of time and space in the modern world posed mighty problems of classification, problems complicated by the massive demographic shift of the Great Migration.

The legal struggle to keep "the Negro" affixed to the soil of the turn-of-the-century New South had been a calculated social and economic risk, and the freedom of movement and search for opportunity of African Americans in the wake of the Great War had realized the worst fears of many white folks. Bigger Thomas's stuffed-shirt attorney, Mr. Max, professed:

> The Negro comes of a people who have lived under queer conditions of life, conditions thrust outside the normal circle of our civilization. But even in living outside of our lives, he has not had a full life of his own. We have seen to that. It was convenient to keep him close to us; it was nice and cheap. We told him what to do; where to live; how much schooling he could get; where he could eat; where and what kind of work he could do. We marked up the earth and said, "Stay there!" But life is not stationary.[1]

By the 1930s "the Negro question," popularized in nearly every aspect of American culture, from art to advertising, from minstrel shows to movies, from song lyrics to public scientific exhibitions, had nearly eclipsed all other racial quandaries, offering an increasingly easy solution to those immigrants who sought whiteness, or Americanism, or both.

The wildly popular dramatic epic *Gone with the Wind* (both the 1936 novel written by Margaret Mitchell and the 1939 film) captured the role of a new mass culture in foregrounding "the Negro problem." Therein, the narrative of the fall of the Old South, echoing that of the Roman Empire, is presented as a human tragedy. At the center of the protracted disintegration of this lost "civilization" is a love story, and at the center of that love story is young Scarlett O'Hara, daughter of a wealthy southern planter. From the very first scene, the O'Hara family is both quintessentially southern and unmistakably Irish. "Katie Scarlett O'Hara," as her father calls her, is reminded by the O'Hara patriarch (who speaks with "the brogue of County Meath still heavy on his tongue") that her appreciation of the family plantation—named after the old Gaelic stronghold of Tara—should grow out of her inherently Irish love of the land, out of her potent "drop of Irish blood." As Margaret Mitchell described it, the face of Scarlett's irascible father, Gerald O'Hara, was indelibly marked as Irish: "His shrewd face was unlined and his hard little blue eyes were young with the unworried youthfulness of one who has never taxed his brain with problems more abstract than how many cards to draw in a poker game . . . His was as Irish a face as could be found . . . round, high-colored, short nosed, wide mouthed, and belligerent."[2]

The O'Hara family's intrinsic southernness—the chivalrous, upper-class Victorianism that complicates their Irishness—is most particularly displayed in the horrified reaction of Scarlett's mother upon learning that a hired hand ("a Yankee man") has sired an illegitimate child with, as Mr. O'Hara puts it, "a white trash girl" (71). The elder O'Haras are aghast. But expressions of Irishness persist as "ethnic" memories of a racial past. Soon after learning of the unseemly behavior of their hired hand, the entire aristocratic O'Hara family gather in a small room and, on their knees and with heads bowed, share a Catholic prayer to the Virgin Mary—the "Litany of the Virgin" (71).[3] Irishness and southernness—two very different sensibilities—are thus woven together in the lives of the O'Haras. Gerald O'Hara recalls:

> He liked the South, and he soon became, in his own opinion, a Southerner. There was much about the South—and Southerners—that he would never comprehend; but, with the wholeheartedness that was his

nature, he adopted its ideas and customs, as he understood them, for his own—poker and horse racing, red-hot politics and the code duello, States' Rights and damnation to all Yankees, slavery and King Cotton, contempt for white trash and courtesy to all women. He even learned to chew tobacco. There was no need for him to acquire a good head for whiskey, he had been born with one. (44)

As a born Irishman, Gerald O'Hara is naturally drawn to the lifestyle of the Old South, becoming the perfect embodiment (as both Mitchell and the film would have it) of all that is noble and glorious in the "moss-hung kingdoms" of Georgia (45). Gerald's marriage to a woman of aristocratic French parentage—whose family "fled Haiti in the Revolution of 1791"— completes his movement into the southern pale and raises the disturbing specter of racial revolution (40). There were, then, important cues for immigrant Americans in *Gone with the Wind*—a blueprint for nearly total assimilation.

"Slavery and King Cotton"—two elements of southern life cherished by Gerald O'Hara—are at the center of *Gone with the Wind*. The O'Haras are surrounded by slaves, by slavery, and by the coming war of northern aggression. Their absolute whiteness is assured by their mastery and ownership of black folks as well as by their aristocratic refinement. Gerald O'Hara's "three most prized possessions" are his wife, his plantation, and his valet, named Pork, whom he describes as "shining black, dignified and trained in all the arts of sartorial elegance" (45). In the movie version, while taking an early nap with several other young women at a neighboring plantation, Scarlett and her sisters are fanned by slave children (young girls, of course) holding elegant fans composed of ostrich feathers. Later, after sneaking out of the grand bedroom to listen in on the gentlemen's conversation—an argument, really, about the coming war with the North and about southern manhood—Scarlett descends a long staircase while the audience hears her father, the old Irishman in a room of Anglo-Saxons, offer the loudest and angriest defense of the South and of slavery. Scarlett's "magnolia-white skin" (a phrase reminiscent of Madison Grant's veneration of the "ivory whiteness" of the Nordic race) is thus enhanced permanently and powerfully by her family's remarkable southernness, and by the overwhelming presence of slaves in her world (3).[4]

The "real significance" of *Gone with the Wind*, one historian has argued, lay in its pervasive "reaffirmation" of faith in the American way of life: in individual struggle and triumph over the terrible odds of the Depression.[5] More important, *Gone with the Wind* catered to the deeper racial fears and anxieties of its audience, and reflected a near-permanent shift in American culture. In an age defined by the Scottsboro trial, by the looming importance of radical politics, and by the gunpowder violence of the Depression South, *Gone with the Wind* was of a piece with the blazing racial hatreds of American labor, and part of a nationalist culture predicated on racism and white unity that would hinder the emergence of a fully unified labor movement. In a world where color-conscious international radicalism was embodied by Du Bois and the younger radicals of the NAACP, *Gone with the Wind* depicted black folks as loving slaves selflessly devoted to their masters and incapable of radical protest. In a nation where lingering fears of "the immigrant" were buried just below the surface of the culture, *Gone with the Wind* reminded Americans that "the Negro problem" was *the* overwhelmingly important dilemma of national—and nationalist—significance. African Americans had become an indispensable social attraction, a singular *stella polare* for all that white Americans feared and loathed in themselves and in their nation.

The tragic narrative of the Civil War presented in Mitchell's novel and in the film, and the general fascination with southern culture in the 1930s, would have disturbing consequences for the coming intensification of segregation in America. But the hidden narrative of the whitening process, or of the triumph of color-consciousness, had already become an important part of American culture during the Depression. In "making, losing, and struggling to revive a Southern plantation," writes Michael Rogin, the "Irish O'Haras" in the Old South reveal that "race Americanizes white immigrants."[6] Indeed, the blinding whiteness of the Irish O'Haras in *Gone with the Wind* illustrates the central premise of this book: that the principal social forces responsible for the growing national significance of "the Negro" and the reunification of whiteness—especially in regard to the Irish— can be found in the 1920s and 1930s. A quite popular St. Patrick's Day greeting card from the 1930s, for instance, depicts a small, ambiguously gendered "Negro," with jet-black skin and an impish grin, smiling at the reader and offering a holiday greeting: "Ah aint Irish, but ah sho does wish you de top o' de mornin.'"[7] The pernicious, terrifying "Irish menace" of the nineteenth and early twentieth centuries had, it seemed, been permanently solved by the simple act of replacement: by the deliberate substitution of a Negro for the absent stage Irishman, or "Paddy," of the past. On another level, the late 1920s and the Depression 1930s would witness a revival of social scientific works on "the Negro problem" written by aspiring PhD's, advocates for civil rights, and "objective" Negrophobes. The Irish in America, much like Gerald O'Hara of *Gone with the Wind,* had been "bled white" by the world around them, and found their all-important Irishness recast as "ethnicity."[8]

The lure of whiteness and Americanism would soon encourage a similar reclassification of Jews and Italians as members of "the Caucasian race"—an identity rooted in absolute whiteness and even more inclusive of Europeans than Nordicism. The assimilation of these other groups into whiteness had begun during those same tumultuous decades following the Great War, but had proceeded at a somewhat different pace than that of the Irish. For Jews, the post-Holocaust rejection of anti-Semitism in some quarters of the United States—evident in movies like *Gentlemen's Agreement*—helped to finalize the placement of the color line. But, in the end, many of the same forces were behind the racial bleaching of both Jews and Italians, namely the continued arrival of "the Negro" in the North after the Second World War, the dominance of a national popular culture fixated on skin color and race questions, and the subsequent nationalization of "the Negro problem." The postwar migration of African Americans to the cities would inspire the later European immigrants to take advantage of new opportunities outside the urban enclaves. Encouraged by federal G.I. benefits to leave the cities for the suburbs, immigrants who might have been despised in the early 1920s were, by the end of World War II, eagerly offered a range of white privileges. Jewish Americans, firmly in place in the growing entertainment industry, would attempt a remarkable balancing act between their private lives as Jews and their public celebration of whiteness and Americanism.[9] Immigrant communities in Newark, New Jersey, even as they protested discriminatory anti-Catholic ordinances during the 1950s, would find that beating up on "the Negro" was the surest route to civil rights. Post–World War II antagonism toward "the Negro" in Detroit and Chicago led to a rash of bombings and racialized confrontations that harked back to the summer of 1919.[10] Somewhat like the Irish before them, then, these later, turn-of-the-century arrivals to the United States would eventually find themselves pushed—and just as often pulled—into the charmed circle of white racial identity by the great and lasting national debate over "the Negro."

The assertiveness of African-American civil rights advocates—much like that of the New Negro Movement of the 1920s—also contributed to the final triumph of whiteness and blackness. "Changes wrought in the U.S. social order by the war itself and by the early Cold War," concludes the historian Matthew Frye Jacobson, "helped to speed the alchemy by which Hebrew became Caucasian. From A. Phillip Randolph's threatened march on Washington, to African-American campaigns for Double Victory, to the major parties' civil rights planks in 1944 and the rise of the Dixiecrats in 1948, the steady but certain ascendance of Jim Crow as *the* pressing political issue of the day brought the ineluctable logic of the South's white-black binary into play with new force in national life." In pressing for their own civil rights, and for their own humanity, in the face of massive resistance, those who sought to redeem the soul of America distracted attention even further away from the last few quirks in whiteness.[11]

The uplift of America's many different white peoples came always at the expense of black folks, for whom life would get far worse before it got better. The quickening pace of assimilation, the related growth of Hollywood, and the symbolic emergence of clean-cut, All-American types like Joe DiMaggio came at the expense of "the Negro," who was described—unlike European immigrants—as a problem without solution. "In spite of all race prejudice," summarized Gunnar Myrdal in 1944, "few Americans seem to doubt that it is the ultimate fate of this nation to incorporate without distinction not only all the Northern European stocks, but also the people from Eastern and Southern Europe, the Near East, and Mexico . . . The Negroes, on the other hand, are commonly assumed to be unassimilable." The difference of "the Negro"—what Langston Hughes had once called the "strange un-whiteness of his . . . features"—was, as Myrdal tellingly put it, "fixed to his person much more ineffaceably than the yellow star is fixed to the Jew."[12]

That persistent "un-whiteness" continues to lump together remarkably different groups of people as "black," erasing the lines between rich and poor, light-skinned and dark-skinned, classically educated and streetwise, rural and urban, immigrant and American-born. The increasing flexibility, or inclusiveness, of whiteness that matured in the 1920s thus brought with it an equally inclusive and lasting redefinition of blackness. "The black man," James Baldwin once wrote, "has functioned in the white man's world as a fixed star, as an immovable pillar: and as he moves out of his place, heaven and earth are shaken to their foundations." Today, whiteness and blackness, imbued with the deepest symbolism in a richly varied

America, play key roles in determining a wide range of social and economic privileges. They are also equally important reference points in the human quest for the self and the other. We are, then, still stuck in Jean Toomer's nightmarish world of painful differences, still quite far away from a truly color-blind world where everyone agrees with Baldwin that "the value placed on the color of the skin is always and everywhere and forever a delusion."[13]

NOTES
ACKNOWLEDGMENTS
INDEX

# Notes

## Introduction

1. James Baldwin, "Preface to the 1984 Edition," *Notes of a Native Son* (1955; Boston: Beacon, 1984), xii.
2. Matthew Frye Jacobson, *Whiteness of a Different Color: European Immigrants and the Alchemy of Race* (Cambridge, Mass.: Harvard University Press, 1998), 280.
3. Cornel West, *Race Matters* (New York: Vintage, 1994), xvi.
4. Rayford Logan, *The Betrayal of the Negro: From Rutherford Hayes to Woodrow Wilson* (1965; New York: De Capo, 1997).
5. Lothrop Stoddard, *Re-Forging America: The Story of Our Nationhood* (New York: Scribner's, 1927).
6. Jean Toomer to Suzanne LaFollette, 22 Sept. 1930, Jean Toomer Papers, Beinecke Rare Books and Manuscript Library, Yale University.
7. See Mia Bay, *The White Image in the Black Mind: African-American Ideas about White People, 1830–1925* (New York: Oxford University Press, 2000).
8. See Charles Callan Tansill, *America and the Fight for Irish Freedom, 1866–1922: An Old Story Based on New Data* (New York: Devin-Adair, 1957), 113–449; Terry Golway, *John Devoy and America's Fight for Irish Freedom* (New York: St. Martin's, 1998).
9. Du Bois, *Dusk of Dawn: An Essay towards an Autobiography of a Race Concept* (New York: Harcourt, Brace, and World, 1940), 221.
10. See, e.g., Kevin K. Gaines, *Uplifting the Race: Black Leadership, Politics, and Culture in the Twentieth Century* (Chapel Hill: University of North Carolina Press, 1995); David Levering Lewis, *W. E. B. Du Bois: Biography of a Race, 1868–1919* (New York: Henry Holt, 1993); Manning Marable, *W. E. B. Du Bois: Black Radical Democrat* (Boston: Twane, 1986).
11. See Gail Bederman, *Manliness and Civilization: A Cultural History of Gender and Race in the United States, 1880–1917* (Chicago: University of Chicago Press, 1995).
12. Cynthia Kerman and Richard Eldridge, *The Lives of Jean Toomer: A Hunger for Wholeness* (Baton Rouge: Louisiana State University Press, 1987); Nellie McKay,

*Jean Toomer: Artist* (Chapel Hill: University of North Carolina Press, 1984); George Hutchinson, "Jean Toomer and American Racial Discourse," *Texas Studies in Literature and Language* 35 (1993): 227–250.

13. Neil Foley, *White Scourge: Mexicans, Blacks, and Poor Whites in Texas Cotton Culture* (Berkeley: University of California Press, 1998); Alexander Saxton, *The Indispensable Enemy: Labor and the Anti-Chinese Movement in California* (1971; Berkeley: University of California Press, 1995); Grace Elizabeth Hale, *Making Whiteness: The Culture of Segregation in the South, 1890–1940* (New York: Pantheon, 1998).

14. Peggy Pascoe, "Miscegenation Law, Court Cases, and Ideologies of 'Race' in Twentieth-Century America," *Journal of American History* 83, no. 1 (June 1996): 44–69. Rodolphe Lucien Desdunes, *Our People and Our History,* trans. Dorothea Olga McCants (1911; Baton Rouge: Louisiana State University Press, 1973).

15. Ann Douglas, *Terrible Honesty: Mongrel Manhattan in the 1920s* (New York: Farrar, Straus and Giroux, 1995), 13.

16. On *Battle Cry of Peace* see Kevin Brownlow, *The War, the West, and the Wilderness* (New York: Knopf, 1979). *Irish World,* Jan. 11, 1919. Margaret Mitchell, *Gone with the Wind* (1936; New York: Warner, 1999), 3.

## 1. Salvaging a Shipwrecked World

1. Brooks Adams to Henry Adams, Feb. 2, 1895, Additional Adams Family Correspondence, Houghton Library, Harvard University (hereafter AAFC). Brooks Adams to Henry Adams, March 7, 1896, AAFC. "Nervous force" is from Brooks Adams, *The Law of Civilization and Decay: An Essay on History* (New York, 1896); Max Nordau, *Degeneration* (1895; New York: Appleton, 1912), 2.

2. Adams, *Law of Civilization and Decay,* 60, 61, 336, 61, 349. See Arthur Hermann, *The Idea of Decline in Western History* (New York: Free Press, 1997), 153–174; T. J. Jackson Lears, *No Place of Grace: Antimodernism and the Transformation of American Culture, 1880–1920* (1983; Chicago: University of Chicago Press, 1994).

3. Henry Adams, *The Education of Henry Adams* (1918; Boston: Houghton Mifflin, 1974), 382.

4. "Race," *The Century Dictionary and Cyclopedia* (12 vols.; New York, 1889), vol. 8, 4926. M. Sanson, cited in A. H. Keane, *Ethnology* (Cambridge: Cambridge University Press, 1901), 13. Ibid., 3.

5. William M. Sloane, "History and Democracy," *American Historical Review* 1 (Oct. 1895): 1–3. Charles Rollin Keyes, "The Physical Basis of History," *The Arena* 27 (June 1902): 585.

6. Edward S. Ellis, *The Story of the Greatest Nations: From the Dawn of History to the Twentieth Century* (10 vols.; New York, 1901), vol. 1, 1. Justin McCarthy et al., *The Standard History of the World: A Narrative of Political Events and a Survey of Civilization, Forming a Comprehensive Record of Human Progress and Achievement* (10 vols.; New York, 1914), vol. 10, 13; Israel Smith Clare, *Library of Universal History,*

*Containing a Record of the Human Race from the Earliest Historical Period to the Present Time, Embracing a General Survey of the Progress of Mankind in National and Social Life, Civil Government, Religion, Literature, Science and Art* (5 vols.; New York, 1901), vol. 1, 27, 34.

7. Ridpath, *Great Races of Mankind: An Account of the Ethnic Origin, Primitive Estate, Early Migrations, Social Evolution, and Present Conditions and Promise of the Principal Families of Men* (4 vols.; Cincinnati, 1893), vol. 1, xli–xlii.

8. John Commons, *Race and Immigrants in America* (New York, 1907), 13; "Races of Men," in *The New Practical Reference Library* (6 vols., Chicago, 1910), vol. 4, n.p.

9. See Matthew Frye Jacobson, *Whiteness of a Different Color: European Immigrants and the Alchemy of Race* (Cambridge, Mass.: Harvard University Press, 1998); John Higham, *Strangers in the Land: Patterns of American Nativism* (1955; New York: Atheneum, 1979).

10. Higham, *Strangers in the Land*, 86, 169, 166; David Roediger, *Wages of Whiteness: Race and the Making of the American Working Class* (London: Verso, 1991).

11. In addition to the work of David Roediger, see esp. Alexander Saxton, *The Indispensable Enemy: Labor and the Anti-Chinese Movement in California* (1971; Berkeley: University of California Press, 1995); Rosanne Currarino, "Labor Intellectuals and the Labor Question: Wage Work and the Making of Consumer Society in America, 1875–1905" (Ph.D. diss., Rutgers University, 1999), 143–178.

12. S. Ivan Tonjoroff, "The Clash of Races in Europe," *The Arena* 21 (March 1899): 370–381; John L. Brandt, *Anglo-Saxon Supremacy; or, Race Contributions to Civilization* (Boston, 1915), 4.

13. Frederick Jackson Turner, "The Problem of the West," *Atlantic Monthly* (Sept. 1896): 296.

14. Brooks Adams to Henry Adams, April 7, 1912, AAFC. Roosevelt to Lodge, July 19, 1898, in *Selections from the Correspondence of Theodore Roosevelt and Henry Cabot Lodge*, ed. Henry Cabot Lodge (New York: Scribner's, 1925), vol. 1, 328. Roosevelt, review of *The Law of Civilization and Decay*, in *The Forum* 22 (1896): 588.

15. Joseph Conrad, *Heart of Darkness*, in *Youth, Heart of Darkness, and The End of the Tether* (1902; London: Everyman's Library, 1974), 42.

16. "Impressions and Opinions," *Anglo-Saxon Review* 1 (June 1899): 248.

17. Gail Bederman, *Manliness and Civilization: A Cultural History of Gender and Race in the United States, 1880–1917* (Chicago: University of Chicago Press, 1995), 214.

18. Brooks Adams to Henry Adams, Nov. 12, 1899, AAFC. Brooks Adams, *The New Empire* (New York, 1902), xi, 208. Also see Brooks Adams, *America's Economic Supremacy* (1900; New York: Harper and Brothers, 1947), 63–83.

19. David Starr Jordan, *Imperial Democracy* (1899; New York: Garland, 1977), 32. "Imperialistus americanus" is from Robert Beisner, *From the Old Diplomacy to the New* (Arlington Heights, Ill.: AHM Publishing, 1975), 27.

20. Finis Dunaway, "Hunting with the Camera: Nature Photography, Manliness, and Modern Memory, 1890–1930," *Journal of American Studies* 34 (Aug. 2000); Dennis

Hickey and Kenneth Wylie, "'Heart of Darkness' or 'Mother of Light'? American Perceptions of the African Rainforest," *Centennial Review* 35 (1991): 249–259. Higham, *Strangers in the Land,* 149.

21. Thomas Dyer, *Theodore Roosevelt and the Idea of Race* (Baton Rouge: Louisiana State University Press, 1980), esp. 67–68.

22. Wilhemina Harris, "Brooks Adams with His Family Relics," in *Furnish Report of the Old House* (10 vols.; National Park Service, 1966–1974), vol. 1, 909–938: "If the guests showed a shade of interest in the surroundings, Mr. Adams would begin to recall his family life at the Old House. Yes, the six hitching posts were still there as a reminder of the days of horse and carriage travel, 'before the decline of civilization,' he was apt to remark" (910).

23. John F. Reiger, *American Sportsmen and the Origins of Conservation* (Norman: University of Oklahoma Press, 1986), 114–141; Richard Slotkin, *Gunfighter Nation: The Myth of the Frontier in Twentieth Century America* (New York: Harper Perennial, 1992), 29–62, 198–200. William Temple Hornaday, *Thirty Years War for Wild Life* (New York: Scribner's, 1931), 150–154.

24. Higham, *Strangers in the Land,* 155. Also see E. Digby Batzell, *The Protestant Establishment: Aristocracy and Caste in America* (New York: Random House, 1964), 97; *National Cyclopædia of American Biography* (1930; Ann Arbor: University Microfilms, 1967), vol. 29, 319–320.

25. *Dictionary of American Biography* (New York: Scribner's, 1958), vol. 22, supplement 2, 256. *National Cyclopædia of American Biography,* vol. 29, 320. Madison Grant, *The Passing of the Great Race; or, The Racial Basis of European History* (New York: Scribner's, 1916), 16.

26. Grant, "The Origin of the New York Zoological Society," in *Trail and Campfire: The Book of the Boone and Crockett Club,* ed. George Bird Grinnell and Theodore Roosevelt (New York, 1897), 320. William Cronon, "The Trouble with Wilderness; or, Getting Back to the Wrong Nature," in *Uncommon Ground: Toward Reinventing Nature,* ed. Cronon (New York: Norton, 1995), 76–80.

27. Richard Hofstadter, *The Age of Reform: From Bryan to FDR* (New York: Knopf, 1955). Donna Haraway, "Teddy Bear Patriarchy: Taxidermy in the Garden of Eden, New York City, 1908–1936," in *Cultures of United States Imperialism,* ed. Amy Kaplan and Donald Pease (Durham: Duke University Press, 1993), 237–291. Higham, *Strangers in the Land,* 155.

28. Alan M. Kraut, *Silent Travelers: Germs, Genes, and "the Immigrant Menace"* (New York: HarperCollins, 1994), 167.

29. See Stephen Jay Gould, *The Mismeasure of Man* (New York: Norton, 1981), 158–174; Leila Zenderland, *Measuring Minds: Henry Herbert Goddard and the Origins of American Intelligence Testing* (New York: Cambridge University Press, 1998); Kraut, *Silent Travelers;* Steven Noll, *Feeble-Minded in Our Midst: Institutions for the Mentally Retarded in the South, 1900–1940* (Chapel Hill: University of North Carolina Press, 1995).

30. Edward Alsworth Ross, *The Old World in the New: The Significance of Past and Present Immigration to the American People* (New York, 1914), 285–286; Jacobson, *Whiteness of a Different Color*. The phrase "brutish brute" is from Jack London, *The Chinago and Other Stories* (New York, 1906), 161; Edgar Rice Burroughs, *Tarzan of the Apes* (1914; New York: Viking, 1990), see esp. editor's note 29:2, 281.

31. Grant, *Passing of the Great Race,* 228. See Kristin L. Hoganson, *Fighting for American Manhood: How Gender Politics Provoked the Spanish-American and Philippine-American Wars* (New Haven: Yale University Press, 1998), 201–202; Kirk Savage, *Standing Soldiers, Kneeling Slaves: Race, War, and Monument in Nineteenth-Century America* (Princeton: Princeton University Press, 1997).

32. Grant, *Passing of the Great Race,* 49–50. See Mark H. Haller, *Eugenics: Hereditarian Attitudes in American Thought* (New Brunswick: Rutgers University Press, 1963).

33. Office memo, Whitney Darrow to Maxwell Perkins, Dec. 13, 1933, Charles Scribner's Sons Archive, Firestone Library, Princeton University (hereafter SA: "Grant").

34. Peter J. Bowler, *Evolution: The History of an Idea* (Berkeley: University of California Press, 1989), 271.

35. Grant, *Passing of the Great Race,* 15.

36. Grant, "America for the Americans," *Forum* 74 (Sept. 1925): 348. Grant, "The Racial Transformation of America," *North American Review* 219 (March 1924): 346.

37. Osborn, preface to the 2nd ed. of *The Passing of the Great Race* (New York: Scribner's, 1917), xiii. Grant, *Passing of the Great Race,* 230.

38. William Z. Ripley, *The Races of Europe: A Sociological Study* (New York, 1899). Grant, *Passing of the Great Race,* xv, 200.

39. See Roediger, *Wages of Whiteness;* Noel Ignatiev, *How the Irish Became White* (New York: Routledge, 1996); Eric Lott, *Love and Theft* (New York: Oxford University Press, 1993).

40. Grant, *Passing of the Great Race,* 53–58, 182, 183, and the chart facing 123. Thomas Gossett depicts Grant's work as an attempt to popularize Anglo-Saxon notions of "civilization" through the inclusion of the Irish. See Thomas Gossett, *Race: The History of an Idea in America* (1963; New York: Oxford University Press, 1997), 361.

41. Ibid., 88, 64. Michael Rogin, "The Sword Became a Flashing Vision," in *Ronald Reagan, the Movie, and Other Episodes in Political Demonology* (Berkeley: University of California Press, 1987), 190–235.

42. Grant, *Passing of the Great Race,* xv. Also see Grant to Earnest Sevier Cox, Dec. 14, 1920, Earnest Sevier Cox Papers, Duke University (hereafter ESCP).

43. Grant, "Discussion of Article on Democracy and Heredity," *Journal of Heredity* 10, no. 4 (April 1919): 165. Higham, *Strangers in the Land,* 157. Grant, *Passing of the Great Race,* 200. Grant, "Restriction of Immigration: Racial Aspects," *Journal of the National Institute of Social Sciences* 7 (Aug. 1, 1921): 54.

44. "Ivory whiteness" is from Grant, *Passing of the Great Race,* 24. Bradshaw to

Charles Scribner's Sons, June 3, 1918; Grant to Maxwell Perkins, June 3, 1918—both in SA: "Grant."

45. Bederman, *Manliness and Civilization*, 230. Louise Michele Newman, *White Women's Rights: The Racial Origins of Feminism in the United States* (New York: Oxford University Press, 1998).

46. "The Major," *Hank, His Lies and His Yarns* (New York, 1931), 114, 93–103. Grant's use of the term "queer" is interesting. As George Chauncey has shown, one commonplace meaning of the term in the 1910s and 1920s denoted men who stood outside the bounds of conventional sexuality. But, as Siobhan Somerville has reminded me, Chauncey limits his discussion of this word to men, while Grant is quite clearly referring to women. For more, see George Chauncey, *Gay New York: Gender, Urban Culture, and the Making of the Gay Male World, 1890–1940* (New York: Basic Books, 1994), 12–23 and Siobhan Somerville, *Queering of the Color Line: Race and the Invention of Homosexuality in American Culture* (Durham: Duke University Press, 2000), 142–145.

47. Grant, *Passing of the Great Race*, 227, 29, 20, 228, 66–67, 23.

48. Robert M. Yerkes, "How Psychology Happened into the War," in Yerkes, ed., *The New World of Science* (New York, 1920), 351; Gould, *Mismeasure of Man*, 192–224.

49. The committee was also proposed as the "Section of Anthropology and Eugenics," to be organized under the auspices of the Surgeon General's Office. Davenport to Grant, Jan. 12, 1918, and attachment, Charles Davenport Papers, American Philosophical Society (hereafter CDPAPS).

50. See Grant to Davenport, Dec. 19, 1917, Davenport to Grant, Dec. 21 and Dec. 31, 1917, and Davenport to Grant, Jan. 12, 1918, and attachment, all in CDPAPS; Gould, *Mismeasure of Man*, 224–232.

51. Grant to Stoddard, Oct. 13, 1927, cited in James Robert Bachman, "Theodore Lothrop Stoddard: The Bio-Sociological Battle for Civilization" (Ph.D. diss., University of Rochester, 1967), 236n18. See reviews of *Passing* in the *American Historical Review* 22 (July 1917): 842, and the *Nation* 54 (April 19, 1917), 446. Publication figures from Grant's *New York Times* obituary, May 31, 1937.

52. George Schuyler, *Black No More* (1931; Boston: Northeastern University Press, 1989); Higham, *Strangers in the Land*, 234–300.

53. Grant, *Passing of the Great Race*, xv, 22.

54. Stoddard, *The Rising Tide of Color against White World Supremacy* (New York: Scribner's, 1920), 220. Also see Stoddard, *Revolt against Civilization* (New York: Scribner's, 1922); F. A. Woods, "The Racial Limitation of Bolshevism," *Journal of Heredity* 10, no. 4 (April 1919): 188–190.

55. See Michael H. Hunt, *Ideology and U.S. Foreign Policy* (New Haven: Yale University Press, 1987), 114–124; Higham, *Strangers in the Land*, 194–254; Joan M. Jensen, *The Price of Vigilance* (Chicago: Rand McNally, 1968).

56. Grant, "Racial Transformation of America," 344; Jensen, *Price of Vigilance*.

57. Jensen, *Price of Vigilance;* also see "Defense Society Says U.S. Buys German Planes," *New York Tribune,* June 1, 1920.

58. Grant, "American for Americans," 348.

59. See Grant to Prescott Hall, Oct. 15, 1919, American Defense Society Papers, New York Historical Society, Box "1918" (hereafter ADSP); Minutes, Executive Committee, American Defense Society, Oct. 15, 1919; Prescott Hall to Charles S. Davison, April 30, 1920, ADSP.

60. See ADSP, Box "1919."

61. Stoddard, *Revolt against Civilization,* 233. On Lapouge's speech see "Race War Seen in Clash Class," *Negro World,* Oct. 8, 1921. Also see, e.g., Grant, "Discussion of Article on Democracy and Heredity," 164–165: "In the last analysis, the Bolshevist movement in Russia is a war of the races. The Alpine peasantry, under Semitic leadership, are engaged in destroying the Nordic bourgeoisie, and with it the only racial elements of value in that great sodden welter of quasi-European peoples called 'The Russias'" (165).

62. Nancy Cott, *The Grounding of Modern Feminism* (New Haven: Yale University Press, 1987), 250. Bernhard Stern, "Nazi Spectroscope," *New Republic,* May 29, 1935.

63. Du Bois, "Americanization," *Crisis* (Aug. 1922): 154.

64. Du Bois, "West Indian Immigration," *Crisis* (Dec. 1924): 57. Mark H. Haller, *Eugenics: Hereditarian Attitudes in American Thought* (New Brunswick: Rutgers University Press, 1963), 155–157; Charles C. Alexander, "Prophet of American Racism: Madison Grant and the Nordic Myth," *Phylon* 23 (Spring 1962): 77; Gould, *Mismeasure of Man,* 225–232; Jacobson, *Whiteness of a Different Color,* 82–85.

65. Richard B. Sherman, "'The Last Stand': The Fight for Racial Integrity in Virginia in the 1920s," *Journal of Southern History* 65, no. 1 (Feb. 1988): esp. 77–78. For evidence of Grant's involvement, see the correspondence in "Grant, Madison," CDPAPS. The Virginia legislation deliberately evaded evidence of miscegenation between native Americans and white southerners in the so-called Pocahontas exception, a fact Grant found quite amusing; see Grant to Charles Davenport, April 8, 1924, CDPAPS.

66. Du Bois, "Harvard," *Crisis* (March 1923): 199. Du Bois, "Americanization," *Crisis* (Aug. 1922): 154. See Raymond Wolters, *The New Negro on Campus: Black College Rebellions of the 1920s* (Princeton: Princeton University Press, 1975), 324–331; *Blacks at Harvard: A Documentary History of African American Experience at Harvard and Radcliffe,* ed. Werner Sollors, Caldwell Titcomb, and Thomas A. Underwood (New York: New York University Press, 1993), 195–227.

67. Barbara Jean Fields, "Ideology and Race in American History," in *Region, Race, and Reconstruction,* ed. J. Morgan Kousser and James M. McPherson (New York: Oxford University Press, 1982), 143–178. Du Bois, "The Black Man Brings His Gifts," *The Survey* (March 1, 1925): 657.

68. Du Bois, "Brothers, Come North," *Crisis* 19 (Jan. 1920): 105–106. Florette Henri, *Black Migration: Movement North, 1900–1920* (Garden City, N.Y.: Anchor, 1976); James R. Grossman, *Land of Hope: Chicago, Black Southerners, and the Great Migration* (Chicago: University of Chicago Press, 1989). Stoddard, *Re-Forging America: The Story of Our Nationhood* (New York: Scribner's, 1927), vii, 260.

69. Harold Rabinowitz, *Race Relations in the Urban South, 1865–1890* (Athens: University of Georgia Press, 1996); Saul Dubow, *Racial Segregation and the Origins of Apartheid* (New York: St. Martin's, 1985). Rudolph Fisher, "City of Refuge," in *The New Negro,* ed. Alain Locke (New York: Albert and Charles Boni, 1925), 57–58. Stoddard, *Re-Forging America,* 260.

70. Cyril Briggs, "The Old Negro Goes: Let Him Go in Peace," in *Voices of a Black Nation: Political Journalism in the Harlem Renaissance,* ed. Theodore Vincent (Trenton: Africa World Press, 1973), 64. On the New Negro Movement generally, see Wilson Moses, *The Golden Age of Black Nationalism, 1850–1925* (1978; New York: Oxford University Press, 1988), 220–271; Winston James, *Holding Aloft the Banner of Ethiopia: Caribbean Radicalism in Early Twentieth Century America* (London: Verso, 1998).

71. The third work in the trilogy was *Clashing Tides of Color* (1936). Stoddard, "Butter-Side Down," unpublished autobiography, 106. On Stoddard's Upper East Side apartment and the writing of *Rising Tide of Color,* see ibid., 57, 62. My thanks to Ted Stoddard for sharing this work with me. For more on Stoddard, see Bachman, "Theodore Lothrop Stoddard"; "Lothrop Stoddard, 66, Author and Editorial Writer for Star, Dies," *Washington Star,* May 2, 1950, Morgue File: "Lothrop Stoddard," *Washington Star* Collection, Martin Luther King Jr. Memorial Library, Washington (hereafter *Star* Collection).

72. "Brain proletariat" is from Victor Clark, "The Rising Tide in Japan," *Atlantic Monthly* (March 1920): 397. For West Coast reaction to *Rising Tide of Color,* see Stern, "Nazi Spectroscope." Japan had been the sole "darker nation" at Versailles, and had acted as an anti-racist representative for African Americans and others, urging that the League of Nations adopt a human equality provision. See Paul Gordon Lauren, "White Supremacy at the Versailles Peace Conference: Woodrow Wilson and the Challenge from Japan," manuscript.

73. Stoddard to Maxwell Perkins, July 8, 1926, Charles Scribner's Sons Archives, Firestone Library, Princeton University (hereafter SA: "Stoddard"). Stoddard, "Butter-Side Down," 106.

74. Stoddard, *Re-Forging America,* 281, 305, 276–283. Grant to Earnest Sevier Cox, Dec. 2, 1920, ESCP. Stoddard had proposed a "fairly detailed study of the race-problem in South Africa" to his editor in 1921; see Stoddard to Maxwell Perkins, June 4, 1921, SA: "Stoddard."

75. Northcliffe cited in "An American You Should Know: Lothrop Stoddard Has Hobbies as Well as Works of Fame," *Washington Star,* Feb. 27, 1937, *Star* Collection. The deathbed testimony is taken from a magazine advertisement for

Stoddard's works by Charles Scribner's Sons, ca. 1923 and reportedly from *Time* magazine, given to me by Ted Stoddard.

76. Harding quoted in *New York Times*, Oct. 26, 1921. For reactions see "Rising Tide of Color Sets White World A-Trembling," *Crusader*, July 1920; "The Rising Wave," *Crusader*, June 1920; *Crusader*, Sept. 1920; "Christianity as Propaganda," *Crusader*, Oct. 1920; Emory Tolbert, "Outpost Garveyism and the UNIA Rank and File," *Journal of Black Studies* 5 (March 1975): 240–241; Hubert H. Harrison, *When Africa Awakes: The 'Inside Story' of the Stirrings and Strivings of the New Negro in the Western World* (1920; Chesapeake, Md.: ECA Associates, 1991), 76–83. "The Rising Tide of Color," *Chicago Defender*, July 2, 1927.

77. Jackson Lears, *Fables of Abundance: A Cultural History of Advertising in America* (New York: Basic Books, 1994), 219. David Nasaw, *Going Out: The Rise and Fall of Public Amusements* (New York: Basic Books, 1995); Jacobson, *Whiteness of a Different Color*. Warren I. Susman, *Culture as History: The Transformation of American Society in the Twentieth Century* (New York: Pantheon, 1984), xix–xxx.

78. Jackson Lears, "Beyond Veblen: Rethinking Consumer Culture in America," in *Consuming Visions: Accumulation and Display of Goods in America, 1880–1920*, ed. Simon Bronner (New York: Norton, 1989), 91–96.

79. Manuel Ugarte, *The Destiny of a Continent*, trans. Catherine A. Phillips (New York: Knopf, 1925), 139–140. Bram Dijkstra, *Evil Sisters: The Treat of Female Sexuality and the Cult of Manhood* (New York: Knopf, 1996), 248. "Contributor Takes Issue with Noted Interracial Agitator's Magazine Article," *Philadelphia Tribune*, Feb. 23, 1928.

80. See Michael Adas, *Machines as the Measure of Men: Science, Technology, and Ideologies of Western Dominance* (Ithaca: Cornell University Press, 1989), 199 265, 292–342, 402–418. Stoddard, *Rising Tide of Color*, 90–93. Jacqueline Jones, *American Work: Four Centuries of Black and White Labor* (New York: Norton, 1998), 301–336.

81. Teddy Roosevelt on Haiti, cited in Hunt, *Ideology and U.S. Foreign Policy*, 127; Hans Schmidt, *The United States Occupation of Haiti, 1915–1934* (New Brunswick: Rutgers University Press, 1971). See "Lady Dorothy Mills Loses Race Prejudice after Visit to Hayti: Natives Dance Mad," *New York World*, June 1, 1924; "Santo Domingo and Haiti," *New York Tribune*, Feb. 17, 1921; "Haitians Eat White Men for Courage," *New York Globe*, Jan. 4, 1921.

82. Songbook cover entitled "Jungle Ways," DeVincent Sheet Music Collection, Archives Center, National Museum of American History, Smithsonian Institution. A. Scott Berg, *Lindbergh* (New York: Putnam, 1998), 108, 193; John W. Ward, "The Meaning of Lindbergh's Flight," *American Quarterly* 10 (Spring 1958): 3–16. Ann Douglas, *Terrible Honesty: Mongrel Manhattan in the 1920s* (New York: Farrar, Straus, and Giroux, 1995), 434–461.

83. F. H. Henderson, *Rubber: Its Production and Marketing* (New York: Henderson, Helm, 1926), 17.

84. *What's What in Tires: Being a Reprint of a Series of Talks by H. S. Firestone, President, Firestone Tire and Rubber Company* (Akron, Oh., 1914). Walter LaFeber, *Inevitable Revolutions: The United States in Central America* (New York: Norton, 1993). "Cavernous blackness" is from Llewelyn Powys, *Black Laughter* (1924; New York: Blue Ribbon Books, 1930), 5. On investment in Liberia, see Arthur Knoll, "Firestone's Labor Policy," *Liberian Studies Journal* 16 (1991): 49–75.

85. Advertisement for "Jungle Ways," *Forum* 85 (April 1931): viii; Seabrook, *Jungle Ways* (New York: Harcourt, Brace, 1931).

86. Du Bois, *Darkwater: Voices from Within the Veil* (New York: Harcourt, Brace, 1920), 29–30.

87. See "The Firestone Building," in *Official Pictures in Color: A Century of Progress—1934* (Chicago, 1934), and *How Firestone Gum-Dipped Tires Are Made* (n.d.), both in Warshaw Collection of Business Americana, Archives Center, National Museum of American History, Smithsonian Institution.

88. N. W. Ayer Collection, Archives Center, National Museum of American History, Smithsonian Institution, Box 387, Book 641.

89. Stoddard, *Racial Realities in Europe* (New York: Scribner's, 1924), 230, 243. Du Bois to E. Pearl Bailey, Jan. 13, 1926, Du Bois Papers, University of Massachusetts, Amherst.

90. See correspondence and ephemera in ADSP.

91. Harrison, "The New Race Consciousness," in *When Africa Awakes,* 76.

92. Du Bois, *Dark Princess: A Romance* (New York: Harcourt, Brace, 1928), 7. See Robert A. Hill, "General Introduction," in *The Marcus Garvey and Universal Negro Improvement Association Papers,* ed. Hill (Berkeley: University of California Press, 1983—), vol. 1, lxx–lxxix; James, *Holding Aloft the Banner of Ethiopia,* 185–194. Harrison, *When Africa Awakes,* 76.

93. Grant, publicity comment on pamphlet promoting 2nd ed. of Earnest Sevier Cox's *White America,* SA: "Grant." Grant, *Passing of the Great Race,* 78. Grant to Maxwell Perkins, May 3, 1927, SA: "Grant." Stoddard, "The Pedigree of Judah," *Forum* 75 (March 1926): 320–333.

94. "The Major," *Hank,* 9, 51.

95. The phrase is from Alain Locke, "The Eleventh Hour of Nordicism," *Opportunity* (Jan. 1935): 9.

96. Mark Naison, *Communists in Harlem during the Depression* (Urbana: University of Illinois Press, 1983); Robin D. G. Kelley, *Hammer and Hoe: Alabama Communists during the Great Depression* (Chapel Hill: University of North Carolina Press, 1990).

97. Grant to Cox, June 1, 1932, ESCP. Grant, *The Conquest of a Continent; or, The Expansion of the Races in America* (New York: Scribner's, 1933), 281. Grant, "Closing the Floodgates," in *The Alien in Our Midst; or, "Selling Our Birthright for a Mess of Pottage,"* ed. Madison Grant and Charles Stewart Davison (New York: Galton, 1930), 23. Dike, "Aliens and Crime," in *The Alien in Our Midst,* 83. Grant and

Davison also coedited another volume in support of further immigration restriction: *The Founders of the Republic on Immigration Naturalization and Aliens* (New York: Scribner's, 1928).

98. "Negro Bandits Equip Selves for Jazz Band," *New York Tribune*, Jan. 4, 1920. Nancy Weiss, *Farewell to the Party of Lincoln: Black Politics in the Age of FDR* (Princeton: Princeton University Press, 1983), 3–32, 180–208. Gerald Meyer, *Vito Marcantonio: Radical Politician, 1902–1954* (Albany: State University of New York Press, 1989). Grant to Cox, June 24, 1930, ESCP.

99. Grant, *Conquest of a Continent*, 283. Locke, "Eleventh Hour of Nordicism," 9.

100. David Bennett, *The Party of Fear: The American Far Right from Nativism to the Militia Movement* (1988; New York: Vintage, 1995), 244.

101. Stefan Kühl, *The Nazi Connection: Eugenics, American Racism, and German National Socialism* (New York: Oxford University Press, 1994), esp. 50, 61, 73–64; Bachman, "Theodore Lothrop Stoddard," 274–283.

102. See Leon H. Whitney, unpublished autobiography, in Whitney Papers, American Philosophical Society, 205. Higham, *Strangers in the Land*, 327. Stern, "Nazi Spectroscope."

103. See Grant's obituary in the *New York Times*, May 31, 1937.

## 2. Bleeding the Irish White

1. Cyril Briggs, "The American Race Problem," *Crusader* (Sept. 1918): 12, in *The Crusader*, ed. Robert A. Hill (1918–1920; New York: Garland, 1987). Lothrop Stoddard, *The French Revolution in San Domingo* (New York, 1914), vi.

2. Du Bois, *Darkwater: Voices from Within the Veil* (New York, 1920), 29–30; Stoddard, *Re-Forging America* (New York: Scribner's, 1927); Harrison, "The New Race Consciousness," in *When Africa Awakes: The "Inside" Story of the Stirrings and Strivings of the New Negro in the Western World* (1920; Chesapeake, Md.: ECA Associates, 1991), 76.

3. *Gaelic American*, March 11, 1916.

4. A typescript of the declaration, dated Feb. 25, 1916, is in the Daniel F. Cohalan Papers, American Irish Historical Society, New York (hereafter DFCP); *New York Times*, Nov. 13, 1946; Charles Callan Tansill, *America and the Fight for Irish Freedom* (New York: Devin-Adair, 1957).

5. Thomas Brown, "The Origins and Character of Irish-American Nationalism," *Review of Politics* 18, no. 3 (July 1956): 333.

6. Kerby Miller, "Class, Culture, and Immigrant Group Identity in the United States: The Case of Irish-American Ethnicity," in *Immigration Reconsidered: History, Sociology, and Politics*, ed. Virginia Yans-McLaughlin (New York: Oxford University Press, 1990), 118. Miller, "Assimilation and Alienation: Irish Emigrants' Responses to Industrial America, 1871–1921," in *The Irish in America: Emigration, Assimilation, Impact*, ed. J. Drury (Cambridge: Cambridge University Press, 1985), 107.

7. *Gaelic American,* Feb. 19, 1916. Michael Donahoe to Joseph McLaughlin, Feb. 19, 1916, in Papers of Joseph McGarrity, Maloney Collection of Irish Historical Papers, New York Public Library (hereafter MCNYPL). McLaughlin quoted in Francis Carroll, *American Opinion and the Irish Question, 1910–1923* (Dublin: Gill and Macmillan, 1978), 52.

8. *Gaelic American,* Feb. 25, 1916; *New York Tribune,* March 4, 1916.

9. *Gaelic American,* March 11, 1916.

10. See L. Perry Curtis Jr., *Apes and Angels: The Irishman in Victorian Caricature* (1984; Washington: Smithsonian Institution Press, 1997); and John Higham, *Strangers in the Land: Patterns of American Nativism* (1955; New York: Atheneum, 1975); Gail Bederman, *Manliness and Civilization: A Cultural History of Gender and Race in the United States, 1880–1917* (Chicago: University of Chicago Press, 1995), intro.

11. The phrase is from the first Irish Race Convention's "Declaration of Principles," in John Devoy, *Recollections of an Irish Rebel* (1929; Shannon: Irish University Press, 1969), 452. On the role of race in Irish-American nationalism see Miller, *Emigrants and Exiles;* James P. Rodechko, *Patrick Ford and the Search for America* (New York: Arno, 1968), 256–273; Matthew Frye Jacobson, *Special Sorrows: The Diasporic Imagination of Irish, Polish, and Jewish Immigrants in the United States* (Cambridge, Mass.: Harvard University Press, 1995), 177–216.

12. Patrick Ford, trained as a printer under William Lloyd Garrison, was an outspoken Gilded Age nationalist advocate of the African-American cause, as was John Boyle O'Reilly, editor of the *Boston Pilot.* See Rodechko, *Patrick Ford;* Mark R. Schneider, *Boston Confronts Jim Crow, 1890–1920* (Boston: Northeastern University Press, 1997), 160–169.

13. Eric Lott, *Love and Theft: Blackface Minstrelsy and the American Working Class* (New York: Oxford University Press, 1993); David Roediger, *The Wages of Whiteness: Race and the Making of the American Working Class* (London: Verso, 1991). Iver Bernstein, *The New York Draft Riots: Their Significance for American Society and Politics in the Age of the Civil War* (New York: Oxford University Press, 1990); Gilbert Osofsky, *Harlem: The Making of a Ghetto* (New York: Harper and Row, 1963), 46–50. Matthew Frye Jacobson, *Whiteness of a Different Color: European Immigrants and the Alchemy of Race* (Cambridge, Mass.: Harvard University Press, 1998).

14. Douglas Hyde, "The Necessity for De-Anglicising Ireland," in *The Revival of Irish Literature* (1892; New York: Lemma, 1973). Lady Isabella Augusta Gregory, *Our Irish Theatre: A Chapter of Autobiography* (New York, 1913), 9. Stephen Gwynn, "The Gaelic League and the Irish Theatre," in *To-day and To-morrow in Ireland: Essays on Irish Subjects* (Dublin, 1903), 26. On the "growth of national consciousness," see F. S. L. Lyons, *Ireland since the Famine* (London: Fontana, 1973), 224–259.

15. Pearse quoted in Ruth Dudley Edwards, *Patrick Pearse: The Triumph of Failure*

(London: Faber, 1979), 22; Yeats in James Kilroy, *The "Playboy" Riots* (Dublin: Dolmen, 1979), 83. See C. L. Innes, *Woman and Nation in Irish Literature and Society, 1880–1935* (Athens: University of Georgia Press, 1993), esp. 43–62; Patrick McDevitt, "Muscular Catholicism: Nationalism, Masculinity, and Gaelic Team Sports, 1884–1916," *Gender and History* 9, no. 2 (Aug. 1997): 262–284. Edward Said, *Culture and Imperialism* (New York: Vintage, 1993), 224.

16. Padraic Pearse to John Devoy, 12 Aug. 1914, DFCP. Open letter, marked "dictated by Joseph McGarrity," June 4, 1914, MCNYPL. San Francisco *Leader*, rpt. in *Gaelic American*, Feb. 25, 1916.

17. Devoy to McGarrity, June 10, 1914, and Devoy to McGarrity, June 14, 1914, MCNYPL. Joseph Lee, *Ireland, 1912–1985: Politics and Society* (New York: Cambridge University Press, 1989), 20–21. Ford in *Irish World*, Oct. 17, 1914. For proof of a close German-Irish relationship, see Daniel Cohalan to McGarrity, Oct. 21, 1914, McGarrity, "Memos on the IRB trouble in Ireland," and McGarrity, "German Connections regarding Military help for Ireland," all in the Joseph McGarrity Collection, National Library of Ireland (hereafter JMCNLI).

18. *Gaelic American*, Feb. 12, 1916. *Irish World*, Oct. 17, 1914; *Irish World*, Oct. 3, 1914. Shaw in *The World*, Jan. 12, 1912.

19. Kathleen Donovan, "Good Old Pat: An Irish-American Stereotype in Decline," *Eire-Ireland* 15, no. 3 (Fall 1980): 6–14; John J. Appel, "From Shanties to Lace Curtains: The Irish Image in *Puck*, 1876–1910," *Comparative Studies in Society and History* 13, no. 4 (Dec. 1971): 365–375; Joel Perlmann, *Ethnic Differences: Schooling and Social Structure among the Irish, Italians, Jews, and Blacks in an American City, 1880 1935* (New York: Cambridge University Press, 1988). Michael Paul Rogin, "'The Sword Became a Flashing Vision': D. W. Griffith's Birth of a Nation," in *Ronald Reagan, the Movie, and Other Episodes in Political Demonology* (Berkeley: University of California Press, 1987).

20. See Higham, *Strangers in the Land*, 194–254; Stephen Vaughn, *Holding Fast the Inner Lines: Democracy, Nationalism, and the Committee on Public Information* (Chapel Hill: University of North Carolina Press, 1980); Joan M. Jensen, *The Price of Vigilance* (Chicago: Rand McNally, 1968).

21. On the Von Igel affair, see Alan J. Ward, *Ireland and Anglo-American Relations, 1899–1921* (London: Weidenfeld and Nicolson, 1969), 129–130; "German Interest in Irish Matters," Records of the Office of the Counselor (RG 59), National Archives, File 137, Box 8, Location 250/45/34/01. On Irish-American reaction to repression, see, e.g., McGarrity's memo (dated June 11, 1912, JMCNLI) after a "spy" has been discovered in the Philadelphia branch of the Clan: "Here was the first designate proof I had ever seen of the active spy system of the British with regard to the Clan na Gael; I was aroused to the great pitch of excitement, here was real proof of the importance of our Organization and of its danger to the Great British Empire."

22. Devoy to McGarrity, May 19, 1915, MCNYPL.

23. Open letter marked "Dear Sir and Brother," signed by Devoy, Dec. 29, 1915, MCNYPL.

24. Hughes in "The Irish Crisis," clipping from the *Montreal Star,* in William Bourke Cockran Papers, Rare Books and Manuscripts Division, New York Public Library. See Kathy Peiss, *Cheap Amusements: Working Women and Leisure in Turn-of-the-Century New York* (Philadelphia: Temple University Press, 1986), 61; *Irish-American Voluntary Organizations,* ed. Michael Funchion (Westport, Conn.: Greenwood, 1983), 119–126.

25. See the Call, printed in the *Gaelic American,* Feb. 12, 1916.

26. Kallen, "Democracy versus the Melting Pot," in *Culture and Democracy in the United States* (1915; New York: Boni and Liveright, 1924), 124.

27. Address of Rev. John Cavanaugh at the American Irish Historical Society, "Dr. Thomas Addis Emmet, an Ideal Hyphenated American," rpt. in *The Irish World,* Jan. 15, 1916. Cohalan, fragment, in DFCP. Speech to the League of Foreign Born Citizens, Jan. 24, 1917, DFCP. Randolph Bourne, "Transnational America," in *The Radical Will: Randolph Bourne, Selected Writings, 1911–1918,* ed. Olaf Hansen (New York: Urizen, 1977), 263.

28. See the speeches of the convention in *Gaelic American,* March 11, 1916; "Columbus and Ireland," *Irish World,* Oct. 12, 1918; "Elihu Root versus George Washington," *Irish World,* Feb. 26, 1916; Patrick Ford, *The Criminal History of the British Empire* (1881; New York, 1915); Thomas Mahoney, *Similarities between the American and Irish Revolutions* (New York: Friendly Sons of St. Patrick, 1921); "The Irish Element in Thanksgiving," *Irish World,* Nov. 29, 1919; "Dread Secrets Hid in Muster of 1778," *Philadelphia Ledger,* Nov. 6, 1911.

29. Humphrey J. Desmond, *Why God Loves the Irish* (New York, 1918), 107.

30. *Irish World,* May 20, 1916. Cohalan, speech delivered at Carnegie Hall, 24 Jan. 1917, DFCP.

31. William Thompson, *The Imagination of an Insurrection* (New York: Oxford University Press, 1967); Donal McCartney, "The Gaelic Ideological Origins of 1916," in *1916: The Easter Rising,* ed. Owen Dudley Edwards and Fergus Pyle (London: MacGibbon and Kee, 1968), 44–45.

32. Kelly in *Irish World,* May 13, 1916. Devoy, *Recollections of an Irish Rebel,* 480.

33. *Irish World,* June 17, 1916. Devoy to McGarrity, April 22, 1917, JMCNLI. See Lyons, *Ireland since the Famine,* 381–395.

34. Letters rpt. in Tansill, *America and the Fight for Irish Freedom,* 446–449; FOIF circular dated June 21, 1920, JMCNLI. "Though he paid lip service to it, De Valera never seemed to fully appreciate the notion that Irish-Americans such as Devoy and Cohalan were American citizens." Terry Golway, *Irish Rebel: John Devoy and America's Fight for Ireland's Freedom* (New York: St. Martin's, 1999), 264. Golway details the complete breakup of the "unity" of the Irish; ibid., 255–283.

35. *Irish World*, Aug. 16, 1919; "India, Egypt, and Ireland," *Irish World*, May 31, 1919; "Shall Might or Right Prevail in Egypt," *Gaelic American*, Jan. 17, 1920; "The Outlook for India," *Gaelic American*, July 31, 1920.

36. Untitled fragment, DFCP; FOIF circular written by Dairmuid Lynch, National Secretary, JMCNLI; and see "Voicing Aspirations of the Irish Race," *Irish World*, Feb. 22, 1919.

37. "Report of a Madison Square Garden Meeting," in *The Marcus Garvey and Universal Negro Improvement Association Papers*, ed. Robert A. Hill (Berkeley: University of California Press, 1983— ) (hereafter MGP), vol. 2, 499; *New York Times*, Aug. 3, 1920. The original telegram can be found in the De Valera Papers, Franciscan Archives, Killiney, Co. Dublin, Ireland. My thanks to Mike Lynch for this information.

38. *New York Times*, Aug. 28, 1920; *Sun and New York Herald*, Sept. 3, 1920.

39. *New York Times*, Aug. 28, 1920; *Sun and New York Herald*, Sept. 3, 1920; *Evening Post*, Sept. 3, 1920. Joe Doyle, "Striking for Ireland on the New York Docks," in *The New York Irish*, ed. Ronald Bayor and Timothy Meagher (Baltimore: Johns Hopkins University Press, 1996), 367. "Report by Special Agent P-138," MGP, vol. 2, 12–13. "Report of the Convention, 31 August 1920," MGP, vol. 2, 649.

40. Thomas C. Holt, *The Problem of Freedom: Race, Labor, and Politics in Jamaica and Britain, 1832–1938* (Baltimore: Johns Hopkins University Press, 1992), 346–379. On Dusé Mohamed Ali, see Immanuel Geiss, *The Pan-African Movement: A History of Pan-Africanism in America, Europe, and Africa*, trans. Ann Keep (New York: Africana, 1974), 221–232. On the ITGWU strike, Emmet O'Connor, *A Labour History of Ireland, 1824–1960* (Dublin: Gill and Macmillan, 1992), 83–87. On Garvey, Tony Martin, *Race First: The Ideological and Organization Struggles of Marcus Garvey and the Universal Negro Improvement Association* (Dover: Majority Press, 1976).

41. See Robert A. Hill, "Introduction—Racial and Radical: Cyril V. Briggs, *The Crusader* Magazine and the African Blood Brotherhood," in *The Crusader*, ed. Hill, vol. 1, xx–xxiv. "Interview with Marcus Garvey by Charles Mowbray White, Aug. 18, 1920," MGP, vol. 2, 603; "Report by Special Agent P-138, Jan. 4, 1921," MGP, vol. 3, 125. Robert A. Hill, "General Introduction," MGP, vol. 1, lxviii–lxxvii; Judith Stein, *The World of Marcus Garvey: Race and Class in Modern Society* (Baton Rouge: Louisiana State University Press, 1986), 53n39.

42. Harrison, *When Africa Awakes*, 9. Also see "New Viewpoints of the American Negro," *The Toiler*, July 9, 1921; Barbara Bair, "True Women, Real Men: Gender, Ideology, and Social Roles in the Garvey Movement," in *Gendered Domains: Rethinking Public and Private in Women's History*, ed. Susan M. Reverby and Dorothy O. Helly (Ithaca: Cornell University Press, 1992), 154–166; Martin Summers, "Nationalism, Race-Consciousness, and the Construction of Black Middle-Class Manhood during the New Negro Era, 1915–1930" (Ph.D. diss., Rutgers University,

1996); Michele Mitchell, "Adjusting the Race: Gender, Sexuality, and the Question of African-American Destiny, 1877–1930" (Ph.D. diss., Northwestern University, 1997).

43. "Dedication of UNIA Liberty Hall," MGP, vol. 1, 472. "The Resurrection," *Crusader* (April 1920): 8; also see *Crusader* (Oct. 1919): 10; "Ireland," *Crisis* (Aug. 1916): 166–167.

44. Bederman, *Manliness and Civilization.* Summers, "Nationalism," 75–227.

45. "Fighting the Savage Hun and Treacherous Cracker," *Crusader* (April 1919): 6; political cartoon, *The Messenger* (Sept. 1919): 16; David Levering Lewis, *When Harlem Was in Vogue* (New York: Knopf, 1981), 13; "Returning Soldiers," *Crisis* (May 1919): 14. "Race Riots," *World's Work* (Sept. 1919): 463.

46. Kevin K. Gaines, *Uplifting the Race: Black Leadership, Politics, and Culture in the Twentieth Century* (Chapel Hill: University of North Carolina Press, 1996); Wilson Jeremiah Moses, *The Golden Age of Black Nationalism, 1850–1925* (1978; New York: Oxford University Press, 1988), 156–179; Mitchell, "Adjusting the Race." Epigraph, "Overseas Correspondence," *Crusader* (April 1920).

47. "'Stage Irishwoman' Is Speedily Suppressed," *Gaelic American,* Dec. 6, 1919.

48. See, e.g., the article about African-American John Taylor and the Irish American Athletic Club, "Taylor, Irish A.A.C.," *Colored American Magazine* (Oct. 1907): 250. The second New Negro Movement—the one which we now call the Harlem Renaissance—drew its own powerful connections between Ireland and Harlem. Alain Locke, the short, misogynistic Howard University professor, struck up a correspondence with the Irish playwright Padraic Colum, who had moved to New York in 1915 and secured a teaching position at Columbia. Later Locke would introduce the young poet Countee Cullen to Colum, and Cullen would send the Irish expatriate his poetry from time to time. Claude McKay, James Weldon Johnson, Locke, Du Bois, Willis Richardson, Cullen, and others expressed great admiration for the so-called Irish Renaissance (especially the folk artist J. M. Synge), and drew from that admiration the desire for a "Negro Theatre." See Alain Leroy Locke [misspelled "Loche"] to Padraic Colum, Sept. 7, 1917, and "Countee Cullen, poem sent to Padraic Colum," [n.d.], both in Padraic Colum Papers, Berg Collection, New York Public Library; Colum to Cullen, March 20, 1930, Countee Cullen Papers, Amistad Research Center, Tulane University.

49. See "India's Freedom in American Courts" (1919) and "Back to the Hangman" (1919) in Friends of Freedom for India Vertical File, Tamament Library, New York University. Naeem Gul Rathore, "Indian Nationalist Agitation in the United States: A Study of Lala Lajpat Rai and the India Home Rule League of America, 1914–1920" (Ph.D. diss., Columbia University, 1965), 5, 9, 69, 75, 277; Scott Cook, "The Example of Ireland: Political and Administrative Aspects of the Imperial Relationship with British India, 1855–1922" (Ph.D. diss., Rutgers University, 1987), 427–502.

50. See, e.g., "German Interest in Irish Matters," National Archives, RG 59; "The

Hindu Conspiracy, the Ghadar Society, and Indian Revolutionary Propaganda," Records of the War Department, National Archives, RG 165, File 10560–152; Joan M. Jensen, "The 'Hindu Conspiracy': A Reassessment," *Pacific Historical Review* 46 (1979): 65–81; Tansill, *America and the Fight for Irish Freedom*, 233–240; Emory Tolbert, "Federal Surveillance of Marcus Garvey and the U.N.I.A.," *Journal of Ethnic Studies* 14, no. 4 (Winter 1987): 25–46.

51. On June 14, 1919, Lt. Edward Tinker wrote to the Office of the Naval Inspector of Ordinance: "Many signs point to the fact that all these negro associations are joining hands with the Irish Sinn Feiners, Hindu, Egyptians, Japanese and Mexicans." See "Enclosure," MGP, vol. 1, 433.

52. Ann Douglas, *Terrible Honesty: Mongrel Manhattan in the 1920s* (New York: Farrar, Straus, Giroux, 1995); Henry F. May, *The End of American Innocence: A Study of the First Years of Our Own Time* (New York: Knopf, 1959); Nathan Irvin Huggins, *Harlem Renaissance* (New York: Oxford University Press, 1971).

53. Stoddard, *The Rising Tide of Color against White World Supremacy* (New York, 1920), 309; Cook, "The Example of Ireland," 358, 313–426; Lewis, *Marcus Garvey*, 99–177; Barbara N. Ramusack, "Cultural Missionaries, Maternal Imperialists, Feminist Allies: British Women Activists in India, 1865–1945," in *Western Women and Imperialism: Complicity and Resistance*, ed. Nuper Chaudhuri and Margaret Strobel (Bloomington: Indiana University Press, 1992), 119–136.

54. Du Bois to D. J. Bustin, March 30, 1921, W. E. B. Du Bois Papers, University of Massachusetts Library, Amherst. Alan H. Spear, *Black Chicago: The Making of a Negro Ghetto, 1890–1920* (Chicago: University of Chicago Press, 1967), 201–222; William Tuttle, *Race Riot: Chicago in the Red Summer of 1919* (New York: Atheneum, 1972), 32, 49, 167.

55. "Reports of the Convention," Aug. 15, 1920, MGP, vol. 2, 587–588. "Race First," *Crusader* (March 1920): 8.

56. In *The Messenger* (Sept. 1920).

57. See Jacobson, *Special Sorrows*, 5–6; Michael Hopkinson, *Green against Green: The Irish Civil War* (Dublin: Gill and Macmillan, 1988), esp. 47–51.

58. See Kenneth T. Jackson, *The Ku Klux Klan in the City* (New York: Oxford University Press, 1967), 182.

59. "Our Lone Monopoly," *Crusader* (Oct. 1920): 11.

## 3. Against the White Leviathan

1. Du Bois, "The Conservation of the Races," in *W. E. B. Du Bois: A Reader*, ed. David Levering Lewis (New York: Henry Holt, 1995), 25, 26, 22. For examples of Kallen's and Royce's pluralism, see Kallen, "Democracy versus the Melting Pot," in *Culture and Democracy in the United States* (1915; New York: Boni and Liveright, 1924); Royce, "On Provincialism," in *Race Questions and Other Problems* (New York, 1899).

2. David Levering Lewis, *W. E. B. Du Bois: Biography of a Race, 1868–1919* (New York: Henry Holt, 1993), 160.

3. Du Bois, "Conservation," 21–22. Wilson Jeremiah Moses, *The Golden Age of Black Nationalism, 1850–1925* (Hamden, Conn.: Archon, 1978), 135; Anthony Appiah, "The Uncompleted Argument: Du Bois and the Illusion of Race," in *Race, Writing, and Difference,* ed. Henry Louis Gates Jr. (Chicago: University of Chicago Press, 1986), 23–29.

4. Du Bois, *Dusk of Dawn* (1940; New Brunswick: Transaction Publishers, 1995), 10, 14. Lewis, *W. E. B. Du Bois,* 146. Du Bois, *The Philadelphia Negro: A Social Study* (1899; Philadelphia: University of Pennsylvania Press, 1996).

5. See, e.g., Thomas Nelson Page, *The Negro: The Southerner's Problem* (1904; New York: Johnson Reprint, 1970); Charles Carroll, *"The Negro a Beast," or "In the Image of God"* (St. Louis, 1900). On the raising of social barriers, see C. Vann Woodward, *Origins of the New South, 1877–1916* (Baton Rouge: Louisiana State University Press, 1951); Joel Williamson, *A Rage for Order: Black-White Relations in the American South since Emancipation* (New York: Oxford University Press, 1984).

6. See Thomas Dixon, *The Clansman* (New York, 1906). For song lyrics, see "I Want to Go Back to Birmingham," "When I Hear a Gun, I'm Going to Run Back Home to Tennessee," and "I'm Going Back to Kentucky Where I Was Born," DeVincent Sheet Music Collection, Archives Center, National Museum of American History, Smithsonian Institution.

7. Crummell, "The Attitude of the American Mind toward Negro Intellect," in *Civilization and Black Progress: Selected Writings of Alexander Crummell of the South,* ed. J. R. Oldfield (Charlottesville: University Press of Virginia, 1995), 209. See Louis R. Harlan, *Booker T. Washington: The Making of a Black Leader, 1856–1901* (New York: Oxford University Press, 1972); Harlan, *Booker T. Washington: The Wizard of Tuskegee* (New York: Oxford University Press, 1983).

8. See Wilson J. Moses, "W. E. B. Du Bois's 'The Conservation of the Races' and Its Context: Idealism, Conservatism and Hero Worship," *Massachusetts Review* 34 (Summer 1993): 275–294; Wilson Jeremiah Moses, *Alexander Crummell: A Study in Civilization and Discontent* (New York: Oxford University Press, 1989), 208–221; Lewis, *W. E. B. Du Bois,* 173. William Ferris, *The African Abroad; or, His Evolution in Western Civilization Tracing His Development under Caucasian Milieu* (New Haven, 1913).

9. Lewis, *W. E. B. Du Bois,* 278.

10. See Moses, *Golden Age,* 136.

11. Lewis, *W. E. B. Du Bois,* 248. Du Bois, "To the Nations of the World," in *Writings by W. E. B. Du Bois in Non-Periodical Literature,* ed. Herbert Aptheker (Millwood, N.Y.: Kraus-Thomson, 1982), 11.

12. Du Bois, *Souls of Black Folk* (1903; New York: Bantam, 1989), 10.

13. See Harlan, *Wizard of Tuskegee,* 247–253; August Meier, *Negro Thought in Amer-*

*ica, 1880–1915: Racial Ideologies in the Age of Booker T. Washington* (1955; Ann Arbor: University of Michigan Press, 1966), 112–114.

14. Booker T. Washington, *Up from Slavery,* in *Three Negro Classics,* ed. John Hope Franklin (1899; New York: Avon, 1965), 148, 147.

15. Moses, *Golden Age,* 98. Harlan, *Making of a Black Leader,* 210, 220.

16. Lewis, *W. E. B. Du Bois,* 230–231.

17. Du Bois to Oswald Garrison Villard, March 24, 1905, in *The Correspondence of W. E. B. Du Bois,* 3 vols., ed. Herbert Aptheker (Amherst: University of Massachusetts Press, 1973), vol. 1, 102; Lewis, *W. E. B. Du Bois,* 233–237, 275, 238–296.

18. The phrase is from J. Douglas Wetmore to Du Bois, Oct. 20, 1903, in *Correspondence,* vol. 1, 60.

19. See Obherholtzer to Du Bois, Jan. 25, 1904, and Feb. 16, 1904, in *Correspondence,* vol. 1, 63, 65; Herbert Aptheker, *The Literary Legacy of W. E. B. Du Bois* (White Plains, N.Y.: Kraus International, 1989), 87 93; Lewis, *W. E. B. Du Bois,* 357–362.

20. Du Bois, *John Brown: A Biography* (1909; London: M. E. Sharpe, 1997), 193, 194. Du Bois, "The Color Line Belts the World," in *Writings by W. E. B. Du Bois in Periodicals Edited by Others,* 4 vols., ed. Herbert Aptheker (Millwood, N.Y.: Kraus-Thomson, 1982), vol. 1, 330.

21. To I. M. Rubinow, Du Bois wrote on Nov. 17, 1904: "While I would scarcely describe myself as a socialist still I have much sympathy with the movement and I have many socialist beliefs." *Correspondence,* vol. 1, 81.

22. "The Significance of History," in *Frontier and Section: Selected Essays by Frederick Jackson Turner,* ed. Ray A. Billington (Englewood Cliffs, N.J.: Prentice-Hall, 1961), 17.

23. Du Bois, *Black Folk: Then and Now* (1939; Millwood, N.Y.: Kraus-Thomson, 1975), vii; Franz Boas, "Commencement Address at Atlanta University," *Atlanta University Leaflet #19,* May 31, 1906, partly rpt. in *The Health and Physique of the Negro American: Report of a Social Study Made under the Direction of Atlanta University,* ed. W. E. B. Du Bois (Atlanta, 1906), 19.

24. Baker, *From Savage to Negro: Anthropology and the Construction of Race, 1896–1954* (Berkeley: University of California Press, 1998), 125. Boas, cited in *Health and Physique,* 19. Michael Adas, *Machines as the Measure of Men: Science, Technology, and Ideologies of Western Dominance* (Ithaca: Cornell University Press, 1989).

25. Du Bois, *Dusk of Dawn,* 67. Du Bois, "The Souls of White Folk," in *Writings in Periodicals Edited by Others,* vol. 2, 25; Lewis, *W. E. B. Du Bois,* 469.

26. Du Bois, "A Litany of Atlanta," in *Du Bois: A Reader,* 443; Lewis, *W. E. B. Du Bois,* 387.

27. Du Bois, *Dusk of Dawn,* 94. Du Bois, *The Autobiography of W. E. B. Du Bois: A Soliloquy on Viewing My Life from the Last Decade of Its First Century* (1968; New York: International Publishers, 1991), 254. See Charles Flint Kellogg, *NAACP: A History of the National Association for the Advancement of Colored People* (Baltimore: Johns Hopkins University Press, 1967), 3–88; James M. McPherson, *The*

　　*Abolitionist Legacy: From Reconstruction to the NAACP* (Princeton: Princeton University Press, 1975), 368–393; Lewis, *W. E. B. Du Bois,* 386–407.

28. Du Bois, *Autobiography,* 259.

29. "South Africa," *Crisis* 6 (Sept. 1913): 231; "The World Problem of the Color Line," *Crisis* 7 (March 1914): 233. See, e.g., "The African Situation," *Crisis* 3 (Nov. 1911): 13–14; "The Cuban Revolution," *Crisis* 4 (Oct. 1912): 300–302; "The Saddest of Rebellions," *Crisis* 4 (July 1911): 124; "Self Righteous Europe and the World," *Crisis* 4 (May 1912): 34–37.

30. Gardiner, "Golden Fleece," cited in Aptheker, *Literary Legacy,* 113; Aptheker, editorial comment, in *Correspondence,* vol. 1, 128; Aptheker, *Literary Legacy,* 110; Lewis, *W. E. B. Du Bois,* 445, 447.

31. Du Bois, *The Quest of the Silver Fleece* (1911; Boston: Northeastern University Press, 1989), 266.

32. Lewis, *W. E. B. Du Bois,* 439.

33. Du Bois, "The First Universal Races Congress," in *Du Bois: A Reader,* 44. Du Bois, "The Races Congress," in *Selections from The Crisis,* 2 vols., ed. Herbert Aptheker (Millwood, N.Y.: Kraus-Thomson, 1983), vol. 1, 18, 26. Lewis, *W. E. B. Du Bois,* 439; Mary White Ovington, *The Walls Came Tumbling Down* (1947; New York: Feminist Press, 1997), 132.

34. Paul Rich, "'The Baptism of a New Era': The 1911 Universal Races Congress and the Liberal Ideology of Race," *Ethnic and Racial Studies* 7, no. 4 (Oct. 1984): 534. Elliot Rudwick, "W. E. B. Du Bois and the Universal Races Congress of 1911," *Phylon* (Winter 1959): 372–378. Lewis, *W. E. B. Du Bois,* 439–444. For evidence of later enthusiasm for the Races Congress, see Du Bois, *Dusk of Dawn,* 229–231; Du Bois, *Autobiography,* 258.

35. Du Bois, "World War and the Color Line," *Crisis* 9 (Nov. 1914): 28. Du Bois, "The African Roots of the War," in *Du Bois: A Reader,* 650.

36. Du Bois, *Black Reconstruction in America, 1860–1880* (1935; New York: Atheneum, 1992), 728.

37. E. T. H. Shaffer, "A New South—the Negro Migration," *Atlantic Monthly* (Sept. 1923): 403. Du Bois, "Migration," *Crisis* 12 (Oct. 1916): 270.

38. Du Bois, "The Passing of 'Jim Crow,'" in *Writings in Periodicals Edited by Others,* vol. 2, 107. See Robert Higgs, *Competition and Coercion: Blacks in the American Economy* (Cambridge, Mass.: Harvard University Press, 1977); Florette Henri, *Black Migration: Movement North, 1900–1920* (New York: Anchor, 1975), 49–53.

39. Du Bois, "Of Work and Wealth," in *Darkwater: Voices from Within the Veil* (1920; New York: Schocken, 1969), 89; Darlene Clark Hine, "Black Migration to the Urban Midwest: The Gender Dimension, 1915–1945," in *The Great Migration in Historical Perspective: New Dimensions of Race, Class, and Gender,* ed. Joe William Trotter (Bloomington: Indiana University Press, 1991), 127–146; Irma Watkins-Owens, *Blood Relations: Caribbean Immigrants in the Harlem Community* (Bloomington: Indiana University Press, 1996).

40. Meier, *Negro Thought in America*, 274–276; David Levering Lewis, *When Harlem Was in Vogue* (New York: Knopf, 1981), 20–23; Theodore Kornweibel Jr., "Apathy and Dissent: Black America's Negative Responses to World War I," *South Atlantic Quarterly* 80, no. 3 (Summer 1981): 322–338.

41. Grant, *The Conquest of a Continent* (New York: Scribner's, 1933), 353.

42. Lee E. Williams and Lee E. Williams II, *Anatomy of Four Race Riots: Racial Conflict in Knoxville, Elaine, Tulsa, and Chicago, 1919–1921* (Jackson: University and College Press of Mississippi, 1972), 21–37, 56–73; Alan H. Spear, *Black Chicago: The Making of a Negro Ghetto, 1890–1920* (Chicago: University of Chicago Press, 1967), 201–222; William M. Tuttle Jr., *Race Riot: Chicago in the Red Summer of 1919* (New York: Atheneum, 1970); Constance McLaughlin Green, *The Secret City: A History of Race Relations in the Nation's Capital* (Princeton: Princeton University Press, 1967), 191–192; St. Clair Drake and Horace Cayton, *Black Metropolis: A Study of Negro Life in a Northern City* (1945; Chicago: University of Chicago Press, 1993), 64, 58–76; Theodore Kornweibel, *Seeing Red: Federal Campaigns against Black Militancy, 1919–1925* (Bloomington: Indiana University Press, 1998); Robert A. Hill, "'The Foremost Radical among His Race': Marcus Garvey and the Black Scare," *Prologue* 16, no. 4 (Winter 1984): 215–231.

43. Du Bois, "A Plan for the Southern Migrant," *Crisis* (Sept. 1917): 217. Du Bois, "Of Work and Wealth," 93.

44. Letter rpt. in Du Bois and Martha Gruening, "The Massacre at East St. Louis," *Crisis* (Sept. 1917): 221; Du Bois, "Of Work and Wealth," 93. See Elliot Rudwick, *Race Riot in East St. Louis, July 2, 1917* (New York: Atheneum, 1972); Henri, *Black Migration*, 265–267; Lewis, *W. E. B. Du Bois*, 536–542.

45. Du Bois and Gruening, "Massacre of East St. Louis," 220; Du Bois, "Of Work and Wealth," 95; Lewis, *W. E. B. Du Bois*, 540.

46. *Bee* Clipping and NAACP Bulletin, July 24, 1917, in National Association for the Advancement of Colored People Papers, Manuscript Division, Library of Congress (hereafter NAACP).

47. Allan Spear, "The Origins of the Urban Ghetto, 1870–1915," in *Key Issues in the Afro-American Experience*, ed. Nathan Huggins, Martin Kilson, and Daniel M. Fox (New York: Harcourt, Brace, 1971), 157–166; James R. Grossman, "The White Man's Union: The Great Migration and the Resonance of Race and Class in Chicago, 1916–1922," in *Great Migration in Historical Perspective*, ed. Trotter, 83–105; Gilbert Osofsky, *Harlem: The Making of a Ghetto: Negro New York, 1890–1930* (New York: Harper and Row, 1963), 105–123.

48. Du Bois, "World War and the Color Line," 28–30; Adam Lively, "Continuity and Radicalism in American Black Nationalist Thought, 1914–1929," *Journal of American Studies* 18 (1984): 221–222; Du Bois, "Close Ranks," in *Du Bois: A Reader*, 697.

49. Gunner to Du Bois, July 25, 1918, Du Bois to Gunner, Aug. 10, 1918, and Du Bois to L. M. Hershaw, Aug. 5, 1918, in *Correspondence*, vol. 1, 228–229.

50. Mark Ellis, "'Closing Ranks' and 'Seeking Honors': W. E. B. Du Bois in World War I," *Journal of American History* 79, no. 1 (June 1992): 96–124; Lewis, *W. E. B. Du Bois,* 551–560.

51. Du Bois, *Darkwater,* 29–30. Eric Sundquist, *To Wake the Nations: Race in the Making of American Literature* (Cambridge, Mass.: Harvard University Press, 1993), 545, 591, 540–625.

52. Du Bois, *Darkwater,* 41, 49. Moses, *Golden Age,* 220–271; Arthur Herman, *The Idea of Decline in Western History* (New York: Free Press, 1997), 187–220. George Luther Cady, *Race Values and Race Destinies* (New York: American Missionary Association, n.d.), 11.

53. Du Bois to Gertrude E. Winslow, March 22, 1922, W. E. B. Du Bois Papers, University of Massachusetts Library, University of Massachusetts, Amherst (hereafter Du Bois Papers).

54. Lothrop Stoddard, *The Rising Tide of Color against White World Supremacy* (New York: Scribner's, 1921), 11; Aptheker, *Literary Legacy,* 143–149, 157–163; Kornweibel, *Seeing Red;* "Darkwater," *Crusader* (Nov. 1920): 15, 19, in *The Crusader,* ed. Robert A. Hill (New York: Garland, 1987). Eric Walrond, "The New Negro Faces America," *Current History* (Feb. 1923): 787.

55. Judith Stein, "Defining the Race, 1890–1930," in *The Invention of Ethnicity,* ed. Werner Sollars (New York: Oxford University Press, 1989), 103; Moses, *Golden Age,* 249. Abram Harris, "Negro Migration to the North," *Current History* (Sept. 1924): 925.

56. John M. Barry, *Rising Tide: The Great Mississippi Flood of 1927 and How It Changed America* (New York: Simon and Schuster, 1997), 412–422. Lothrop Stoddard, *Re-Forging America: The Story of Our Nationhood* (New York: Scribner's, 1927).

57. Garvey, Address in New York, Nov. 12, 1921, in *The Marcus Garvey and Universal Negro Improvement Association Papers,* 10 vols., ed. Robert A. Hill (Berkeley: University of California Press, 1983–1999) (hereafter MGP), vol. 4, 180; Garvey, Address in Washington, July 4, 1920, MGP, vol. 2, 456–457.

58. Du Bois, *Darkwater,* 9. Marcus Garvey, "Purity of Race," in *Philosophy and Opinions,* 2 vols., ed. Amy Jacques-Garvey (1923, 1925; New York: Atheneum, 1992), vol. 2, 37.

59. Joel Williamson, *New People: Miscegenation and Mulattoes in the United States* (Baton Rouge: Louisiana State University Press, 1995); Lawrence Otis Graham, *Our Kind of People: Inside America's Black Upper Class* (New York: HarperCollins, 1999). Caroline Bond Day listed Du Bois's family tree as a perfect example of a finely evolved people in *A Study of Some Negro-White Families in the United States* (Cambridge, Mass.: Peabody Museum of Harvard University, 1932).

60. Claude McKay, "A Negro Extravaganza" (1921), in Nathan Huggins, ed., *Voices of the Harlem Renaissance* (1976; New York: Oxford University Press, 1995), 134. Wallace Thurman, *The Blacker the Berry* (1929; New York: Scribner's, 1996), 143–144.

61. Garvey, "W. E. B. Du Bois as a Hater of Dark People," in *Philosophy and Opinions*, vol. 2, 310, 312. Wheeler Sheppard, *Mistakes of W. E. B. Du Bois, Being an Answer to Dr. W. E. B. Du Bois' Attack upon the Honorable Marcus Garvey* (n.d.: n.p.), 19.

62. Du Bois, "A Lunatic or a Traitor," in *Du Bois: A Reader*, 342. Du Bois, "Back to Africa," *Century Magazine* 105 (Feb. 1923), 541. Garvey in *The Negro World* (May 10, 1924). The elevator incident is related in Tony Martin, *Race First: The Ideological and Organizational Struggles of Marcus Garvey and the Universal Negro Improvement Association* (Dover, Mass.: Majority Press, 1976), 305.

63. Robert Bagnall, "The Madness of Marcus Garvey," *Messenger* (March 1923): 638. See David J. Hellwig, "Black Leaders and United States Immigration Policy, 1917–1929," *Journal of Negro History* 66, no. 2 (Summer 1981): 110–127.

64. *Negro World*, Oct. 8, 1921; editorials in the *New York Amsterdam News*, Oct. 26 and Nov. 16, 1921, in NAACP, Marcus Garvey clippings folder.

65. See Martin, *Race First*, 299–302; Du Bois to B. Young, Aug. 8, 1925, in *Correspondence*, vol. 1, 317–318; Earnest Lyon to Du Bois, July 10, 1924, Du Bois Papers. A draft of the letter to the attorney general, complete with marginalia, is in the NAACP papers; see Chandler Owen et al. to Hon. Harry M. Daugherty, Jan. 15, 1923, NAACP, folder labeled "Marcus Garvey Jan. 15–Dec. 19, 1923." On the Department of Justice investigation, see Kornweibel, *Seeing Red*; Martin, *Race First*, 325–333.

66. Du Bois, "A Second Journey to Pan-Africa," *New Republic* 29 (Dec. 7, 1921): 39.

67. Du Bois to Ramsey McDonald, Sept. 3, 1923, and Du Bois to T. A. Marryshaw, n.d., Du Bois Papers; Immanuel Geiss, *The Pan-African Movement: A History of Pan-Africanism in America, Europe, and Africa*, trans. Ann Keep (New York: Africana, 1974), 163–262; Clarence G. Contee, "Du Bois, the NAACP, and the Pan-African Congress of 1919," *Journal of Negro History* 57 (1972): 13–28. Lewis, *W. E. B. Du Bois*, 9.

68. Du Bois, *The Gift of Black Folk: The Negroes in the Making of America* (Boston: Stratford, 1924), 320; Du Bois to Edward McSweeney, July 13, 1923, Du Bois Papers; Aptheker, *Literary Legacy*, 165–182.

69. Du Bois, "The Negro Mind Reaches Out," in *The New Negro*, ed. Alain Locke (New York: Albert and Charles Boni, 1925), 385; Lewis, *W. E. B. Du Bois*, 504. *To the World (Manifesto of the Second Pan-African Congress)*, in *Pamphlets and Leaflets by W. E. B. Du Bois*, ed. Herbert Aptheker (New York: Kraus-Thomson, 1986), 197.

70. Stoddard, *The French Revolution in San Domingo* (New York, 1910). "Haiti," *Crisis* 20 (Oct. 1920): 261. Claude McKay, *Home to Harlem* (1928; Boston: Northeastern University Press, 1987), 134. My thanks to Michele Stephens for sharing this McKay quote. See Michele A. Stephens, "Black Transnationalism and the Politics of National Identity: West Indian Intellectuals in Harlem in the Age of War and Revolution," *American Quarterly* 50, no. 3 (Sept. 1998): 592–608.

71. Brenda Gayle Plummer, "The Afro-American Response to the Occupation of Haiti, 1915–1934," *Phylon* (June 1982): 125–143. *Occupied Haiti: Being the Report of a Committee of Six Disinterested Americans Representing Organizations Exclu-*

*sively American Who, Having Personally Studied Conditions in Haiti in 1926, Favor the Restoration of the Independence of the Negro Republic,* ed. Emily Greene Balch (New York: Writer's Publishing Co., 1927). Du Bois, "Haiti," in *Du Bois: A Reader,* 466. Du Bois, "The American Congo," NAACP, folder labeled "Speech and Article File—W. E. B. Du Bois." On eugenic thinking among African Americans see Michele Mitchell, "Adjusting the Race: Gender, Sexuality, and the Question of African-American Destiny, 1877–1930" (Ph.D. diss., Northwestern University, 1997).

72. Cyril Briggs's *Crusader* often cited Stoddard as an expert in support of its opinions, and used quotes from Grant as epigraphs for the editorial page. See "Rising Tide of Color Sets White World A-Trembling," *Crusader* (July 1920); "The Rising Wave," *Crusader* (June 1920); *Crusader* (Sept. 1920); "Christianity as Propaganda," *Crusader* (Oct. 1920). Garveyites in Los Angeles were encouraged to read Stoddard and Earnest Sevier Cox; see Emory Tolbert, "Outpost Garveyism and the UNIA Rank and File," *Journal of Black Studies* 5 (March 1975): 240–241.

73. Harrison, "The Rising Tide of Color against White World Supremacy," in *When Africa Awakes: The "Inside" Story of the Stirrings and Strivings of the New Negro in the Western World* (1920; Chesapeake, Md.: ECA Associates, 1991), 143–144. Harrison to Stoddard, Nov. 13, 1920, cited in Jeffrey Babcock Perry, "Hubert Henry Harrison, 'The Father of Harlem Radicalism': The Early Years—1883 through the Founding of the Liberty League and *The Voice*" (Ph.D. diss., Columbia University, 1986), 402.

74. Cox, *Black Belt around the World* (Richmond, Va.: n.p., 1963). Edith Wolfskill Hedlin, "Earnest Sevier Cox and Colonization: A White Racist's Response to Black Repatriation, 1923–1966" (Ph.D. diss., Duke University, 1974). Grant to Cox, March 18, 1924, cited in William A. Edwards, "Racial Purity in Black and White: The Case of Marcus Garvey and Earnest Cox," *Journal of Ethnic Studies* 15, no. 1 (1987): 125.

75. Cox, cited in Martin, *Race First,* 344. See Nancy MacLean, *Behind the Mask of Chivalry: The Making of the Second Ku Klux Klan* (New York: Oxford University Press, 1994); Barbara Bair, "True Women, Real Men: Gender, Ideology, and Social Roles in the Garvey Movement," in *Gendered Domains: Rethinking Public and Private in Women's History,* ed. Susan M. Reverby and Dorothy O. Helly (Ithaca: Cornell University Press, 1992), 154–166.

76. Garvey, "Who and What Is a Negro," in *Philosophy and Opinions,* vol. 2, 21. *Philosophy and Opinions,* vol. 2, advertisement following 412; Garvey to Cox, Aug. 27 and Aug. 8, 1925, both in Earnest Sevier Cox Papers, Special Collections Library, Duke University.

77. Du Bois, "Back to Africa," 547; also see NAACP Press release, Jan. 25, 1923, in NAACP, folder labeled "Marcus Garvey, Jan. 15–Dec. 19, 1923." *Messenger* cited in Judith Stein, *The World of Marcus Garvey: Race and Class in Modern Society* (Baton Rouge: Louisiana State University Press, 1986), 161. See Stein, *World of Marcus*

*Garvey,* 161–170; Martin, *Race First,* 346; Theodore Kornweibel Jr., *No Crystal Stair: Black Life and the Messenger, 1917–1928* (Westport, Conn.: Greenwood, 1975), 132–175.

78. James Robert Bachman, "Theodore Lothrop Stoddard: The Bio-Sociological Battle for Civilization" (Ph.D. diss., University of Rochester, 1967). Frederick Lewis Allen, *Only Yesterday: An Informal History of the 1920s* (New York: Harper and Brothers, 1931), 94. Garvey, Speech in New York, Nov. 12, 1921, MGP, vol. 4, 181. Stoddard, *Re-Forging America,* 303–305.

79. Du Bois to Jackson, Sept. 20, 1923, Du Bois Papers. Du Bois, "Back to Africa," 548. See clipping file labeled "Lothrop Stoddard," Schomburg Center for Research in Black Culture, New York Public Library; Tolbert, "Outpost Garveyism." Madison Jackson to Du Bois, Aug. 31, 1923, Du Bois Papers.

80. *Report of a Debate Conducted by the Chicago Forum: Shall the Negro Be Encouraged to Seek Cultural Equality? March 17, 1929* (Chicago: Chicago Forum Council, 1929), 9.

81. Durant to Du Bois, July 25, 1925, and Aug. 14, 1925, Du Bois Papers. Grant to Stoddard, Sept. 28, 1927, cited in Bachman, "Theodore Lothrop Stoddard," 231n14.

82. Henry Goddard Leach to Du Bois, Aug. 23, 1927, Du Bois to Leach, Sept. 5, 1927, and E. C. Aswell to Du Bois, Sept. 10, 1927, Du Bois Papers; Alain Locke, "The High Cost of Prejudice," and Lothrop Stoddard, "Impasse at the Color-Line," *Forum* (Oct. 1927): 500–519.

83. See George White to Walter White, March 19, 1929, NAACP; "'Cease Your Demand for Social Equality and We'll Recognize Your Culture,' Stoddard Tells Du Bois in Debate," Associated Negro Press release, in Claude A. Barnett Collection, Chicago Historical Society, folder labeled "Du Bois, W. E. B. clippings and pamphlets"; "Du Bois Shatters Stoddard's Cultural Theories," Chicago *Defender,* March 23, 1929. Du Bois would later suggest that one-third of the audience was white; Du Bois, "The Chicago Debate," in *The Crisis* (May 1929): 167.

84. Enclosure, Du Bois to Margaret Sanger, Feb. 14, 1925, in *Correspondence,* vol. 1, 302. Du Bois, "Black Folk and Birth Control," *Birth Control Review* 16 (June 1932), 166–167, in *Writings in Periodical Literature Edited by Others,* vol. 2, 320–321.

85. E. C. Aswell to Du Bois, Sept. 10, 1927, Du Bois Papers. Du Bois to Fred A. Moore, Feb. 18, 1929, Du Bois Papers. Du Bois wrote to Moore: "It is quite possible that Stoddard will not appear, so that you ought to have something up your sleeve to fill out the program."

86. Moore, in *Shall the Negro Be Encouraged to Seek Cultural Equality,* 10. Chicago *Defender,* March 23, 1929. Ted Stoddard to Matthew Pratt Guterl, May 31, 2000.

87. Du Bois, *Dark Princess* (New York: Harcourt, Brace, 1928), 257, 297.

88. Ibid., 7.

89. Lawrence Levine, "American Culture and the Great Depression," in *The Unpre-*

*dictable Past: Explorations in American Cultural History* (New York: Oxford University Press, 1993), 209. See, e.g., Warren Susman, *Culture as History: The Transformation of American Society in the Twentieth Century* (New York: Pantheon, 1984), 180, 150–183.

90. See Patricia Sullivan, *Days of Hope: Race and Democracy in the New Deal Era* (Chapel Hill: University of North Carolina Press, 1996); Harvard Sitkoff, *A New Deal for Blacks* (New York: Oxford University Press, 1979).

91. Dan T. Carter, *Scottsboro: A Tragedy of the American South* (1969; Baton Rouge: Louisiana State University Press, 1992); Robin D. G. Kelley, "Afric's Sons with Banner Red: African-American Communists and the Politics of Culture, 1919–1934," in Kelley, *Race Rebels: Culture, Politics, and the Black Working Class* (New York: Free Press, 1994), 103–121; Kelley, *Hammer and Hoe: Alabama Communists during the Great Depression* (Chapel Hill: University of North Carolina Press, 1990).

92. Carter, *Scottsboro*, 103, 51–103. Kelley, *Hammer and Hoe*, 159–192. "Left Wing of McCarthyism," from Manning Marable, *Race, Reform, Rebellion: The Second Reconstruction in Black America* (1984; Jackson: University of Mississippi Press, 1991), 32. Carol Anderson, "Bleached Souls and Red Negroes: The NAACP and Black Communists in the Early Cold War," in *America's Dilemma: Civil Rights, Foreign Relations, and the Cold War,* ed. Brenda Gayle Plummer (Chapel Hill: University of North Carolina Press, forthcoming).

93. Du Bois, "The Negro and Communism," in *Selections from The Crisis,* vol. 2, 637, 635, 639. Lewis, "Introduction," in *Du Bois: A Reader,* 6.

94. Du Bois, "The Union of Color," in *Writings in Periodicals Edited by Others,* vol. 3, 46; Von Eschen, *Race against Empire.* Stoddard, "The Impasse at the Color Line," *Forum* (Oct. 1927): 518–519.

95. Du Bois, "Segregation," in *Du Bois: A Reader,* 557–558.

96. Du Bois, "On Being Ashamed of Oneself," in *Du Bois: A Reader,* 79. Du Bois, "A Negro Nation within the Nation," *Current History* (June 1935): 268. Du Bois himself sometimes portrayed "the Negro" as a solution to the labor problems of the urban North or corporate America—see, e.g., "The Hosts of Black Labor," *Nation* 116 (May 9, 1923): 539–541, and Du Bois to Harvey Firestone Jr., Oct. 26, 1925, in *Correspondence,* vol. 1, 320–323.

97. Du Bois, "A Negro Nation within the Nation," 270; Du Bois, "The Negro College," in *Du Bois: A Reader,* 75.

98. Du Bois, "On Being Ashamed of Oneself," 78–80.

99. Ibid. Du Bois, "A Negro Nation within the Nation," 268–269.

100. Du Bois, "Miscegenation," W. E. B. Du Bois Small Collection, Schomburg Center for Research in Black Culture, New York Public Library (hereafter Small Collection).

101. Typescript of question-and-answer session following Du Bois's speech "Basic Phi-

losophy and Policies for Negro Life in the North," given in Milbank Chapel, Teachers College, Columbia University, March 25, 1936, Small Collection.

## 4. The Hypnotic Division of America

1. Toomer, "Book X," Jean Toomer Papers, James Weldon Johnson Memorial Collection, Beineke Rare Book and Manuscript Library, Yale University (hereafter JTP). All references are to final draft.
2. Toomer, "America and Problems," n.d., JTP.
3. Jean Toomer to Suzanne LaFollette, Sept. 22, 1930, JTP.
4. Robert A. Bone, in one of the first attempts at a "recovery" of *Cane*, suggests that Toomer's failure to produce another novel can be blamed on the poor sales of *Cane*—an interpretation that avoids any mention of Toomer's post-*Cane* discontent with blackness. See Bone, *The Negro Novel in America* (1958; New Haven: Yale University Press, 1968), 89. For a considerate analysis of claims that Toomer "passed" see Henry Louis Gates Jr., *Figures in Black: Words, Signs, and the "Racial" Self* (New York: Oxford University Press, 1987), 196–224. On "racelessness" see Toni Morrison, review of *The Wayward and the Seeking: A Collection of Writings by Jean Toomer*, ed. Darwin T. Turner (Washington: Howard University Press, 1980), cited in Gates, *Figures in Black*, 221–222.
5. George Hutchinson, "Jean Toomer and American Racial Discourse," *Texas Studies in Literature and Language* 35 (1993): 227; also see David Bradley, "Looking behind *Cane*," *Southern Review* 21 (1985): 682–694.
6. Gates, *Figures in Black*, 197. Cynthia Kerman and Richard Eldridge, *The Lives of Jean Toomer* (Baton Rouge: Louisiana State University Press, 1987), 27–28, 26–51. See S. P. Fullenwider, *The Mind and Mood of Black America: Twentieth Century Thought* (Homewood, Ill.: Dorsey, 1969), 137–144. On Pinchback, see James S. Haskins, *Pinckney Benton Stewart Pinchback* (New York: Macmillan, 1973).
7. See Rayford Logan, *The Betrayal of the Negro: From Rutherford B. Hayes to Woodrow Wilson* (New York: Collier, 1965); Joel Williamson, *A Rage for Order: Black-White Relations in the American South since Emancipation* (New York: Oxford University Press, 1984).
8. Willard B. Gatewood, *Aristocrats of Color: The Black Elite, 1880–1920* (Bloomington: Indiana University Press, 1990); Constance McLaughlin Green, *The Secret City: A History of Race Relations in the Nation's Capital* (Princeton: Princeton University Press, 1967); Kevin K. Gaines, *Uplifting the Race: Black Leadership, Politics, and Culture in the Twentieth Century* (Chapel Hill: University of North Carolina Press, 1996). Haskins, *Pinckney Benton Stewart Pinchback*.
9. Toomer, "Book X," JTP.
10. William Faulkner, *Light in August* (1932; New York: Vintage International, 1985), 34. Toomer, "Book X," JTP.

11. Kerman and Eldridge, *Lives of Jean Toomer*, 72.

12. Ibid. Herbert Croly, *The Promise of American Life* (New York, 1909). "The Blue Meridian" (1936), in *Wayward and the Seeking*, 214–234.

13. Toomer, "Book X." Charles Scruggs and Lee VanDemarr, *Jean Toomer and the Terrors of American History* (Philadelphia: University of Pennsylvania Press, 1998), 58–108. On the radicalism of the wartime and postwar literary scene, see Edward Abrahams, *The Lyrical Left: Randolph Bourne, Alfred Stieglitz, and the Origins of Cultural Radicalism in America* (Charlottesville: University Press of Virginia, 1986); Daniel Henry May, *End of American Innocence: A Study of the First Years of Our Own Time, 1912–1917* (1959; New York: Columbia University Press, 1989).

14. Toomer, "The Negro Emergent," in *A Jean Toomer Reader*, ed. Frederick L. Rusch (New York: Oxford University Press, 1993), 91.

15. Harrison, "The New Race Consciousness," in *When Africa Awakes: The "Inside" Story of the Stirrings and Strivings of the New Negro in the Western World* (1920; Chesapeake, Md.: ECA Associates, 1991), 76.

16. David Levering Lewis, *When Harlem Was in Vogue* (New York: Knopf, 1981); Nathan Irvin Huggins, *Harlem Renaissance* (New York: Oxford University Press, 1971); George Hutchinson, *The Harlem Renaissance in Black and White* (Cambridge, Mass.: Harvard University Press, 1995); Ann Douglas, *Terrible Honesty* (New York: Farrar, Straus, Giroux, 1995).

17. Douglas, *Terrible Honesty*, 115. Langston Hughes, "The Negro Artist and the Racial Mountain," *Nation* (June 23, 1926): 692. Lewis, *When Harlem Was in Vogue*; Huggins, *Harlem Renaissance*; David Nasaw, *Going Out: The Rise and Fall of Public Amusements* (New York: Basic Books, 1993). Stoddard, *Revolt against Civilization: The Menace of the Under Man* (New York: Scribner's, 1922), 125–141.

18. Konrad Bercovici, "Rhythm of Harlem," *Survey Graphic* (March 1925): 679; James Weldon Johnson, "Harlem, the Culture Capital," in *The New Negro*, ed. Alain Locke (New York: Albert and Charles Boni, 1925), 309. Rudolph Fisher, "The Caucasian Storms Harlem," in *The Portable Harlem Renaissance Reader*, ed. David Levering Lewis (New York: Viking, 1994), 117.

19. Locke, "Foreword," in *The New Negro*, xxvi. Du Bois, "Can the Negro Serve the Drama?" *Theatre Magazine* (July 1923): 68. "Racial aptitude" is from Harlem's preeminent theater critic, Theophilus Lewis; *Messenger* (Sept. 1924): 291.

20. Locke, "The New Negro," in *The New Negro*, 7; Locke, "The Drama of Negro Life," in *The Critical Temper of Alain Locke*, ed. Jeffrey Stewart (New York: Garland, 1983), 90. Floyd Dell in *The Liberator* (March 1918): 33, referring to Synge's work of ethnography, *The Aran Islands* (1907). Johnson wrote: "What the colored poet needs to do is something like what Synge did for the Irish, he needs to find a form that will express the racial spirit by symbols from within rather than by symbols from without, such as the mutilation of English spelling and pronunciation. He needs a form . . . expressing the imaginary, the idioms, the peculiar turns of thought, and the distinctive humor and pathos, too, of the Negro." James Weldon

Johnson, Preface to *The Book of American Negro Poetry* (New York: Harcourt, Brace, 1921), 41.

21. Scruggs and VanDemarr, *Jean Toomer*, 139. George Chauncey, *Gay New York: Gender, Urban Culture, and the Making of a Gay Male World* (New York: Basic Books, 1994); Siobhan S. Somerville, *Queering the Color Line: Race and the Invention of Homosexuality in American Culture* (Durham: Duke University Press, 2000). For close readings of *Cane*, see Scruggs and VanDemarr, *Jean Toomer*, 135–207; Barbara Foley, "Jean Toomer's Washington and the Politics of Class: From 'Blue Vein' to Seventh-Street Rebels," *Modern Fiction Studies* 42, no. 2 (Summer 1996): 289–318; Darwin T. Turner, *In Minor Chord: Three Afro-American Writers and Their Search for Identity* (Carbondale and Edwardsville: Southern Illinois University Press, 1971), 14–30.

22. Toomer to Waldo Frank, 1923?, JTP.

23. Charles S. Johnson, "The Vanishing Mulatto," *Opportunity* (Oct. 1925): 291. Joel Williamson, *New People: Miscegenation and Mulattoes in the United States* (New York: New York University Press, 1984), 91–186; F. James Davis, *Who Is Black? One Nation's Definition* (University Park: Pennsylvania State University Press, 1991), 11–13.

24. Toomer, untitled fragment, "written for publication a few days before my marriage," JTP. Toomer to Frank, n.d., JTP. As David Bradley wrote, Toomer "has been accused of denying his blackness; in fact, he was guilty of refusing to deny everything else"; Bradley, "Looking behind *Cane*," 693. Also see Charles Scruggs, "Jean Toomer: Fugitive," *American Literature* 47, no. 1 (March 1975): 86–87; Hutchinson, "Jean Toomer and American Racial Discourse"; George Hutchinson, "The Whitman Legacy and the Harlem Renaissance," in *Walt Whitman: The Centennial Essays*, ed. Ed Folsom (Iowa City: University of Iowa Press, 1994), 209–303.

25. Bederman, *Manliness and Civilization: A Cultural History of Gender and Race in the United States, 1880–1917* (Chicago: University of Chicago Press, 1995), 25. See George W. Stocking, "Lamarckianism in American Social Science," in *Race, Culture, and Evolution: Essays in the History of Anthropology* (1968; Chicago: University of Chicago Press, 1982), 234–269.

26. Waldo Frank, "Foreword" in Jean Toomer, *Cane*, ed. Darwin T. Turner (1923; New York: Norton, 1988), 138, 140. *The Dial* (Jan. 1924): 92. Paul Rosenfeld, *Men Seen: Twenty-Four Modern Authors* (New York: Dial Press, 1925), 233. William Stanley Braithwaite, "The Negro in American Literature," in *The New Negro*, 44. For responses to *Cane*, see Henry Louis Gates Jr., *Jean Toomer and Literary Criticism* (Washington: Howard University Press, 1987), 20–50; Charles R. Larson, *Invisible Darkness: Jean Toomer and Nella Larson* (Iowa City: University of Iowa Press, 1993), 25–27; Kerman and Eldridge, *Lives of Jean Toomer*, 108–109.

27. Locke, "The New Negro," in *The New Negro*, 14.

28. Du Bois, "The Negro Mind Reaches Out," in *The New Negro*, 412. Du Bois, *Dark Princess: A Romance* (New York: Harcourt, Brace, 1928); George Schuyler, "Black

Internationale," and "Black Empire," in *Black Empire,* ed. Robert A. Hill and R. Kent Rasmussen (Boston: Northeastern University Press, 1991).

29. Toomer to Frank, Summer 1923?, JTP. Kerman and Eldridge, *Lives of Jean Toomer,* 373–374.

30. Toomer to Liveright, n.d., in Rusch, ed., *Jean Toomer Reader,* 94. Toomer to Frank, 1923?, JTP.

31. Toomer to Suzanne LaFollette, Sept. 18, 1930, JTP.

32. See, e.g., Jon Woodson, *To Make a New Race: Gurdjieff, Toomer, and the Harlem Renaissance* (Jackson: University Press of Mississippi, 1999), 1–46.

33. Toomer, "Book X"; Toomer, "The Americans," Brown Composition Book, JTP.

34. Bederman, *Manliness and Civilization.* Walker, "The Divided Life of Jean Toomer," in *In Search of Our Mother's Gardens* (New York: Harcourt, Brace, 1984), 63.

35. Nasaw, *Going Out;* Jackson Lears, *Fables of Abundance: A Cultural History of Advertising in America* (New York: Basic Books, 1994), 162–234; Melvin Patrick Ely, *The Adventures of Amos 'n' Andy: A Social History of an American Phenomenon* (New York: Free Press, 1991).

36. E. E. Cummings, *The Enormous Room* (1922; New York: Boni and Liveright, 1978), 197. See Ellen Kay Trimberger, "Feminism, Men, and Modern Love: Greenwich Village, 1900–1925," in *Powers of Desire: The Politics of Sexuality,* ed. Ann Snitnow, Christine Stansell, and Sharon Thompson (New York: Monthly Review Press, 1983), 131–152; Joseph Singal, "Towards a Definition of American Modernism," *American Quarterly* 39 (Spring 1987): 7–26; May, *End of American Innocence;* Douglas, *Terrible Honesty,* 31–176; Lewis, *When Harlem Was in Vogue,* 98–100; Huggins, *Harlem Renaissance,* 84–136.

37. See, e.g., Kevin J. Mumford, *Interzones: Black/White Sex Districts in Chicago and New York in the Early Twentieth Century* (New York: Columbia University Press, 1997); Hazel Carby, "Policing the Black Women's Body in an Urban Context," *Critical Inquiry* (1992): 738–755; Chauncey, *Gay New York,* 248–267.

38. *New York Herald* (March 4, 1916); *New York Tribune* (March 4, 1916).

39. Bernarr Macfadden, *Vitality Supreme* (New York, 1915), xii. Toomer, "Book X." See Ann Fabian, "Making a Commodity of Truth: Speculations on the Career of Bernarr Macfadden," *American Literary History* 5, no. 1 (1993): 51–76; Lears, *Fables of Abundance,* 162–195.

40. Ibid.

41. Lears, *Fables of Abundance,* 169. Michael Anton Budd, *The Sculpture Machine: Physical Culture and Body Politics in the Age of Empire* (New York: New York University Press, 1997), 82.

42. See Diana I. Williams, "Building the New Race: Jean Toomer's Eugenic Aesthetic," manuscript.

43. Toomer, "Book X." See E. Anthony Rotundo, *American Manhood: Transformations in Masculinity from the Revolution to the Modern Era* (New York: Basic Books, 1994); John S. Haller and Robin Haller, *The Physician and Sexuality in Victorian America* (Carbondale and Edwardsville: Southern Illinois University Press, 1995);

Peter G. Filene, *Him/Her/Self: Gender Identity in Modern America* (Baltimore: Johns Hopkins University Press, 1998).

44. Toomer, "Book X"; Toomer to Frank, n.d., Waldo Frank Papers, Van Pelt Library, University of Pennsylvania (hereafter WFP).

45. Frank to Toomer, 1923?, JTP. Toomer, "Book X." Kerman and Eldridge have suggested that Toomer was bipolar, or manic-depressive; *Lives of Jean Toomer,* 373–374.

46. "Just Americans," *Time,* March 28, 1932. See Scruggs and VanDemarr, *Jean Toomer,* 214–219; Kerman and Eldridge, *Lives of Jean Toomer,* 194–198, 201–204; Larson, *Invisible Darkness,* 120–136. This was not the first time Toomer's public classification as a "Negro" had posed a problem; see, e.g., Toomer, "Outline of an Autobiography," in *Wayward and the Seeking,* 105. Nor was this the only time race had mattered in a relationship. Toomer referred to his relationship with Mae Wright—a dark-skinned African-American girl—as a "complete tragedy of color"; Toomer to Frank, n.d., WFP.

47. Toomer, untitled essay, n.d., JTP. Also see Toomer, untitled fragment, "written for publication a few days before my marriage," JTP.

48. See esp. Cecelia Tichi, *Shifting Gears: Technology, Literature, Culture in Modernist America* (Chapel Hill: University of North Carolina Press, 1987); Miles Orvell, *The Real Thing: Imitation and Authenticity in American Culture, 1880–1940* (Chapel Hill: University of North Carolina Press, 1989), 141–197.

49. Toomer to Ridge, [Dec. 1922], in Rusch, ed., *Jean Toomer Reader,* 17.

50. Ibid. Toomer to Frank, 1923?, JTP.

51. Toomer, "Outline of an Autobiography," 123. Toomer, "On Being an American," in *Wayward and the Seeking,* 129.

52. Toomer to Frank, 1923?, JTP. Lewis, *When Harlem Was in Vogue,* 90. Toomer, "On Being an American."

53. Toomer, "Race Problems and Modern Society," in *Problems of Civilization,* ed. Baker Brownell (New York: Van Nostrand, 1929), 108. Toomer, "On Being an American"; Williams, "Building the New Race." Toomer, "Outline of an Autobiography," 123; see Fullenwider, *Mind and Mood of Black America,* 140–141.

54. Du Bois to Toomer, May 5, 1931, JTP. Toomer, "Race Problems and Modern Society," 98.

55. Toomer, "America and Problems." Toomer, "The Americans," Brown Composition Book, n.d., JTP.

56. Toomer, "America and Problems."

## Epilogue

1. Richard Wright, *Native Son* (1940; New York: Perennial Classics, 1998), 393–394.

2. Margaret Mitchell, *Gone with the Wind* (1936; New York: Warner, 1999), 30. Subsequent citations appear in the text.

3. In the movie version the O'Hara family does not offer the "Litany of the Virgin";

instead, they offer up "the *Confitior*," an ancient prayer of confession and a more subtle demonstration of their ardent Catholicism. This slight shift is in keeping with the slight blurring of the Irishness of the O'Haras in the film—prayers to the Virgin Mary were an immediate sign of Catholicism.

4. Madison Grant, *The Passing of the Great Race; or, the Racial Basis of European History* (New York, 1916), 22. Matthew Frye Jacobson writes: "In 1936 Margaret Mitchell described Scarlett O'Hara, who was to become the most famous Irishwoman in American history, as possessing 'magnolia white skin—that skin so prized by Southern women and so carefully guarded with bonnets, veils and mittens against hot Georgia suns.' The notion that Irishness, like other 'ethnic' whitenesses, was a cultural trait rather than a visual racial cue became deeply embedded in the nation's political culture between the 1920s and 1960s." Jacobson, *Whiteness of a Different Color: European Immigrants and the Alchemy of Race* (Cambridge, Mass.: Harvard University Press, 1998), 96.

5. Lawrence Levine, "American Culture and the Great Depression," in *The Unpredictable Past: Explorations in American Cultural History* (New York: Oxford University Press, 1993), 218.

6. Michael Rogin, *Blackface, White Noise: Jewish Immigrants in the Hollywood Melting Pot* (Berkeley: University of California Press, 1996), 164.

7. Rostcraft Slide #93–10999 RC, 1930, Ethnic Imagery Project, Archives Center, National Museum of American History, Smithsonian Institution.

8. See Franz Boas, "Race," in *The Encyclopedia of the Social Sciences,* ed. Edwin R. A. Seligman and Alvin Johnson (New York: Macmillan, 1935), vol. 13, 25–34; Melville Herskovitz, "Race Conflict" ibid., 36–43; Abram Harris and Sterling Spero, "Negro Problem," ibid., vol. 11, 335–355; Charles S. Johnson, *Shadow of the Plantation* (Chicago: University of Chicago Press, 1934). Also see James B. McKee, *Sociology and the Negro Problem: The Failure of a Perspective* (Urbana: University of Illinois, 1993); Werner Sollars, "Introduction: The Invention of Ethnicity," in Werner Sollars, ed., *The Invention of Ethnicity* (New York: Oxford University Press, 1989), iv–xx.

9. Rogin, *Blackface, White Noise;* Neal Gabler, *An Empire of Their Own: How the Jews Invented Hollywood* (New York: Crown, 1988); Karen Brodkin, *How Jews Became White Folks and What That Says about Race in America* (New Brunswick: Rutgers University Press, 1998), 25–42.

10. See Arnold R. Hirsch, "Massive Resistance in the Urban North: Trumbull Park, Chicago, 1953–1966," *Journal of American History* 82, no. 2 (Sept. 1995): 522–550; Thomas J. Sugrue, "Crabgrass-Roots Politics: Race, Rights, and the Reaction against Liberalism in the Urban North, 1940–1964," ibid., 551–570. On the Cold War civil rights coalition in Newark, see G. Kurt Piehler, Matthew Guterl, and Sidney Pash, interviews with Alan Victor Lowenstein, Alan V. Lowenstein, Esq., Oral History Project, Alexander Library, Rutgers University.

11. Jacobson, *Whiteness of a Different Color,* 188.

12. Gunnar Myrdal, *An American Dilemma: The Negro Problem and Modern Democracy* (1944; New Brunswick: Transaction, 1996), 53, 117. Langston Hughes, "The Negro Artist and the Racial Mountain," in *The Portable Harlem Renaissance Reader,* ed. David Levering Lewis (New York: Viking, 1994), 95.

13. James Baldwin, *The Fire Next Time* (1962; New York: Vintage International, 1993), 9, 104.

# Acknowledgments

There is nothing quite like the joy that accompanies the writing of one's acknowledgments . . .

At Rutgers University, David Levering Lewis was a true scholar and gentleman, taking time away from his biography of W. E. B. Du Bois to suggest possible approaches to the topic and to read every version of this book. I owe David much more than I could ever repay. Likewise, Michael Adas, Jackson Lears, and Mia Bay were extraordinarily helpful. Very generous assistance came from John Aveni, Norma Basch, Herman Bennett, Jenny Brier, Kim Brodkin, Robert Churchill, Will Cobb, Rosanne Currarino, Sara DuBow, Finis Dunaway, Chris Fisher, Justin Hart, Nancy Hewitt, Rick Jobs, Dan Katz, Richard Keller, Melissa Klapper, Peter Lau, Jan Lewis, Patrick McDevitt, Lucia McMahon, Neil Miller, Khalil Muhammad, Annie Nicolosi, Liam O'Brien, Philip Pauly, Jennifer Pettit, Clem Price, Liz Smith, Todd Uhlman, Chris Warley, and Deborah G. White.

The larger academic community supplied equally valuable criticism. Matthew Frye Jacobson was, quite simply, amazing. I am likewise especially grateful for the sage counsel of James Bachman, JoAnne Brown, Genevieve Fabre, Mandy Frisken, Charlie McGovern, Michele Mitchell, Robin Muncy, Louise Newman, Jeanne Petit, Heather Munro Prescott, Fath Davis Ruffins, Siobhan Somerville, Jonathan Peter Spiro, and Diana Williams.

Ted Stoddard answered difficult questions with grace and a remarkable openness of heart, sending me a photocopy of his father's unpublished autobiography and sharing the photograph used here.

The financial support of the Department of History, Rutgers University, made this book possible, as did a timely fellowship at the National Museum of American History, Smithsonian Institution. Help from librarians at Alexander Library at Rutgers University, the Library of the American Philosophical Society, the Rare Books, Manuscripts, and Special Collections Library of Duke University, the Amistad Research Center at Tulane University, the Beinecke Library at Yale University, the National Library of Ireland, the Moorland-Spingarn Research Center at Howard University, the Schomburg Center for Research in Black Culture of the New York Public Library, the Archives Center at the National Museum of American History, Van Pelt Library at the University of Pennsylvania, Firestone Library at Princeton University, Houghton Library at Harvard University, the Massachusetts Historical Society, the New York Historical Society, the main branch of the New York Public Library, the Library of Congress, and the Martin Luther King, Jr., Library in Washington, D.C., was priceless. Kelly Cobble of the Adams National Historic Site, Quincy, Massachusetts, and William Cobert, director of the American Irish Historical Society, were wonderful hosts and insightful guides.

Professional wordsmiths left their mark on this work. Aïda Donald guided me through the revisions and sharpened my argument immeasurably. Margaret Hunt of Purdue University Press worked miracles with an early draft of one chapter. Jerry Bentley, editor of the *Journal of World History*, did the same. Anonymous readers at Harvard University Press and at the *JWH* were shrewd, tough, generous, and brilliantly constructive. At Harvard, Camille Smith humbled me, and schooled me again in the art of writing.

Heartfelt thanks to good friends and family: Todd Uhlman and Anne Dobmeyer, Neil Miller, Jane and Michael Adas, Rosanne Currarino and Chris Warley, Finis Dunaway and Dana Capell, Patrick and Sheila McDevitt, Kim Brodkin and Rick Jobs, Jack Kroll and Lucia McMahon, Ruth Ann Stewart and David Levering Lewis, John Kaim, Milton and Pat Latcha, Hugh, Indira, and Johann Hamilton, Rajindra Latcha, and Tom and Jeanne Pratt. William Guterl and Peter Henning put me up in their D.C. apartment for one summer, while I worked at the NMAH. My wonderful parents, Robert and Sheryl Guterl, did everything they could to help. Lastly, my siblings lived this project in ways that I can hardly imagine. Love, then, to Kyung Ok Kim, Willie James Walker, Kyung Ja Kim, Mark Gerard Guterl, and Mohammad Brown—we are bound more tightly together than some would think.

Sandra Latcha put her own dreams on hold for six long years to make this book possible. But she also insisted that we continue to "live" even as I was writing. Her dogged determination and inability to compromise on the things that really matter are precious. So, too, is her unflagging faith in me. I could not have written this book without her in my life, nor could I have done just about anything else. For these and many other reasons, this book is dedicated to her, and also, at her insistence, to my deserving parents.

# Index